FALLING OFF HORSES

A Memoir

BY

KAREN DONLEY-HAYES

MILSPEAK BOOKS

An imprint of MilSpeak Foundation, Inc.

Library of Congress Cataloging-in-Publication Data
Donley-Hayes, Karen
Library of Congress Number: 2022942949
ISBN: 979-8-9857941-4-4 (paperback)
ISBN: 979-8-9857941-5-1 (epub)

Editing by: Ann Wicker
Cover & Design: Michelle Bradford Art

MilSpeak Foundation, Inc.
5097 York Martin Road
Liberty, NC 27298
www.MilSpeakFoundation.org

Contents

Acknowledgments

I would like to acknowledge literary journal, *The Quotable,* for first publishing "Under Cover," an essay derived from this book's chapter, "The Thaw," and for nominating the essay in 2013 for a Pushcart Prize in nonfiction; *The Healing Muse,* for first publishing "Road Trip" an excerpt from this book's chapter, "Altered States"; Holy Cow! Press for first publishing the chapter, "Buying the Farm, Part B," in the anthology, *The Heart of All That Is: Reflections on Home*; and the Lerner College of Medicine journal *Stethos* for first publishing "The End and Forever After," adapted and excerpted from this book's chapter of the same name.

I have so many to thank for helping me write this book: Anton Habsburg for open willingness to share; Bill and Janeen Carrell, for steadfast encouragement and enthusiasm; my parents, for always nurturing the storyteller, writer, and minute adventurer in me; Arnold, for sharing his life with me and holding my hand; Indy, for carrying me, literally and figuratively, through all these years; Jon Kerstetter for his support, insightful suggestions, and close reads; my Ashland University classmates; Steve Harvey, Bob Cowser Jr., Robert Goolrick; my agent Tracy Crow, who championed this book, forged through pandemic challenges, and whose tenacity and enthusiastic support guided it to a home; Ann Wicker for her thorough and insightful copyediting; and last but most important: my best friend, confidant, sister I never had and true soul mate, Ashley Byrd Carrell Habsburg, without whom there would not have been a story to tell.

chapter one

Falling Off Horses

For Lash's thirty-sixth, and final, birthday, I gave her a bullet-point list chronicling our lives together. Not a typical gift, but this wasn't a typical birthday. And what do you give your best friend when she's dying, anyway?

I had spent weeks jotting notes, instances I remembered and wanted to include. Those jottings unburied tangential memories that triggered other recollections and the bullet-point list grew. It revisited our growing up, our adolescent angst, our educations and adventures and loves found and lost. Our tenacious battles-of-the-bulge. And it revisited all the horses Lash and I had known and ridden and loved over the years. The bullet-list delved back into our childhoods when Lash and I first met and then bonded over horses.

Actually, her name wasn't Lash then. It was Leslie. Leslie Anne Carrell. She cited any number of reasons for legally changing her name to Ashley Byrd Carrell when she was a high school senior, the primary reason being she didn't like the name Leslie and *did* like the name Ashley. I could swear she told me once that because her birth mother had named her Leslie and had then died at thirty, "Leslie" was bad luck, and she wanted rid of it. But when I mentioned this story to Lash decades later, not long before she herself died, she looked at me as if I were speaking in tongues and said I must not be remembering right. Perhaps, but I still don't think I imagined that one.

Whatever her reasons for changing her name, I'd known her all through our school years as Leslie. She was Leslie when we met. She was Leslie when our relationship evolved from summertime playmates to genuine friends, spending our summers riding or dreaming about horses, ogling boys, or weekends at Geauga Lake, leaping from the barely stopped cars of the Big Dipper right back into the line, ducking under the serpentine railings to avoid wasting time and steps. She was Leslie when she was still a lanky pre-adolescent and I was already chubby. She was Leslie when she herself developed curves. She was Leslie while in high school art class we stooped over a map of the United States, smoothing it out and tracing with our fingers how, once we both graduated, we would ride our horses across the country, starting in the fall from Ohio, riding south with the warmer weather, then we would "hang a right at Georgia," and head westward. She was still Leslie when I was in my second year of college and she was finishing high school as a Rotary International exchange student in Sweden. I was *used* to "Leslie."

She didn't dither about changing her name. She decided on it and her parents accompanied her to the courthouse to handle whatever legalese name changing mandated. Maybe I was offended she made such a change without asking or even telling me ahead of time; more likely, I was stubborn and thought it was just silly to change your name.

Lash was committed, however, calmly correcting anyone who called her Leslie ("My name is Ashley"), so eventually I acquiesced. More or less. One day, I admitted the difficulty I was having adjusting to her new name. "I'm gonna call you Lash–mixing the two, you know—until I get used to calling you Ashley." I said this as a declaration, expecting her to argue, but she didn't.

And thus was born "Lash," a name no one planned and yet to me became as much Ashley's name as Ashley.

I gave Lash the bullet-point list, those short snippets that coasted over the events of our lives together on August 23, 2002, her last birthday. I had printed the list, hole-punched the sheets of paper, and put them in a three-ring binder. I had wrapped it up so I could present it to her like any other birthday gift.

Lash opened the present as soon as I handed it to her and read it cover-to-cover right then and there. I sat off to the side in the living room, feeling off-kilter and self-conscious. I could hear Lash turn the pages; every now and then, she snickered, or even guffawed outright, and I had to resist the urge to leap up, scurry over, ask her to show me where she was, what it was that made her laugh. I sat and didn't move and let her read it, and when she finally closed the cover, she erupted into keening sobs. I did leap then and scurry over to her side, apologizing, and feeling the blood rushing to my face. But she just grabbed me and hugged, and pretty soon, we were laughing and snuffling, and passing the binder around the room for whomever else was there to peruse. Lash put the binder with her photo albums and other documents. I don't know if she ever looked at it again.

I, however, have looked through that bullet-point list many, many times over the several years. It starts in "1978-ish" and ends, abruptly, on August 23, 2002. As often as I look at it, I'm always a little disconcerted that no bullet points come after August 23, 2002. Then I remember—the list was for Lash's birthday. And even though she lived another two months and even though I could have added another thousand bullet points about our lives together *after* August 23, 2002, that date is where that list ends.

A psychiatrist once asked if I remembered the first time I ever fell off a horse. I was flustered by the question and what Freudian correlations he might attach to my answers. I never really gave thought to the actual question until many years later, in midlife, when something triggered a dusty fragment of memory, long archived and untouched, about that first fall off a horse. I'm confident it was the *first* time because I think it was also the first time I'd ridden a horse. A pony, actually. A small, silver-dappled Shetland pony named Misty.

I often went with my mother to the Luckys' farm that had gardens, chickens, and cows, and the Luckys themselves, of course, but no horses. Mrs. Lucky would meet us with a body-wide smile and show us her garden or her preserves, and if she hadn't collected the eggs yet, I could go with her to the henhouse to get them. She picked up each egg with the wonder of a newfound treasure. Sometimes she found a double-yolker, weighing it in her knowing hand before holding it out and laying it, hen-warm and heavy, in my cupped palms.

In the evenings, Mr. Lucky drove the cattle up the lane to the barn, walking behind them with a stick, which he said was for him to lean on. He let us sit with him when he milked, his hands working a rhythm like knitting, foamy milk filling the bucket. "Watch this," he'd say, and send a stream of milk out behind the cow, where kittens sat mewling and expectant, open-mouthed and squint-eyed, to catch the milky fountain.

One summer evening, Mr. Lucky left the table in the kitchen and didn't go to the barn, but led us to Misty, tethered on a picket in the row of pine trees by the previously unremarkable alfalfa field. I was spellbound. I stared at the pony's gray coat, his splotchy dapples, his cream-colored mane and tail. I think I can still smell the summer evening, the tang of cows, the pine sap and needles, and the dusty, summer scent of a pony. Mr. Lucky saddled Misty, and then someone hoisted me into the air. I saw the saddle coming toward me between my red cloth tennis shoes, and then I was sitting on the pony. His muzzle didn't leave the ground. I looked down his bushy-maned crest; his mane shook and quivered with each mouthful of grass he tore.

I was seven or eight years old and in love. Misty was in love, too, and not just with the grass under his nose. He also was in love with the horses in a pasture on the far side of the alfalfa field, and when Mr. Lucky let go of him, the pony promptly galloped to them, tearing into the field, where I fell off. I sat in the field, unhurt, whimpering, and looked at the riderless pony now cropping grass next to the fence and his neighbors. Someone retrieved Misty from his friends, and me from the alfalfa, and back into the saddle I went. "Grab hold of that mane," someone said, and I did, hunkered over the saddle horn, clutching wadded handfuls of thick pony mane, pony under me, pony in my hands, pony in my eyes, my nose, my ears, pony all around me.

Every time Mr. Lucky let go, Misty bolted into the field, and I, wailing and tilting, clung to his mane and his round churning back, each of his rapid-fire strides jouncing me just a shade farther ground-ward until I tilted too far and fell off. The small cluster of adults laughed the whole time and told me to get back on. I cried and cried, terrified and exhilarated, and never thought of *not* getting back on. And each time, Misty took me into the field where I came off. I didn't get dumped, bucked off, or thrown, all of which would have implied intent on the horse's part. I simply came off. And Misty came home with us. A flesh and blood pony. Heaven.

I never came off Misty again, but I have subsequently been dumped, thrown, bucked off, come off, taken spills, and fallen from many other horses. I am not a brave equestrienne. I have, in fact, an overdeveloped sense of self-preservation. If I think I may fall off, I don't get on. But then there is this irrefutable fact: every time I have fallen from a horse, I first mounted that horse.

Lash and I used to nod sagely and intone, "If you're going to ride, you're going to fall."

We rode, and we fell. Always, we would get back on. We were there for each other in the days and weeks after those falls, when we first stuck foot in stirrup and climbed aboard again, small victories over the quivering infinite undercurrent of fear.

We also said, "If you're going to work with horses, you're going to get hurt." In fact, my worst horse-related injuries have not involved actual riding. Over the years, I've had broken bones and multiple knee surgeries. I've left emergency departments with slings or crutches or a head full of staples. Lash, too, collected a bevy of non-riding injuries. A mare Lash had when she was a child kicked her in the chest; that mare also nearly bit off Lash's father's thumb and thrashed the barn goat to death. As adults, Lash and I escorted each other to the emergency department after we'd been stepped on, or squashed against barn walls, or trampled, bitten, or kicked. We were fortunate not to have incurred really serious injuries. Horses can be lethal.

Not withstanding having his thumb nearly swallowed by that recalcitrant mare, Lash's father Bill actively participated in and shared in her equine endeavors. Lash's mother, Janeen, adopted a more hands-off position, but always enthusiastically supported her daughter's pony passion.

Strictly speaking, Janeen wasn't Lash's mother. She was her stepmother, although as far as both of them were concerned, that was a minor technicality. "She was a child of my heart, not of my body," Janeen would say. Paula, Lash's birth mother, died of Hodgkin's disease when Lash was very young (Lash referred to Paula as her "first mother" to provide clarification in situations where confusion was likely, such as weddings or other gatherings with extended family from all sides).

During Paula's illness, Lash and Bill skipped between their home in Nashville, Paula's parents' home in Amarillo, Texas, and Hiram, Ohio, where Bill was part of Hiram College's faculty. Bill was the traveling long-distance husband and spent his time and efforts between his young daughter and dying wife in Texas and Tennessee, and his teaching job at Hiram, which is where he and Janeen met.

By the time I met Lash a few years after Paula died, Bill had married Janeen, and it wasn't long before Lash's and my mutual horse-craziness inexorably drew us together, at first mostly during summers to keep each other company and out of trouble. From there, our friendship evolved and over the years, our lives entwined, braiding together.

That "issue" of horses and girls—specifically the premise that there is an inherent link between girls' love for horses and girls' sexuality—has ridden alongside us as long as I can remember. Lash and I grew up horse nuts, and neither of us was oblivious to the Freudian theories. I admit now that theories discomfited, made me vaguely wonder what really was the basis of my love.

So, why *do* girls love horses? And if I had no ready answer, even for myself, to dispel the horses-are-to-girls-as-sex-is-to-women notion, did I then validate that notion? And what other explanation did I have then, or have I now, that satisfies?

Woven throughout my entire life with Lash are horses, soft and strong and constant, different horses striding in and striding out through the years, a shimmering, sentient carousel, breathing, pulsing, rhythmic. I'm sure Lash and I must have discussed the girls/horses topic but I don't recall any such conversations. When we discussed it, it was probably with a wry humor and along the lines of wrapping our legs around horses *and* boys, but certainly not forgoing the former for the latter. Quite the contrary. We both multitasked on that front. Neither of us ever traded in horses for men—in fact, a requisite for the men in our lives was at least an open-ended tolerance for, if not whole-hearted, immersion in our equine lives. My husband Arnold supported all my equine ventures, content to cheer from the sidelines. Lash's husband Anton actively participated in Lash's equestrian life. I don't think either man would have even dabbled in the horse world independent of Lash and me and our equine obsessions.

I was not brave; Lash was braver. But neither of us were reckless daredevils, and we both yearned for, yet feared, the dangers of racing and jumping, the speed, the power, the risk. Both of us occasionally exercised racehorses before easing to calmer, safer pursuits with regret and relief. I blamed my weight, creeping higher every year; Lash blamed her height (and the weight that came with it). To each other, we obliquely confessed our fears.

Officially, I said fear of riding racehorses was due to my healthy sense of self-preservation, but if that were true, I would have foregone horses altogether because there are no safe horses, just some that at times are safer than others.

Lash and I shared in welcoming, loving, buying and selling, attending birthings and grieving the deaths in a long line of horses. Some came into our lives only fleetingly, others stayed for decades. Misty, that first pony, gone after a year; I don't recall why or to whom. Moonlight Bay was not tall enough for long-and-lanky Lash, nor were Major, Cara, or Amber. Cara's foal Strider died mysteriously when he was a few months old. After Misty, my mother got her very own first horse, Trousseau's Pride, a thoroughbred gelding who fell and broke his hip, his death my first true grief. Then there were Shelly, Gallant Witch, Palantir, Relatively Educated, Warlock, Bellstone, Enchanted Scholar. And Gaudior, the first horse Lash ever had that was big enough to fit her long, long legs, but who colicked and died gruesomely while Lash was away visiting her birth mother's parents in Amarillo. There were Ancalagon, Tabriz, and Cully, Castamir, Cappuccino, and Othello's Treasure, Iago's Quicksilver, and my beloved Indy who still nuzzles my palm and warms my heart today. There were Steorling, William, Island Lilly, Kalinka, Silver, Mysty, Johanniter, Kurant, Roanoke, Mackinac, Savannah. And poor Sandusky and Cyprus, my Y2K catastrophes, both born healthy, both dead soon after with broken legs. There were Sukhoi, Rainier, Venice, Alberta, Rodanthe, and dapple-gray Sampson, Lash's last horse, one that was finally tall enough for her and that she rode defiantly the spring and summer she was dying. And there was Monterey, born late on a sunny May morning while Lash, too weak to stand, sat in a chair in the stall doorway watching this new life slip into the world as her life was slipping out.

If there is a genetic link to the love of horses, Lash inherited hers from Bill, and I inherited mine from my mother, who was a singular anomaly in her own family, passionately in love with horses from her own earliest memories. When she read Marguerite Henry's *Misty of Chincoteague*, she pleaded with her mother to get a pony. She reasoned they could keep it in their house in Shaker Heights, Ohio, and put its hay in the fireplace, just as the characters had done for Misty in the book.

I don't remember if my mother told me this snippet before or after my own father had sat on my bed in the evenings, reading to me first *Misty of Chincoteague*, then *Stormy, Misty's Foal*. We didn't have a pony (yet), but we did have a dog and a cat, which was more than my mother had as a child. She had desperately wanted a pet, puppy-napped the neighbor's dog and squirreled it away in her bedroom. When my grandmother found out and made her return her abductee, my mother, all of eight years old, ran away, taking Cleveland's Rapid Transit system downtown, where she moped at Cleveland Municipal Stadium until some police officer corralled her, sulky but unscathed, and my grandfather came and retrieved her. She never did get a pet until she married and moved out of her parents' home in the late 1950s. Then she bestowed the animal-love gene to her children. And to me, she gifted a special love for horses.

Horses filled my daydreams and lulled me to sleep, my mother's voice singing to me of ponies.

Hush-a-bye, don't you cry,
Go to sleep my little baby.
When you wake, you'll have cake,
And all the pretty little horses.

I wonder if my mother gained as much comfort, angora soft and velvety, as she gave, wrapping that lullaby around me like a quilt. Now, decades later, I can google the lyrics, listen again to the old folk tune, but in my heart, the voice is my mother's, riding with me into dream.

A few years ago, I asked her about the lullaby, and if her own mother had sung it to her. She laughed as she said no, she'd learned it at camp, probably, singing and hiking and sometimes riding horses. Had she, I asked, sung this lullaby to my brothers?

"No."

"Why not?"

"Because they didn't respond to it. You did." And she smiled at me with a knowing look.

I'm middle-aged now, and I don't ride anymore. What the wear and tear of years of obesity and years working with horses have not given to osteoarthritis, rheumatoid arthritis has commandeered. That autoimmune disease snarls at my joints and sucks at the energy in me till I feel like a straw collapsing on itself.

Sometimes, I say I should find another home for Indy, even though I have had her for her entire life, owned both of her parents. I was with Indy at her own conception, at her birth eleven months later, and her growing up, then in the dark of a late March night when she pushed her first foal, steaming, onto the straw, where Lash had been squatting next to me, whispering to Indy to push. I was with Indy again the next year, a bright Good Friday afternoon, to welcome her second colt, delivered onto warm spring grass, and Lash looked at him and laughing said, "Hey, you got the one I was supposed to get," and so we traded Steorling's filly for Indy's colt. And I was with Indy a breezy May noontime when she brought her third foal into the world in the same stall where she'd delivered her first, but Indy and I were alone that time, because by then Lash had been some time in her grave.

If I don't ride, how can I justify keeping a horse?

I think I'm the only one asking me that question, but I do ask.

I press my hand to Indy's forehead, smooth the hair of her cowlick—an odd sort of cowlick, long and straight like a part—and she closes her eyes a little. I brush my hand off the right side of her cowlick—my right, her left—and run my hand over her left eye. She squints a little, and with my thumb I nudge a pearl of sleep from the corner by her third eyelid before I slide my palm down her face, over her short, silky brown hair, and across the ridge of her cheekbone—her hair cool on the surface, but the warmth of her solid and pulsing up from beneath. She blinks her eye back open and watches me.

She has gray hairs now on her forehead, just a smattering, fanning out from the top of that odd cowlick and flecking their way toward her forelock. She has more now than she did last summer, when I first noticed a few. If she's like her mother and her mother's mother, by the time she's in her mid-twenties, her entire golden bay face will have turned gray.

I straighten her forelock, sleek and black, pluck away a crooked wisp of hay, comb the hair with my fingers down over her forehead and arrange it fan-like over her face. She presses her muzzle into my belly, fiddles at my shirt with her prehensile lips. She sucks a breath deep into her body, holds it for an instant, then pumps it back out so it blasts against me, her core to mine, her nostrils vibrating for a second through cotton against my skin, droplets dampening my shirt.

"Hello, my beauty," I say. "I love you Indy. I love you. I love you."

I kiss her on that straight, strange cowlick, and she leans her face, just a touch, against my lips, pushing them into my teeth. When I pull back, I take with me like a veil her scent, the smell of a horse, sweet and deep and delicate.

So, again, back to *why do girls like horses?* Because... have you ever smelled a horse? I mean, pressed your nose against her neck and inhaled her essence, clean and sweet? Have you ever run your hands down her legs, felt her cool, sleek hair and under your palms, how the bone and sinew and tendon shift to maintain her posture as she bends her neck around to lay her muzzle on your back? Have you ever heard the low, purring nicker she sighs out when you enter the barn, because she knows you're there before she sees you and she's calling you to her? Have you ever sat on the ground near her as she grazes, watching how she bites the grass, hearing the soft tear, chew, tear, chew, smelling the grass and her breath, feeling the cool of the earth and the warmth of the sun?

Horses, I think, smell like God.

Maybe, sometimes a girl just loves a horse. She rides and she falls; yet always, she pulls herself back up again, her hands on the horse, and she claws through her fear and pain, because she's breathing that golden smell, feeling the quiver of muscle and stock of bone under sleek soft hair; she pulls herself back up onto the animal, wrapping her life around her horse and all that horse is, its primal physicality and exquisite tenderness, its bone-heavy power and crystalline fragility. She wraps her life around the horse, committing all she has to give. She commits her life, her pain and fear, her awe and reverence, her pride and shame.

Perhaps that's why a girl loves a horse. Perhaps that's reason enough.

chapter two

Gravity

The last time I fell off a horse I really meant business. I came off a tall gelding and at speed. It seemed the force of gravity had increased exponentially along with my age, so I fell much harder, and didn't spring up to scramble right back on the horse as I had in my younger days but rather stayed splayed on the ground. The gelding, Chino, bolted from the arena and down the adjoining barn's aisle, leaving me at the mercy of whatever had spooked him.

I knew I was in trouble, in part because as I coasted through the air, there was time to catch a glimpse of Anton leaping to his feet, and to hear Lash screaming, and because it took so damn long to hit the ground. When that happened—with enough force to bloody my elbow through my sweatshirt and winter jacket—I plowed a furrow in the dirt, probably triggered seismometers in Cleveland forty miles away, and didn't get up out of my rut for quite some time. I lay in the arena dirt, listening to the clatter and skid of Chino's steel shoes on the barn's cement aisle, and the wailing of a geriatric barn cat not alert or agile enough to evade his flight.

The acrid odor of his steel shoes sparking against cement mixed with the smell of the soil under my nose, and when Lash knelt by my head, I begged her to get the horse, make sure he was uninjured by his mad scrambling. She vanished from my side. I could still hear the gelding at the end of the barn aisle ricocheting off the walls of the stall he'd leapt into, and then Lash's voice, soothing, calming him, and still the ongoing wailing of the cat, wailing that tapered to a mewling sort of whimper. I wanted to get up, to help, to assess the damage, but my body felt smashed and unreliable; I remained inert, evaluating my condition, determining if I could move my arms and legs, if I was bleeding profusely, if my limbs were bending in directions they weren't designed to.

Lash and Anton secured Chino in his stall, and headed back down the aisle toward where I remained in a crumpled heap; they stopped at the arena's edge.

"I think he killed her," Anton said.

"No, I'm OK," I said, alarmed that I appeared in such bad shape, and impelled to try and sit up, to swivel and look at them to prove Chino hadn't killed me.

Lash and Anton were huddled shoulder-to-shoulder at the edge of the barn aisle with their backs to me, scrutinizing a rumpled clump of grey fur.

"I'm afraid she's dead," Anton said again, this time reaching down to gently lift and cradle the ancient cat in his mammoth hands.

"I'm not dead," I said, louder this time. I had made it all the way to my hands and knees, my concern for the cat tempered with a twinge of annoyance that even though I wasn't dead, I was still kneeling in the dirt, and no one was huddled over me in concern.

Lash did come to my aid then, leaving Anton to tend to the fractured feline. I refused to let Lash call an ambulance, but also wasn't convinced I didn't have some significant injury lurking behind a cloak of adrenaline. Within a few minutes, we decided Lash would take me to the emergency room, and her husband would take the cat to the vet to be put out of her misery, which happily wasn't necessary because the cat recovered and continued on with her geriatric life. Lash pulled my truck into the arena; I hobbled to it and we shoveled my bashed-up body into the passenger seat. She drove me to Robinson Memorial Hospital's ER, where they x-rayed everything between my neck and knees, plus my head, declared me extensively contused but otherwise un-fractured, and sent me home with a handful of pain-killers, muscle-relaxants, and admonitions not to ride again until I had recovered.

Recovered? Recovered what? My physical health? Or the sense not to climb onto the back of a half-ton horse in the first place? Within a week, I had swung my leg over the same horse that sent me helicoptering to the ground a few days earlier. The ride was short, heart-pounding, and entirely uneventful, but I flinched and cringed with any sudden movement and my anxiety level plumed into the thinner atmospheric layers. Yet, I knew I had to do this, get back on, and sooner rather than later, because the longer later took, the harder it would be to fend off the fear, the easier to procrastinate, until that fear had rallied an army of excuses—gravity, age, time, aches, pains, work, cats to feed, must-see TV—to permanently detour my route back into the saddle.

While it's true the forces of gravity, the hardness of the ground, and my fear of falling all seem to have increased as I've gotten older, it's not as if that gut-twist trepidation were new to me or to Lash. We were never *eager* to fall off when we were younger, but it seemed we did it more often then, and it was so much easier to rebound in those days. Not to say we didn't get hurt, because we did, but not seriously, and I don't remember feeling the fear of falling as acutely back then. Or maybe just youth's exuberance trammeled the fear, swaddled it in ignorance, and harnessed it. Or maybe we just had greater strength and agility and reflexes and so remained top-side when otherwise we'd have been earth-bound. Perhaps gravity was kinder and less disciplined, or children just bounce better. When we were younger, we possessed not only greater resiliency after falling, but a capacity for spring-loaded remounting too. Usually.

I have never been a limber person. Strong, yes, but not flexible. I've never been able to touch my toes without bending my knees. The last time I seriously attempted a cartwheel was probably in junior-high and looked more like a drunken frog impression than a cartwheel. I stopped even trying to sober up my inner-amphibian because my classmates' lithe cartwheel demonstrations only highlighted my ineptitude. I could stand on my head for longer than anyone else in my class, but that was a matter of balance, not flexibility, and who cared, anyway? I could beat them all in a 100-yard dash. But I was not bendable. I could not master even a single pseudo-cartwheel.

Lash, by contrast, could cartwheel across the playground, bend over backward to make a bridge of her body, or fold herself in half, pressing her forehead against her knees. She could out-thumb-wrestle any challenger because she simply contorted her bendy thumb back out of reach, then snapped it back in for the thumb-pin and win.

Her flexibility and elasticity extended to practical applications as well, like scaling furniture and door frames to reach lofts or attics—or mounting horses without the benefit of saddle and stirrups or even a mounting block. At twelve or thirteen, she'd perfected the "Indian-style" mount, and could stand next to any horse in a field, swing her leg and leap so that in one fluid movement she was astride bareback, sitting upright, her long, long legs dangling on either side of the horse. I, meanwhile, would be searching out a ditch or gully in which to park the horse, or more likely something on which I could stand, maybe an over-turned bucket, a mounting block, a log, a stump, fence railing, truck tailgate, even an anthill or very steep slope. Anything that decreased the height between the horse's back and whatever platform I'd found. From my perch, I coiled up, launched myself, and belly-flopped broadside across the horse's back, then shimmied and squirmed my way to an upright, astride sitting position. If I didn't have enough propulsion in my first lunge at the horse—enough at least to hook my elbows into an equine spine to anchor myself—then no amount of grunting or wriggling saved my effort from gravity and I'd slither down the horse's side and to the ground.

The effort was physically energy-expensive, not to mention more often demoralizing than not. Moreover, most horses didn't appreciate my elbowing or writhing and were disinclined to placidly stand still for additional attempts. Lash either rode off, or impatiently milled in circles while I tried to ferret out a bigger, better mounting block.

I wanted to be able to mount Indian-style like Lash. I wanted to master the leaping mount for practical reasons, but I would be lying if I said pride and the competitive spirit were not factors. Compared to Lash's flying mount, my body-slamming leap-and-squirm approach seemed only slightly more effective—and measurably less attractive—than my cartwheel attempts.

Lash tried to teach me. In fact, she made a concerted effort. She illustrated every move she made, where she put her feet and hands, how she stood, how she moved, how she bent her joints just so to generate the coiled-spring thrust required to move from a standing position to swinging astride a horse with one leap. There was no reason I should not have been able to do this. I was certainly strong enough. I was a good deal stronger than most women, a fact of secret pride. I was at least as strong as Lash, although at six-foot-one, even as an adolescent, she had a six-inch height advantage, which also shouldn't have mattered, but I was willing to milk excuses.

Practicing on Gaudior, the broadest and tallest horse at our disposal, was also probably not the wisest approach. Even Lash sometimes seemed to have a hitch, just the slightest pause and indication of stretch or effort, when she swung onto Gaudior's back. The chestnut gelding's kind, forgiving, and stoic temperament may have figured into our decision to use him as my practice mount, but I don't think that was all. Gaudior was Lash's first truly "big enough" horse—a horse with the height and body to fill out her thirty-six inch inseam legs. She was proud of him, proud to have the biggest horse, proud of how well they fit, pleased with her ability to ride him well, a pleasure that certainly included her ability to also mount him in a single leap without the aid of a mounting block or even a saddle or bridle. I would have been proud too.

Lash demonstrated step-by-slow-motion-step her technique. Stand on the horse's left side, she explained, next to his shoulder and facing his hind end.

"Put your left hand on his withers," she said, turning her head to look back at me as she reached up by her ear and grasped the top of Gaudior's shoulder, latching onto the arched ridge where his neck met his back. His chestnut mane must have prickled between her fingers. "That'll help you pull yourself up."

I watched intently. I nodded.

"Bend your left knee and bring your right leg back," she said, and stretched her right leg far behind her; she looked as if she were in a fencing tournament, not about to mount a horse. "Then, you're going to swing your right leg forward and up, jumping at the same time with your left leg, and pulling yourself up with your hand on the withers." She slow-motioned each movement, including lifting her right leg nearly over her head and simultaneously hopping on her left leg to show the sequence of movement, the swing and thrust that lifted her in an airy arc like a ballerina. She was still watching me, squinting in the summer sunshine, her brown eyes serious and intent in her pale face. "See? See what you need to do? Hand here, leg back, step, kick off, swing over, pull yourself up."

I nodded. I did see.

"OK, good. Now watch," she said, and demonstrated real-time. I watched. I scrutinized. Scrutinized the hand, the step back, the swing, the jump, the leg reaching through the air, clearing the horse's back when Lash's body was parallel to the ground, the pulling-up-with-the-hand-on-the-withers, the right leg disappearing over the other side of the horse, Lash leaning along the chestnut spine, then pushing herself upright. I watched and nodded. Gaudior stood relaxed and at ease under Lash, sitting in the middle of his back. She looked down at me and nodded back. "OK, you ready?"

I was. The sun heated my back, and the tang of mown grass and warm horse seemed to carry the essence of possibility. Lash jumped down and stood at Gaudior's head, holding his halter, and began talking me through the process. I stood next to the chestnut's shoulder, my back to Lash, and reached up with my left hand to grasp Gaudior's withers; I tried to grasp a scant handful of mane poking through my fingers. My elbow was nearly straight. I bent my left knee and swung my right leg as far back behind me as I could. Gaudior's shadow loomed around and above me, blocked the light and my field of vision so all I saw was his brown flank; a couple flies trolled around his belly, and he swished his tail and idly kicked a hind foot at them. I didn't get as much bend in my knee as I really wanted, because when I bent it I couldn't reach Gaudior's withers anymore and his mane slipped from my fingers. Behind me, Lash's voice coached, encouraging and enthusiastic.

I coiled my muscles, compressed them like a spring, focused on channeling my physical strength, and swung my right leg forward and up. I unleashed the spring in my bent left leg and launched into the air. I kept my hand anchored on Gaudior's withers. I had never moved with such thrust and power. It felt seamless, weightless. My right leg kept swinging up, arcing aloft; I stared into the gelding's chestnut side and felt my body following my leg, all of me moving up and skyward, and for a breathless instant I was flying, nothing in the world but this horse and me floating through the air.

My leg's arc topped out not in a graceful curve over Gaudior's back but about midway up his side, so I body-slammed into his chestnut flank, planted my face in his ribs, and flopped to the ground. Not enough thrust. Or power. Or leap. Or height. Gaudior sidled away, surprised at having been kneed in the flank for no reason. Still holding the halter on his head, Lash dissolved into an apoplexy, laughter peeling from her in shrieks. I stood up, laughing too, and brushed off the dirt.

When we had regrouped, we tried again. And again. Sweat poured down my face in runnels; grit and horse hair stuck to my dry tongue. Finally, Lash held Gaudior at the base of a steep incline to counter the handicap of his height, and when I still couldn't swing aboard Indian-style, we resorted to my tried (and sometimes true) broadside belly-flop technique. I ran down the slope full speed, my feet pounding the hard-packed earth. I launched into the air like Wonder Woman, arms outstretched, missile-guided, committed, reaching for the elusive chestnut back. My arms actually crossed the horse's back, but my elbows found no spine to lock onto; my fingers clawed at hide and hair while gravity sucked me writhing down Gaudior's shrinking side, and I slid off like Wile E. Coyote down a cliff face. Gaudior twisted his body away from me, his tolerance and generosity tapped out, and we decided in the horse's best interest to call it a day.

I don't remember ever accomplishing an Indian-style mount on another horse, although I believe I succeeded at least once or twice, but I never tried to mount Gaudior again without full tack and even a mounting block to reach the stirrup swinging on a level with my nose. I believed Lash genuinely wanted me to master the Indian-style mount; I also suspected she felt some degree of private satisfaction that I never achieved it on Gaudior, that she alone was capable of that feat.

For me—for most riders—mounting a saddled horse is a simple process, rote muscle memory taking much of the thought out of the process. My failures at Indian-style and otherwise bareback mounting notwithstanding, I was pretty adept at getting aboard, even on a moving, skittish horse. If I could get toe in stirrup, I could move with the animal and routinely climbed atop moving targets. I was more tolerant when I was younger. As I got older, I began insisting on the horse's immobility when I mounted, a status achieved through reward and also aids like mounting blocks to reduce the heavy pull against the horse's spine and eliminate toe-poking into equine ribs while swinging aboard. Now that I think about it, by the time we were in our twenties and thirties, Lash had foregone Indian-style for full-tack, mounting-block assisted mounting, as well.

And when we got on horses, we didn't intend to come off until we intentionally dismounted at the end of the ride. Or intentionally jumped off our mounts' backs while those horses were still moving. Which we did, with legitimate reason: to practice the "flying dismount." As members in our local Pony Club and 4-H groups, we were told to master the flying dismount so as to safely remove ourselves from out-of-control steeds charging headlong for the nearest freeway or other imminent catastrophe. In theory, the flying dismount wasn't all that different from the standard, stationary dismount. You kicked your feet out of the stirrups, placed your hands on the horse's neck and withers, leaned forward over your horse's neck, swung your right leg behind you and over the horse's rump, then used your hands to balance, and landed gracefully on your feet. Practice this, our instructors mandated, at the walk, trot, and canter. Master it so if you ever need to use it in an emergency situation, the skill is engrained and you will not even need to think about it—you'll just do it.

And as pre-teens and maybe even as teenagers we did practice, which often resulted in more than just our feet landing in the dirt, and we'd get up laughing, brushing the dirt off our butts, to climb back on and throw ourselves off again. Our departures from horseback then were intentional and intrepid, courage fueled by the knowledge we could always choose *not* to leap off, *not* to practice.

I do not think boredom or having perfected technique had anything to do with the fact that the older we got the less we practiced flying dismounts until eventually we stopped practicing altogether.

I performed a bona fide *emergency* flying dismount only once, and it ended badly. A junior high school friend and I were taking turns riding her pony Dino—bareback, helmetless, and using only a halter and lead-rope—up and down her driveway, down by the road where the driveway was broad and smooth, before it passed the house and devolved from driveway into more of a mountain-goat path clinging like a ribbon to the side of a cliff-like hill. The pony's barn squatted in the woods, out of sight at the far end of the path.

As I sat on Dino's back, trotting up the driveway, the family's Great Dane loped across the yard, swung in next to Dino, and the race was on. The pony bolted barn-ward with the dog galumphing alongside, her flapping, spittle spritzing lips right at my eye level. It looked as if she were smiling.

I was *not* smiling; my tugs on Dino's lead shank didn't affect the pony's mad dash in the slightest. As we clattered across the concrete apron by the garage, I knew pony and dog weren't stopping until they reached the barn on the other side of the trail threading the near vertical cliff, which surely wasn't wide enough to accommodate a pony and a Great Dane abreast. They may as well have been heading for the nearest freeway. Almost as a reflex, I performed a flying dismount; I felt my feet touch the ground, then my momentum sent me flying again before my head smacked the cement and I ground to a halt. The dog and pony show continued full tilt to the barn without me. I lay on my back on the ground for a long time, my eyes clamped closed and my hands clamped on the back of my throbbing head, cradling a burgeoning goose egg.

Our Pony Club and 4-H instructors were right; if you practiced the flying dismount before you needed to do one, you just performed one instinctively. I didn't remember thinking about doing a flying dismount; I didn't remember going through the motions, grasping the pony's withers and neck, leaning forward, swinging my right leg over his churning rump, using my hands on his neck to balance and to land gracefully on my feet. All I remembered was the snap decision to bail, and then my feet made first contact with the ground for an instant before my head made second contact. I wasn't wearing a helmet, thereby breaking a cardinal rule along with my head, and I was admonished for breaking both. I would not ride again, my parents informed me, without donning a helmet, and they—or others they recruited—would be watching. I didn't plan on forgetting a brain bucket again, but I was ready and wanted to start riding again before my concussed head was. It was a solid six weeks before the swelling decreased enough that I could shoehorn my dome into headgear again.

It may be all fun and well and good for resilient youngsters to fling themselves from the backs of their trotting or cantering or even galloping horses, but at some point in life, one stops actually *helping* gravity bring one to the ground. That point came for me earlier than for most, with that wicked crack of my skull against cement. What person in her right mind would intentionally and *for fun* throw herself from the relative safety of her horse's back and give herself to gravity? Not I. Not at a canter, or a trot, or even a walk. After a half century considering life from the back of a horse, I learned to appreciate pain, the potential for injury, what activities are likely to increase that potential, and to avoid them whenever possible, which perhaps makes me a boringly sensible person.

Or a hypocrite. Because even though I feared falling off, still I put myself ten or twelve feet above the ground, relying on my ability to stay aboard a half ton of reactive, reflexive prey animal. And between the horse's back and the hard ground was all that insistent gravity, just waiting to capitalize on my slightest loss of balance, to team up with inertia and coax me farther from the security of saddle or mane or reins, until my body slammed into the dirt like a football in the end-zone. Every time I mounted a horse, that fall to the ground was on my mind; the older I got, the more it stayed front and center in my grey-matter.

I knew Lash had the same anxious under-current, and if she endured years of frustration at being unable to find or ride horses big-bodied and tall enough to fit her, at least we could laugh that in some ways, smaller horses had advantages—they were closer to the ground so one had not so far to fall. We were both well aware, however, that small horses could harbor big bucks. A small horse could fling you into the air higher than the back of most any big horse, and it hurts just as much hitting the ground from that height regardless of whether you came off a small horse or a big horse. And because Lash ended up with mostly too-small-for-her horses, that's what she mostly fell off of. Over the years, she sobered to the understanding that little horses concealed big falls (Dino had already taught me that years earlier), and any complacency left over from youth shriveled and withered over time.

Impetuous, indestructible youngsters did things with horses that make adults recoil, that impelled us to admonish childish foolishness or spy with distain and maybe a touch of envy on their silliness and ignorance. They did amazingly harebrained things like riding bareback with only lead-ropes (or not even halters on the horses at all), or not wearing helmets, or sitting backward, or riding double, or standing on their horses' hindquarters, and they probably didn't give the constant threat of falling much more than a cursory second thought.

But *I* do. I think of it all the time, from the moment I climb onto the mounting block, swing my leg over my horse, and settle into the saddle. Falling is always just gravity and a little opportunity away. So, I tighten the girth, secure my feet in the stirrups, adjust my helmet. I lean forward and pat my horse's neck. I look at the ground, and think *not today*. I take a deep breath. And I ride.

chapter three

Rhetorical Questions

Most little girls love horses. Lash and I were no exceptions. Neither of us traded in the love for horses for boys or clothes or any of the other typical adolescent girlie preoccupations. We both continued with our horse endeavors right along with boys and sports and whatnot. Although, to be completely honest, neither of us managed the boy part nearly as effectively as we would have liked. I was shy and naïve. Lash was taller than most boys by the time she was in middle school, and neither of us was waif-like.

Neither Lash nor I were ever poor; we both grew up in solid middle-class families, daughters of PhDs, successful professionals. But by falling in love with horses very early in our childhoods, we grew up with an expensive passion. When we were in school, our parents helped finance our expensive horse habit as much as their professorial paychecks permitted. I dreamed of farm life; for some of her youth, Lash actually lived on a small farm with a few acres and limited room for an animal or two. When a lightning strike and fire severely damaged their old farmhouse, Lash and her parents moved into an apartment complex in town. My family lived smack in the middle of the quaint little village of Hiram, where my parents both worked for Hiram College. I considered Hiram my home as much as anywhere, but there was no room within those village limits for anything more than a cat, a dog, and my pipedreams.

All this mandated farming out, literally, the housing and care of any horses that might trot into my life. And even in the relatively inexpensive rural hills of Northeast Ohio, horse-keeping came at a cost. I was fortunate that I was able to barter the cost of a horse's board for mucking stalls—"manure management," I called it—from junior high all the way through college. If my parents weren't able to chauffer me around, or at least make the family car available once I had my license, I found creative ways to find my way to the farm and my *job* and the horses. I begged or hitched rides, hiked or biked, and became pretty adept at ensuring I ended up where I wanted to be.

After college, both Lash and I entered the work-a-day life with jobs, and rent, and utilities, and car payments, and student loans, and all the other accoutrements the adult world offers. And while neither of us was poised to set corporate America ablaze, we did each find a series of roles that revolved around our interests and aptitudes. I was an English major (after trying on and foregoing both art and psychology), so although I did work professionally as a paramedic for a while, most of the positions I landed involved some communications aspect, and ranged from medical, legal, and technical writing to teaching, training, and education.

Lash's interest in psychology led her to an advanced degree in counseling, and she used that insight along with her perception, candor, and keen intellect in a number of roles that frankly, I never really understood, even though she tried to explain them to me. Things like project manager. Eventually, we both worked at Penske Logistics where Lash blossomed into roles increasing beyond my comprehension—things to do with IT and quality and transportation logistics. I worked as a technical writer and documentation specialist.

While we certainly weren't rich, we also certainly weren't poor. Regardless, I never seemed to take the prudent route and live below my means. For that matter, I rarely even lived within my means. I look back now and regret my fiscal irresponsibility, but when I try to imagine how I might have done it otherwise, I can't seem to come up with any more tenable approach.

So, there we were with our expensive horse habits and other impediments to making all our dreams come true.

And taller horses—ones with enough height and girth to really fit Lash's long legs—were often even more expensive. The price of a *good* horse could be enough to send a child to a private college for four years, or buy a house, for example. A horse being *big* might bump that price up even more.

Lash's height and long inseam factored significantly into how she fit with horses and how she fit with men. Lash was attracted to tall men; so when she was in high school and told me about a new crush she had on one Anton Habsburg, who was a year older and *five* full inches taller, I at first assumed she was blinded simply by the sun. It was in her eyes because she had to look up to see his face. When she also informed me he was quasi-royalty, being a Habsburg of the Austrian Habsburgs, I believed she was not just smitten with his height but also his lineage. I'd never met him and immediately disliked him.

My prejudice was bolstered by the fact that Lash had met him through a church function, which he attended as part of his drug rehabilitation program at a monastery in Hiram. Or something to that effect; I don't remember the exact details. I remained dry-eyed when Lash wept and told me Anton had left for California, telling her he was too messed up for her. Whatever his true reasons for leaving, and whatever frivolous basis upon which I thought Lash thrust her love, Anton always remained her true first love, "the one that got away."

Some years later, Anton showed up on Lash's doorstep. Literally—she called to say, "Guess who showed up on my doorstep?" Anton had moved back from California, boarded a twitter-pated love train with Lash, and I revised my opinion of him, but not until after he saved an abandoned kitten from a dumpster. Lash tried to sway me, extolling his now very sober virtues, but I was skeptical and perhaps reticent to share my best friend. I remained dubious. After all, Lash wasn't exactly impartial. But when a kitten in distress impels a man to climb into a trash bin behind Giant Eagle to rescue said kitten, I consider that man's virtues to be self-evident. He took the sick and starving feline, matted yellow fur draped over frail bones, to the vet, and then brought him home. Fieval survived and, in fact, outlived Lash by years.

If I was jealous of Lash and Anton's relationship, it was not only that I didn't want to share Lash, but also that their match cast my own paucity of relationships in bass relief. Aside from a brief, intense relationship with Arnold in college, I was alone. I blamed my manlessness on obesity, although my weight had never been an issue for Arnold. He had always been everything I ever said I wanted in a man: talk, dark, handsome, plus intelligent, kind, and at six feet, he was heavier than I was and tall enough that he probably always would be. And he was interested in my horses, even if he didn't get personally involved. When I bred my mare, he wanted to understand what was happening, what we were doing and why. When the mare was confirmed in-foal, he celebrated with me, happy for my excitement.

In addition to being everything I said I wanted in a man, Arnold was also intense, sometimes brooding, and an alcoholic—a combination that frightened me and made me question my commitment to our relationship, even though I knew I loved him. Coming into our senior year in college, we amicably agreed to "just be friends" for a while, and revisit the boyfriend-girlfriend status later. And we did remain friends, although every time Arnold suggested we give our relationship another try, I felt panicky and always said I wasn't ready. I didn't know how long I thought it would take me to be ready, but some arrogant part of me assumed Arnold would always be there, waiting, for whenever that time came.

So I was stunned when he called me one afternoon, a couple years after we'd graduated college, and told me he'd gotten married. Moreover, he told me his wife was "terrified" of me, and I probably shouldn't send him letters, or even birthday or Christmas cards, anymore. I sat in a chair in my parents' dining room and told Arnold he could assure his new wife I was no threat, that married men were off my list. As if I *had* a list, as if I were in any position to pick and choose. I told him I was happy for him, and really I was, and that his wife was a very lucky woman. I remember saying this and feeling very disconnected, as if the words were coming from someone else, someone some distance away from me.

When we hung up the phone, I sat in the chair for a while and stared out the window. I didn't wail or sob or sink into a profound depression. I just felt deflated. I admitted to Lash my shame at having assumed Arnold would always be available to me. I hadn't even been particularly bothered when he'd told me he was dating; if anything, in my arrogance, I was relieved I hadn't crushed him. Now I was ashamed of my conceit, and the seeming impossibility of any other man being interested in me, of seeing more than my obesity, left me burning with humiliation. I had lost Arnold, and even Lash's support and understanding couldn't change reality.

As I'd promised, I ceased all contact with Arnold, but over the years I read news about him and about his wife in Hiram's alumni magazine. We'd all graduated in the same class, so we had a common connection to the college. And sometimes, my mother would tell me she'd seen Arnold when he'd been on campus for some kind of alumni event; she said he always asked after me and asked her to say "hi" to me. After several years though, Arnold stopped coming to campus, or at least didn't see my mother, and I didn't hear or know any news of him.

For a long time, Lash urged me to seek Arnold out again, to look him up, reinitiate contact. "That relationship reminds me of me and Anton," she had said once. I always refused, reminding her Arnold had married someone else. For years, that was excuse enough, even when something—I don't recall what—hinted he could be single again. It wasn't until I was in my mid-thirties, living alone on my farm and nearly a hundred pounds overweight, that I took the risk, tracking him down through our college's alumni relations department. I sent him a Christmas card, innocent enough if he were still married, yet still nudging ajar a door it had taken me a decade to crack open.

That nudge was all it took for Arnold to respond to my first contact, confirm his single status, and for us to revisit our old relationship, rekindling the flames I thought had long died. He and I got back together only a few months before Lash found a lump in her breast. Sometimes, I think the timing must have been more than fortuitous. "You'd better make me your matron of honor when you get married," Lash said, and I would have if she'd lived long enough. As it was, we had her picture on the altar and a vase of periwinkle irises; we put the flowers on her grave after our wedding ceremony over a year and a half after she died.

In 2000 when I lost two of my four foals to broken legs, I struggled to find what good could have come of such tragedy; I believed something positive must come from tragedy, even if I couldn't see what that was. Lash and I talked about this once, and to prove the point, pondered the question: What good came of her birth mother Paula's death, and what good could possibly result from a young woman dying of cancer, leaving a husband and small child? The simple, selfish answer: Lash and I. If Paula had not gotten ill, had not died, Bill would not have married Janeen and come permanently to Ohio. Lash and I would never have met. So from a purely self-regarding standpoint, Paula's death enabled the gift of my life with Lash.

And a primary question that kept percolating to the top of my mind when I thought of that silver-lining philosophy: What good had come of Lash's death? I don't have an answer for that one.

I didn't try to write about Lash for years, though Janeen encouraged me to do so even before Lash died. Janeen, and many others. But it took years, not because I didn't want to write about Lash. I wasn't sure I knew *how* to. Or that I even could. Or should. Because how could I tell *her* story without turning it into *my* story? And both our stories, collectively and individually, were always in the constant, sentient, and immortal company of horses.

chapter four

Buying The Farm

PART A

O ne early spring evening I was with my mother when we stopped at the home of family friends and work colleagues of my parents. I was probably eleven or twelve and my world revolved around horses; the fact that the Andersons lived on a small farm with a couple horses made them likeable by default, regardless of any preexisting connections.

While my mother went to the house, I made a beeline to the barn to visit the horses. I rested my chin on top of the stall wall and looked in at Princess, a liver-chestnut Morgan mare who was eleven months pregnant and due to foal any day. I was familiar with Princess and it didn't take me too long to realize something was different about her this day. She seemed restless and milled around her stall, muzzle to the straw as if searching for something. Sweat dampened her neck and shoulders and a gossamer veil of steam followed her as she moved. Though the evening was cool, the air in Princess's stall grew warm and damp with the smell of a hot horse.

I watched breathless, never having witnessed a mare foaling before. Keen for the chance, I waited and watched Princess for an eternity (at least a minute or two) until I was convinced this was *it* before I bolted to the house, wide-eyed and just this side of frantic, to alert the adults who all stood chatting in the kitchen. I didn't wait for their response, turned and leapt off the porch, and was halfway back to the barn before I heard the kitchen screen door slam shut behind me. I was back on foal-watch by Princess's stall eons before my mother and the Anderson family ambled out of the kitchen, crossed the yard, and entered the darkening barn. Princess lay down, and without any drama, other than what I had brought myself, delivered a big, healthy, liver-chestnut colt the Andersons named Pegasus.

I did not want to ever leave that stall or that barn or that experience, and when my mother finally towed me out into the night to drive home with her, the road ahead of us—well, ahead of me at least—had a new bending curve into it, a long serpentine of twists and arcs, into a new land of mares and stallions and breeding and foals and unexpected outcomes.

I guess after that high of my first foaling experience, I was a one-hit addict, even if I didn't know it then. Not that I would have done a damn thing to change it if I had known. I mean, why would I? I had always known I wanted my own farm someday, and you had to start somewhere to build a dream like that. Having a *drug of choice* at least gave the dream some early direction. Which in its infancy aimed at loving and breeding Morgans and/or thoroughbreds or crosses of those breeds; I liked those breeds probably because they were primarily the breeds populating the facilities where I took riding lessons and began to hone my addiction.

Over the years, I refined my focus toward sports horses bred for dressage and jumping sports, but I always kept that early affection for thoroughbreds, which could positively influence conformational refinement, add some drive to the engine, and add quality—the latter being very much determined by whomever is defining such characteristics.

Suffice to say, the influence of the first thoroughbred stallion I really knew, and that I invested in financially and otherwise, was a prominent figure in my evolving definition of *quality;* Sindarin was the maternal sire of Cassie and Silver, who were the dams of Cappuccino and Indigo, respectively, the two first Swedish Warmblood horses I bred, both of them being sired by Johanniter. Whether through dumb luck or calculated consideration or some happy composite of both, for me, it resulted in a combination of bloodlines that enabled me to truly build up my dream over the years.

For a few years in the mid-1990s, I leased an old farm in Garrettsville, Ohio; it was only four miles from my apartment in Hiram, and I could manage the place and my horses the way I wanted. Lash eventually brought her horses there, and Nettie, who we'd grown up with in the horse world, kept her mare there too. It was a good situation I could take advantage of indefinitely, until I was able to buy or build my own place, a life-long pipedream I didn't really believe I'd ever have the money to truly realize. But for years, Lash shared the same fantasy, and she was not as inclined as I to accept the status quo. We both wanted land and farms, but where I whined about not having or being able to realize my dream, Lash went out and investigated, contemplated, and worked to make dreams a reality.

One early spring Saturday at the barn, Lash mentioned, almost conversationally, that she and Anton were going to spend the afternoon perusing local real-estate availability.

"Where are you going?"

"All around. Geauga County mostly, I think. We're just going to drive around and look at for-sale signs. You should come with us." Lash stood looking down at me; there was a teasing lilt in the way she spoke, in the pointed way she looked at me, like she knew I'd refuse and was challenging me to loosen up, to join them as they took to the hills and woods and valleys of Northeast Ohio, where we'd all grown up. We knew the four seasons here, and perhaps a fifth—lake effect—the weather phenomenon born of the Great Lakes. We lived in the snow belt, and Geauga County could pick up a foot of lake-effect snow while Portage County, just to its south, basked under sunny skies. But winter weather woes aside, Northeast Ohio could be an extraordinarily beautiful part of the country. In the fall, with the trees blushing vibrant, with the rolling hills and steep valleys, you might think you were standing in upstate New York or New England instead of Chardon or Parkman.

"No," I said and looked away from her and down the barn aisle. "I'm going to hunt down some hay. We're almost out. You guys go ahead. Let me know when you find our farms. Then I'll fire up the printing press in the basement so we can crank out the fake money to buy 'em."

I recruited Nettie in my search for hay worth buying to feed our horses, and Lash and Anton cruised through Geauga County, looking at for-sale signs. Nettie and I succeeded in finding a good source, packed the bed of my truck full, and arranged to pick up the rest of our purchase the next day.

Later that evening, Lash called to tell me that she and Anton found the perfect land in southern Geauga County, in Parkman, twenty-some-odd acres, mostly wooded with fields and ravines with another twenty-some-odd acre lot right next to it that was perfect for me. I snickered into the phone. Told her I couldn't afford anything that was up to her standards—or my own standards, for that matter.

"Tell me about your land though," I said, partly to deflect her insistence that I could afford more than I thought I could. But she happily diverted onto the topic of *her* land and told me about it, breathless and animated. I pictured her in her kitchen in Mantua, pacing back and forth, the phone cord tethering her to the wall, arcing her arm through the air as she described the woods and the little stream and the ravine and the fields and the magnificent beech tree, so old and huge and regal that she and Anton, each bellied-up to opposite sides of the hoary trunk, could not touch each other's outstretched fingers.

I sat in the dark in my little efficiency apartment in Hiram and smiled.

That night, I dreamed of their farm. Lash and Anton walked, hands clasped between them and swinging like a hammock, gesturing beyond them with their free hands, and their enthusiasm was palpable, poured off them and rolled across the grass. I walked along behind them, pulled by their ebullience. Pale, dried grass lay at their feet, and wan sunlight filtered through tree branches still clinging to end-of-year leaves.

We came into a little wooded gully, anchored by a tractor path that led up an easy slope and out of the trees to a sunny field beyond. "Up in this field," Anton said, glancing at me over his shoulder then pointing with his chin toward the field, "is where we'll put the barn."

"The house will be up there," Lash said and waved her left arm in the other direction, her right hand still encased in Anton's huge mitt. Her voice was like porcelain tinkling along the ground; a chuckle rumbled from Anton, and he swung their joined hands in a swooping arc. They were like bookends, looking to either side, their dream nestled snug between them.

"It's beautiful," I said, and it was. They kept walking, arms swinging pendulum-like, and they looked so fluid, but I couldn't seem to make my legs move the way I wanted. So I stopped and watched them climbing the tractor path toward the field, and the woods drifted away from me. When I came fully awake to my dark room, and left the dream farm behind me in sleep, I could still smell the subtle tang of old wood and sun-dried grass.

"There's a mirror image parcel right next to it," Lash said, dark eyes sparkling, when I told her about the dream. "You need to come look at it."

"I told you, it's too expensive." We'd already had this conversation. So Lash told me about her land again.

Later that morning, Lash, Anton, Nettie, and I combined our efforts and vehicles and hauled several loads of hay that Nettie and I'd arranged for the day before while Lash and Anton were driving around Geauga County playing land baron. Although the hay was really for my horses and Nettie's one horse, Lash and Anton came along to help. Being involved in horses was more than simply riding together. Lash, Nettie, and I had known each other most of our lives, and we helped each other out with our horse-related grunt-work, even if said grunt-work had nothing to do with our own horses. In this case, Lash and

Anton were pitching in to help move a bunch of hay for my and Nettie's horses. Grateful, I'd promised to buy them lunch at Blazin' Bill's afterward.

A chilly drizzle was falling by the time we finished with the hay and were settled in the restaurant, gnawing on ribs, but the dismal weather didn't dampen Lash's mood, or keep her from suggesting that we go look at their dream land after we were done eating. "It's only about ten minutes from here," she said.

"It's raining," I said, stating the obvious.

"It'll stop," Lash replied.

Truthfully, I was cold and tired and really didn't feel like trekking around looking at this land they'd found—I was sure I'd either be underwhelmed or overwhelmed by it, and I didn't want to be either. I glanced hopefully at Nettie—maybe she had obligations she needed to get home for. Nettie knew Lash could be demanding, but she wouldn't hesitate to speak up if she had something else to do.

"I'm game," Nettie said.

I wilted. I whined. I sulked.

Anton laughed, a deep rumbling chortle. "You'll love it," he said.

"And there's an adjoining lot where you can put your farm," Lash said. She nodded vigorously.

I slapped my palm on the table, on the edge of annoyed. "I *know* there's an adjoining lot. You have such an easy time spending money I don't have," I said.

Lash pouted. Nettie focused intensely on her ribs and seemed to shrink.

"Well, at least you could come look at *our* land," Lash said.

Anton rumbled some more, leaned back in his chair, and reached out to Lash. "Yeah," he said and grinned as his fingers worked on the cords in his wife's neck. "After we nearly killed ourselves helping haul hay for *your* horses…"

"I bought you lunch!"

"So?"

"Fine. We'll go look at your land."

Lash perked up, and Nettie returned to normal size.

We left Blazin' Bill's, all four of us wedged into the cab of my truck. "You've got the four-wheel drive," Anton had reasoned, holding his hand out for the keys. "I get to drive." I gave him the keys.

We headed east on Rt. 422 into Parkman, then turned down Farmington Road. After a mile or so, we pulled off the dirt road and into the end of a tractor path at the edge of a field. Anton stopped. We clamored out of the cab.

"Our land starts up there," Lash said, looking up to a line of trees topping a steep hill. "But there's no access from the road up there yet, so we have to come in down here." I looked around me—young alfalfa curling up from the ground, the hay fields rolling up hill on either side of us. The dirt road dipped between the hills; across the road, a dairy farm, expansive barns and silos empty and unused, looked out over the fields where we stood. Somewhere beyond the hills, rhythmic clopping of hooves and rattle of wheels told of an Amish buggy on the road.

"Our land opens up back there," Anton said, tilting his head toward the woods at the back of the field.

Lash, Nettie, and I sat, legs swinging, on the tailgate of my truck as Anton drove down the tractor path. Farmington Road shrank behind us as Lash pointed to her right up the hill, chattered about the space and the trees and the fields and the community. I wrapped my fingers around the tailgate, steadying myself as the truck eased over the bumps and ruts of the tractor path. The air was cool and fresh, and I looked up at Lash, her pale cheeks flushed and the enthusiasm vibrating from her, and I smiled. It wasn't drizzling anymore, and by now, I was actually intrigued to see the land they'd found—the area was more beautiful than I'd expected—it seemed clear that I would be overwhelmed and not underwhelmed.

Anton stopped the truck, and the three of us hopped off the tailgate, the ground solid and sure underfoot. We walked around to the front of the truck and joined Anton. He'd parked on the tractor path, just at the edge of the woods where it dipped into a little ravine; a stream meandered in front of us. The tractor path crossed the stream, then curved its way up the far side of the wooded ravine and out into a bright field beyond.

The hair on the back of my neck prickled and stood on end; I sucked in a breath, tingling, and pointed up the tractor path. "That's my dream!"

Lash looked down at me, a slow smile spreading across her face. I looked back at her, bug-eyed. "That's my dream!" I was still pointing at the ravine. "That's what I dreamed last night, the dream I was telling you about." I stomped my foot for emphasis. "That ravine right there is what I dreamed. Anton was walking up the other side on the tractor path…" I exhaled, hard. Lash smiled even more, if that were possible. Nettie leaned forward a little bit, looked tentatively up the path, then back at me.

Anton started to laugh, grabbed Lash's hand, and led her down the path toward the ribbon of stream. I followed, and it felt like I was stepping over a threshold into my dream, or perhaps it was from my dream into reality.

We crossed the little creek, Nettie and I following Lash and Anton up the tractor path into the field beyond. I followed them through the woods, into the field, up and down the hills, and continued the tour we had started in my dream. I saw the fields, walked amid the trees, my arms outstretched, young sapling branches sweeping my hands. I met the magnificent beech tree, whose circumference was still greater than the reach of Lash and Anton's outstretched fingertips. I stood on the leafy ground while Lash paced out the perimeter of their house, and I stood, hands on my hips, assessing the drainage of the site for their barn.

When Lash said we might as well look at "my" adjoining land while we were here, I didn't resist. Lash and Anton led the way, and Nettie and I clambered up the slope after them. And already, Lash was planning where my house and barn would be, and how we would walk out our doors anytime we wanted, amble down to our barns, or swing up onto the broad back of a mare, grazing in her pasture, because she was there, and we felt like it and we could, just like when we were kids.

That evening, I went to visit my parents in Hiram. We sat in their living room, warming by their fire, and I told them about the day's events and that I'd found the land I wanted to buy.

It had been a couple decades in the making, but by the end of that month, with my parents' help, I was a property owner. And so were Lash and Anton. It was 1997; I was thirty-four years old that year; Lash and Anton were thirty-one and thirty-two, respectively. We were young and healthy and saw our futures unfolding right before us. We laughed about "buying the farm," delighted in the double entendre, at new life promised in those empty fields just now waking after winter and the woods just donning new spring garb.

The spring after we actually bought our adjoining parcels of land, my dream farm started growing up out of the timothy and alfalfa hay fields. While Lash and Anton would wait longer to save money and "stick build" their own dream house, I was impatient, I didn't want to wait. Which meant instead of a stick-built house, I purchased a modular home; it arrived in two pieces, on two tractor-trailers, a few weeks after I'd ordered it to my specifications: three bedrooms, two full baths, a wood-burning fireplace, central air, a washer and dryer, extra windows and sliding doors where I wanted them, drywall throughout its 1,500+ square feet—all items I wanted in a home, but which also gave this particular prefabricated structure more of a "real house" and less of a double-wide feel. While I couldn't afford the basement I'd hoped to have under my house, I did spring for multiple rebar tie-downs set three feet deep into the concrete slab foundation to ensure once it was installed on its foundation, my modular home wasn't budging. It was a comfortable, attractive, affordable, and very efficient house.

The barn actually cost more to build and took longer to take shape than did the house. As the beams and trusses and walls went up, the barn's sheer size stunned me, even though they built it to my specifications: fifty-two feet by thirty-six feet, a center aisle, with four twelve by twelve foot stalls, two twelve by sixteen foot foaling stalls, a tack room, a feed room, an attached run-in shed, and a hayloft over it all under the gambrel roof. Purchasing and installing the fencing I'd selected (a combination of white poly-vinyl and rubber-coated high-tensile wire) specifically because I was satisfied with its safety as well as its aesthetics itself cost half as much again as the house. One new vet visiting the farm laughed, commenting you could tell the true horse-people because they invested more time, money, and effort into designing housing for their horses than for themselves. I laughed with her, even though I wasn't quite sure I wasn't offended.

In the late summer, in one fell swoop, I moved out of my apartment in Hiram, packed up my four mares from the farm I leased in Garrettsville, and moved us all in one day to the new place in Parkman. So with the arrival of two-year-old Indy, her mother Silver, Roanoke, and Mysty—the only of the mares actually in-foal for the following spring—Donley Farm East became an operating horse-breeding farm. Some day, years down the road, I would stand a stallion here, too, when one of my mares produced that rare, outstanding quality colt.

Over the years, I had vacillated over the breeds of horses I wanted to produce. Modified my focus is maybe a better way to put it. Originally, because I learned to ride and took lessons on Morgan horses and thoroughbreds or crosses therein and because English was the style of riding on which I cut my teeth, those were the breeds and disciplines around which my early farm and breeding dreams revolved.

Some of those original ideas stayed with me, particularly dressage and/ or jumping horses, and sticking with the thoroughbreds as a large part of the gene pool in all my years of planning matches. Eventually, I settled on what, as a general category, is often referred to *sports horses*, typically meaning a breed, breeds, or crossbreds intended for dressage, show jumping, three-day eventing, and sometimes combined driving. Often sports horses are *warmbloods*, a definition that encompasses a slew of specific breeds, many originating long ago in Europe. These were more all-purpose horses, and landed somewhere in the middle of the spectrum occupied on one pole by the so-called *cold bloods*—the draft horses—and at the other pole the *hot bloods*—Arabians and thoroughbreds. The cold blood draft horses were heavily built for heavy work and had relatively unflappable, stoic temperaments, whereas the hot blood Arabians or thoroughbreds were much lighter-built, very athletic, often high-strung temperamentally, and often used in sports such as racing.

Not surprisingly, warmbloods fall somewhere between the two poles, but there's more to it than simply breeding a cold blood to a hot blood, although such crosses are not uncommon. But that would produce a single hybrid offspring, and a hybrid bred to a hybrid tends to produce unpredictable results; many generations often go into making a predictable type before that type becomes a breed or even a registry. Today, there are many, many official warmblood registries that reflect many years and generations of selective breeding to produce specific desired characteristics. And few of these are closed registries, meaning they're open to outside blood (even if selectively), which technically means they aren't really breeds, per-se. Not like thoroughbreds or Arabians, for example, that *are* breeds and only by breeding a purebred mare to a purebred stallion can one get a purebred registerable offspring.

I spent two summers while I was in school at Valhalla Farm in Florida, where the owner, Jean Brinkman, bred, showed, and sold warmblood sport horses, primarily Trakehners (a German breed, old enough and developed enough to actually *be* a breed as well as maintain a close registry) and Swedish Warmbloods, technically a registry open to select other breeds (such as thoroughbreds or Trakehners) or other warmblood registries. Jean had imported the Swedish warmblood stallion Johanniter ("Joho" for short) from Europe a year or two before the first summer I went to Valhalla, and I instantly fell in love with him.

For a long time, I had preferred the idea of a breed and a closed registry, which to my mind implied exclusivity and quality. But this left me with a problem if I wanted to breed warmblood sports horses using my thoroughbred mare. Which I did. But if I bred to one of Jean's Trakehner stallions, while I would probably get a nice baby, I could only register it as half-Trakehner, and if I wanted to build a breeding program and someday my own stallion, this would be a problem.

However, the Swedish warmblood registry would register foals out of thoroughbred mares if that foal was sired by an approved Swedish stallion. Johanniter was approved. And I had already seen and been impressed by the foals he had produced out of thoroughbred mares at Valhalla. That word *approved* helped address some of what I had considered drawbacks to an open registry. Open did not mean lack of selectivity. A stallion not only had to be of approved parentage, but had to be approved himself for his offspring to be registerable. The approval process is rigorous and requires not only high scores on specific conformation criteria, but also that the stallion-candidate demonstrates his athletic apptitude by proving himself competitive in both dressage and three-day eventing. This quality standard is consistent in the USA and Europe, and the same Swedish judges who comprise the inspection committee in Europe come to North America every other year to conduct inspection tours here, ensuring consistent evaluation and quality of Swedish warmblood horses internationally. During these inspection tours, mares of accepted non-Swedish breeds can also be inspected for scores and possible inclusion in the official studbook, a requirement for a mare's offspring to be considered a stallion candidate.

This satisfied the quality standard I had previously believed mandated a closed studbook. In fact, these inspections surpassed that in some ways, ensuring quality standards while recognizing the potential value outside blood could bring. For instance, thoroughbred blood could refine the conformation of a heavier, older style Swedish stallion, or contribute some extra drive of athleticism.

Which is why I liked my thoroughbreds. And why I bred two of my thoroughbred mares to Johanniter, giving me first Cappuccino, and a couple years later, my beloved Indigo. Really, what was not to like?

I'd only been on the farm a couple of months, not even long enough for the grass seed in the front to take over the sparse straw mulch and pretend to be a lawn, when an idle afternoon of browsing through horse magazines changed all my plans' timelines.

Nothing forewarned me that this day would usher in a monumental phase in my life: sex on the farm. Specifically, horse sex on the farm. And all because I saw an ad for Johanniter in a horse magazine. That stallion I'd first met at Valhalla Farm in Florida, where I learned his Swedish name was pronounced "Yohan-EEtah," or "Yoho" for short. That stallion I'd fallen in love with during my two summer internships at Valhalla during college. That stallion who had sired, via transported semen, the first two big horses I'd bred: first Cappuccino, then two years later Indigo—my beloved Indy, who was a smaller, compact, feminine version of her father. I was used to seeing ads for Joho in magazines—ads publicizing his significant competitive accomplishments, ads touting the quality of his offspring and the ease of breeding one's mares to him via shipped semen.

But I had never seen a for-sale ad for Joho.

"They're selling Joho!" I said, dismayed. I envisioned some European buying him and spiriting him away, maybe back to Germany, or Sweden where he'd been born, regardless beyond my reach. I'd never see him again.

Lash looked up, distracted from her game of throwing toys for Bristol. The dog crouched, focused, watching the toy in Lash's hand with her Border Collie intensity. Lash crawled across the floor to me, dog toy still in hand, Bristol herding it herky-jerky across the floor until Lash had grabbed the magazine from me.

She sat down, scrutinized the page for a moment.

"You should buy him," she said, without looking up.

"Yeah, right." I rolled my eyes. "I wish."

"I'm serious."

I laughed. "Lash, I don't have $15,000."

"Yes, you do," she said with a straight face, and she did look at me then, unflinching.

I gaped. "You are so full of shit. I'm so broke it's not even funny. And no, there's nothing left over from Chino." Maybe she assumed I still had some money from selling Cappuccino, but that had all gone toward building the barn, putting up the fencing, and buying the modular home in which we now sat.

"I know," she said with a dismissive wave of her hand. "That's not what I'm talking about."

I crossed my arms and glared at her, both intrigued and annoyed. "Well, what *are* you talking about? Because to the best of my knowledge I don't have a spare $15,000 sitting around."

"Yes, you do. Here," she pointed to the floor, then out the window to the fields. "In the farm. You have a lot more equity in the farm than you owe on it."

Bristol stood between us, tongue lolling, her Border Collie focus snapping back and forth between us as if she were at Wimbledon.

I blinked at Lash, stunned for a moment at the absurdity of what she'd just suggested. "Are you nuts?"

"I don't think it's that crazy," she said, a little sulkily. Nor should she think it crazy. She had gotten a car loan from the bank to buy her mare Tabriz years earlier, a move I thought was impulsive and bordering on fiscally irresponsible then; I didn't think much differently now.

Lash reached over and held the magazine against the window, so the stallion's picture stood out against my pastures. She pursed her lips, tilted her head.

"It's a business opportunity. You probably actually have quite a bit of equity in this place. I would think about it."

"Yeah, *you* would think about it," I said, and snatched the magazine back, looking down at the photo of Joho, that extraordinary stallion, the father of the two best horses I'd ever bred, and my stomach gave a little twist. "You're the queen of creative financing. I'm not that brave."

I was already having panic attacks over taking on a mortgage and jumping into doing this horse breeding thing for real; I'd only been on the farm for a few months. My fulltime technical writing job at Penske Logistics barely paid the bills. Technical writing would earn me a decent living—spell check for the most part rescuing me from my own errors—but it wouldn't get me rich. There was absolutely no wiggle room. At all. But with any luck, within a few years, breeding and selling Swedish Warmblood sport horses would start paying for itself, and the farm. I did have a pregnant horse in the barn, and Indy was booked to make her maiden foray into breeding to Amiral, a two-time Olympic and international champion Swedish stallion no less. Just a year before, I had sold Cappuccino for more than Johanniter, his father, was for sale now. I had always planned to have a stallion one day, but I had planned to raise him from the ground up. Actually *buying* an approved, established, successful stallion simply never entered the picture. It wasn't financially feasible.

Except now Lash had put the bug in my ear. From a completely pragmatic standpoint, it had its merits, even though it appeared nowhere in my original, carefully plotted and scripted business plan for Donley Farm East. Standing my own stallion would save me money because I could breed most of my own mares to him and wouldn't have to pay outside stud fees (or the vet bills associated with breeding via shipped semen). I could actually *earn* some money immediately by selling breedings to Johanniter. He was already well-established with a strong national reputation. He'd been born in Sweden, exported to Germany, and had made a bit of a name for himself in Europe before Jean, Valhalla Farm's owner, bought him and he came to the United States.

Plus, I adored him. I always had, since I had first led him in from pasture one morning at Valhalla Farm, had looked at his chiseled muzzle, at the huge black forelock cascading down his face, had looked into his deep brown eye, looking back at me. He was a lot of horse, but he was twenty-one years old. That's geriatric for a horse, and was also why his asking price was this side of complete and irrevocable insanity.

Within a couple of weeks, I'd talked to my folks, talked to the bank (which seemed to view purchasing an established breeding stallion a perfectly reasonable incentive to take out a second mortgage), and had sent Johanniter to the University of Florida veterinary school in Gainesville for a complete physical exam, including extensive fertility analysis. When that all came back very positive, the bank cheerfully extended me credit based on the equity I had in the farm.

I kept waiting for someone to talk me out of this harebrained scheme, but no one did. No one even tried. The din and hubbub, the excitement of the *possible*, soundly drowned out any little voices in my head begging for reason.

In January of 1999, barely six months after I moved myself and my horses to the farm, with Lash standing by my side, beaming, I led Johanniter off the van from Florida and into his new stall on Donley Farm East in Ohio.

True, I was obese and alone and afraid I'd never have another man in my life. But my personal chastity didn't extend to the farm. No, Donley Farm East was going to see a lot of sex. Horse sex, at least. *That* much I could orchestrate, even if I didn't seem able to orchestrate it for myself.

My farm.
My barn.
My stallion.
My gravid mares.
My foals on the way.
My dream come true.

chapter five

The Birds and the Bees
and Then Some

When Lash turned the corner toward adolescence, Janeen gave her a vibrator for her birthday. Lash pulled it out from under her bed one day when we were sitting in her bedroom, talking about what I don't remember, and held it up for display. The late afternoon light brightened her bedroom, illuminating Lash as she sat on the bed, holding this long cylindrical thing, balancing it in her palms.

"What is it?" I asked. I was three years older than Lash, but in some ways, so much younger, so much more naïve, than she.

"It's a vibrator."

"What's that?" I asked, and Lash told me.

She looked at the vibrator with the expression of a kid just given the keys to a four-by-four dually-quad cab with a heavy-duty towing package, a truck she knew she really wanted to drive but wasn't entirely sure how to put into gear. I asked if she'd ever used the vibrator and she said yes.

What surprised me was not that a psychologist who specialized in sex therapy would give her daughter a sex toy, or even that she gave it to her when Lash was so young, but that such a thing *existed*, that not only were there such things as orgasms ("sort of like a sneeze at the other end"), but they were there for the taking. Sex was nebulous and distant and mysterious. I knew it was there, oh yes, but I had no idea what it was, why it fascinated me, or what I would do if it found me. When I had imagined Janeen in her counseling sessions with her patients, I had seen images of them all giggling, leaning toward each other, talking in urgent whispers, faces flushed.

I was ten when I first got my period, and I wouldn't have known what god-awful thing had befallen me if I hadn't been educated about menarche six months earlier by my neighbor and classmate, Adrienne.

"I got my period," she said, more whispered, one spring afternoon. We were on the street in front of my house. In the yard, my younger brother was riding his bike, popping wheelies on the lawn.

"What's a period?" I asked, and Adrienne hushed me, patting the air with her hands.

"Shhhhh!" she said, and she stamped her foot.

I whispered then. "What's a period?"

On the lawn, Ted rode his bike in circles and took no notice of us.

Adrienne wedged her hands onto her hips. "You know," she said, stretching the last word into two syllables.

I shook my head. So she told me about periods and "maturing" and that when you got your period you could have babies.

I shook my head. "Well, forget it. I'm never gonna have any babies."

"Doesn't matter. You still get periods."

I was stunned, and felt like I had a few summers earlier when a garter snake bit me, and one of my older brother's friends told me I would turn yellow and die. My parents hadn't been home, so I had wandered the streets of Hiram crying, wondering if I could just *go* to Dr. Sprogis's office so he could do whatever doctors did to prevent kids who had been bitten by garter snakes from turning yellow and dying. Eventually, I went to the last house on the cul-de-sac, our veterinarian's home, where I learned I would live.

Now with this news about periods, I ran home and told my mother the disturbing story Adrienne had just used to terrify me. With her back to me, standing at the kitchen counter kneading bread, or maybe she was sitting, working on her dissertation, her focus on the production of gluten or supporting a hypothesis, my mother confirmed what lay ahead for me. She handed over a book with pictures, paper cut-outs of a smiling paper man and a smiling paper woman in a tidy paper bed—at the end of the book, a smiling pink paper baby.

It's not fair to say I led a "sheltered" childhood; blithe is perhaps a better description. Uninformed would also be apt, but not because my parents didn't *want* me to know; they just didn't talk to me about sex and *people*. Birds and bees, yes; people, not so much. I remember "the talk." I remember exactly where it happened: in the car at fifty-five miles-per-hour by Panorama Farm on the curve of Route 82, going from Hiram into Garrettsville.

"Your father and I would prefer you were a virgin when you get married.

But we won't hold it against you if you're not." My mother gripped the steering wheel, her eyes focused straight ahead on the road.

I don't remember my response, or even if I responded at all.

And I remember the time my father watched as the mare we owned was bred to a thoroughbred stallion. I was about thirteen. My mother and I were the horse people in the family; my father's involvement was almost exclusively by-proxy. So why he was there that particular day, I don't know.

Whatever the reason, he stood at the periphery of the activity and watched. Me, holding the mare. The stallion being led by his owner. A lot of horse screaming and nickering and status-checking. The stallion reared forward over my mare's back, thrusting and grunting for perhaps fifteen or twenty seconds before he relaxed, backed off the mare, and his owner led him back to the barn. I led the mare in the other direction, keeping her moving so none of the sperm would fall out, I'd been told.

My father said to my mother—not loud, but a cacophony to my ears— "Wow, that was fast."

I never walked in on my parents having sex, but at that moment I felt like I may as well have. Even now, decades later, I still recall how the grass was starting to worm its green way through sod, how the sunlight was still May, pallid, how I smelled a tang in the air of horse sweat and a new, subtle chlorine scent I suddenly knew was semen.

I walked away from the barn with the mare, and glanced over my shoulder, glanced at my parents standing side-by-side watching me walk away. I turned from them, suddenly acutely self-conscious, and continued walking with the mare, up the lane toward the open, yawning field, and I wondered how I could ever simply walk past my parents again, lit neon, as I now was with this knowledge. I looked into the face of the mare next to me, thought of the fluid coursing in her dark recesses, and I may have blushed. But she seemed unbothered and her brown eye blinked back at me, calm and unperturbed.

Other than during one brief fling in college and my relationship with Arnold, I'd spent most of my life wrapped not in a man's arms but in excess adipose tissue, and I waited until the moments I was thin to make myself approachable. Those times were few and far between, and the longer I was fat, the longer I waited for a diet that worked, to make myself touchable, the harder it became to believe I would ever be in a sexual relationship again, much less a long-term, serious relationship. By the time I bought the farm, I had been alone for over a decade.

I didn't want to have sex just for sex's sake, although that's basically what I'd done with my first boyfriend in college. If I just got virginity out of the way, I thought, sex would not seem so big, so powerful and frightening. Virginity was a liability, so I had sex with my boyfriend before I morphed back into obesity and lost my chance.

Years later, Lash and I would laugh at ourselves, and sometimes cry, about our sexual fiascos, assumptions, and what we did or did not like about sex.

"What I hate," she said, scrunching her nose, "is all that stuff running down my leg afterwards." We both cringed.

"I never had *that* problem," I confessed, then shrugged. "'Course, I was so tense my muscles were like a vise-grip or something."

Lash screwed up her face, before giving me a gentler look. "That probably wouldn't have happened with Arnold," she finally said.

"Probably not," I agreed. Arnold and I had not quite gotten to that juncture before I had panicked at the relationship and bolted. Literally. I dropped out of college in my senior year and moved to Delaware to work on a horse farm. After about ten days I regained my senses, moved back to Hiram, and re-enrolled. By then, I was gaining weight again, walling myself away, although any time I saw Arnold on campus or in class, he didn't seem to mind my weight. But I did, so I stayed alone, barricading myself in fat, sequestering myself away from any life with a man.

When I was growing up, I had always assumed I'd get married, have children, be settled in marriage and motherhood and career by the time I was thirty. It was what my mother had done, raising three children and earning her PhD. I didn't know about the PhD part, but marriage and motherhood. No one said *Karen, you have to do this.* I just always thought I would. Maybe *I* said *Karen, you have to do this.*

Thirty was my worst birthday and my best birthday. My worst because I wasn't married, had no prospects, no children, no lucrative or passion-driven career. I had failed to achieve any of these. It also snowed on my thirtieth birthday, the end of April, and that settled on my depression, God's confirmation of my life as a failure. I had failed in school. I had failed in relationships—all two of them. I had failed as a daughter—their only daughter—to marry, to let my parents give me away, even though I had not lived in their home in years. My older and younger brothers had married. My parents had grandchildren; I had a niece and a nephew. No one labeled me a failure, or asked when I would find a man or have children. Yet alone, at home in the dark with Chinese takeout, or sitting in my living room with Lash, eating our pints of Ben & Jerry's, I teased out my own labels: the fat one, the woman with no children because she has no man to father them. I'd wrangled through bouts of recurring major depression for years; year thirty rolled in with another depressive episode, and I wondered (not for the first or last time) if my burgeoning weight and loneliness caused my depression or if depression caused my burgeoning weight and loneliness, or if they just relished joining forces and ganging up on me.

Sometime during that spring and summer of my thirtieth year, though, something slowly changed in my mind. Maybe because I had stood face-to-face with my failure at all that I thought I was supposed to have accomplished, I began to see possibility. Not the possibility of what I *should* be but of who I was, and what I *could* be. My father had said once, when I was a child spouting off about needing to marry a rich man to have my horse farm, *Why do you need a rich man for that? Why don't you do it on your own?* He had been serious, but I never considered his suggestion viable. I blamed dyslexia or my gender or the forty or fifty or sixty extra pounds I carried for holding me back. But for the first time in my life, I took his words, literal or figurative, as serious. I felt enabled, the quickening of some small, embryonic tenacity. *Do what you want with your life.* And it was only in retrospect, years later, that I saw how my thirtieth birthday was also my best.

"There are worse things than being alone," I'd say to whoever cared to listen, or to justify being single, whether to myself or someone else. And the beauty was I believed it. I still believe it. I did not need a man or children to have a full life. Maybe, I was even better off single and barren, closer to achieving what I wanted without the yoke of resentment or duty or responsibility. I liked my space, was set in my ways. When Greg, my older brother, opined that I would be dissatisfied with one of his cyclist friends because said friend was a doctor and would often be away, I laughed and said that made him all the better a candidate.

Occasionally, I wondered about Arnold, wondered if he was happy, hoped he was. I hadn't known the woman he married when we all attended Hiram, but my roommate had and assured me she was a sweet and kind person. And I felt a touch of relief, as if I'd released him into hospitable territory; but there, too, was the sting of regret, subtle and bitter.

I've wondered at times if my self-imposed relationship exile was, for all I loathed it, a paradox without which I may not have found the time, energy, or commitment to build my dream farm. I often say I believe something good must come as a result of something bad; certainly to me, being obese and alone qualified as bad. So, unless I'm a hypocrite, I have to look at that obese-alone-bad-time and wonder if its particular *badness* created the space in my life to pursue my equine passion. For the years I was alone and obese, I kept my life full attaining my farm-building and horse-breeding dream.

Certainly, I may have accomplished and achieved all that with a man in my life. One might argue a man's utility (not to mention financial input) would have enhanced, not hampered, that dream's realization. That I find this argument unconvincing surprises me a bit, and enough to make me dubious.

I don't know if there's a correlation between the bad of lonely obesity and the good of achieving the dream. But I do know enough to wonder about it.

chapter six

Success is Counted Sweetest . . .

In 1998, Lash and I entered Indy and Steorling, then two-years-old, in the Mid-Ohio Dressage Association's Breed Show. If I was serious about breeding, I needed to put myself and the horses I bred out there. Lash wasn't as serious about breeding, but she did want to compete. This MODA show was a stepping stone into competition for us and our young horses. It was our first recognized show together, competing together with our fillies in the same class. And it would be our last (though neither of us knew it then), but not just because Lash died.

On the three-hour drive from Northeast Ohio to Columbus, we had plenty of time to daydream. Indy, my second serious endeavor into breeding Swedish Warmbloods, was small but truly lovely, I thought. Steorling sported regal bloodlines and was the result of Lash's long, tumultuous, and expensive mission to own a filly by the Trakehner stallion, Martini. Privately, I thought Steorling didn't display the quality of her bloodlines. But I never said as much to Lash, which sometimes felt like dishonesty by omission. But how do you tell someone you love that the baby she loves wasn't, well... quite so good?

When we arrived at the show grounds, we ensconced Indy and Steorling into their stalls. We gave them hay and water, made sure they were settled in. We examined the show program, and saw that over a dozen two-year-old fillies were entered in our class. They represented some of the best breeding in the country, from some of the most reputable and well-known farms within 500 miles of the show. Names I'd only ever seen printed in the pages of my horse magazines adorned the pages of the MODA show program.

Starstruck and a little intimidated, I wondered out loud if we had any business being here with our little home-bred fillies. Lash laughed, echoed my concern, and pointed out what we already knew: we were here to gain experience for ourselves and our fillies, and yes, by the way, we had business being here. Lash could look at the pedigrees listed for the other horses in the program and know that Steorling's breeding—Olympic contenders on both her sire and dam's sides—was every bit as stellar. Indy's was also, at least on her father's side; Johanniter, the son of a Swedish Olympic stallion, himself was an accomplished international competitor. On the other hand, Indy's dam was a thoroughbred mare of nondescript lineage and no competitive history. But as a yearling, Indy had scored well, Class 1 in fact at her Swedish inspection, so I was doing something right with my breeding.

The showground buzzed with activity as other competitors and horses arrived. I was relieved to find Indy unperturbed by the commotion. Meanwhile, I ogled some of the most extraordinary horseflesh I'd seen gathered in one place and felt out of my league.

The next day, when Lash and I took our respective turns showing Steorling and Indy to the judge, our moments in the arena were simply waves in a tide of exceptional horses, washing into and out of the arena. And I wasn't even listening when the announcer reported the placings in our class, but Lash's ears caught some of it, and she socked me in the arm, saying *They said Indy's name*! We made our way across the grounds to the bulletin board where the scores for all the classes were posted, trying to appear nonchalant but barely able to affect a casual amble.

We wormed our way through the others scanning the scores, and found the sheet for our class. Lash saw it first, and with a yelp and a hop, jammed her finger against the sheet, tacking the paper to the bulletin board, fingernail imprinting Indy's name. Right at the top of the long list of horses. Over a dozen extraordinary two-year-old fillies, and Indy had placed second. I saw her name posted there, in the second position, and gaped, amazed and thrilled. Lash grabbed my arms and shook me for an instant before swallowing me in a bear hug, laughing and squealing. My little filly was at the top of the class, second only to one. It was a tangible confirmation that my breeding was measuring up to some of the best horses in the country. I felt validation. I was here for real.

Lash pivoted back to the board, bending for a closer look, searching for Steorling's placing in the class, her finger sliding down the list of names, and I was still hand-over-mouth, hopping in place and looking around me when I realized Lash had grown quiet, and her grin faded as she scrolled down the rankings, leaning over, until she found Steorling's name. At the bottom of the list, second to last. Lash stared for a moment, then stepped back and straightened.

The glow of anticipation on her face was gone. Her mouth twisted. A flush of tears filled her eyes. I reached to her, but she jerked her arm away. Dodging her way out of the crowd, with a stifled sob, she stalked across the grounds toward the barns. I started to follow, called for her to wait, but she ignored me. Around us, I could feel people staring, and I was at once embarrassed and confused and angry.

I stood a little removed from the bulletin board, watched Lash march across the grass, sweep around the corner of the nearest barn, and disappear. I didn't know if I should follow or not. I stood rooted to the spot, feeling rudderless and self-conscious. And when I went to the show office and picked up Indy's ribbon and her score sheet with its glowing comments, I didn't feel excitement or thrill, but rather guilt. And that made me angry.

I don't think I said anything to Lash when I got back to the stalls; she sat on a hay bale, leaning her head against the stall wall, picking at a stem and occasionally glancing into the stall at Steorling before dropping her gaze again to the hay bale. Anton stood nearby, silent and unmoving. I felt decidedly awkward. I exchanged a look with Anton; I gave a little shrug to his little shrug, and slipped into Indy's stall. I hugged her and leaned my cheek against her neck, and whispered to her how much I loved her, how proud I was of her.

But I didn't hang her big ribbon on her stall front like all the other winners did. I stuffed it and her score sheet with its glowing comments out of sight into the grooming box next to her brushes and fly spray.

Eventually, Lash looked in at Steorling again, and said, "Well, *I* think you're beautiful." And we all started to breathe again then, but I felt an almost searing discomfort for the rest of the show and the trip home. There was no celebration for me after those first few seconds of seeing Indy's success before it was entirely eclipsed by Steorling's bottom placing. Lash's reaction, her black focus on failure, seemed to rob me of the right to celebrate my success.

Even though I knew Lash's poor sportsmanship was rooted in the intensity of her love for and investment in Steorling, her reaction had hurt me. And I didn't say anything to her about it. I never said anything. Instead, I vowed in my mind that I would never compete in another class with her again, that I wouldn't give this situation the opportunity to arise in the future.

But of that day's consternation, to me the greatest was that I never told Lash how hurt I was. This has always bothered me because she and I had worked so hard to recognize the petty little things that bothered us, to talk about them and clear the air, and to ensure those petty little things couldn't expand into emotional infestations. But I never had the courage to tell Lash what

I felt that afternoon at the show, and I had a few years in which to do it before she died. But I didn't. And really, I can't help feeling that was a failure, which left me the biggest loser coming out of that day.

I never did compete in a show against Lash again. I went with her to shows, supported her when she was competing, and she came with me to shows and inspections for support, but Indy and Steorling never had occasion to step foot in the same arena in the same class again. I never had to screw up the courage to tell Lash I did not want to compete against her. I was battling my ever in-creasing weight, which gave me a prime excuse not to ride, so after starting Indy lightly under saddle when she was three, I bred her.

Although she'd been crushed by Steorling's basement placing at the MODA show, and even more crushed when the filly scored poorly at her offi-cial American Trakehner Association breed evaluation, Lash forged ahead with her original plans to ride, train, and show Steorling in dressage. And if she continued with her plans with a harder, more jaded attitude, she nevertheless succeeded in training and riding Steorling well—very well in fact. Lash invested in professional coaching and committed herself to accomplishing the most she could with Steorling. And when she entered Steorling in her first show under saddle, her first low-level competition where she rode and competed in front of a national level judge, she won both her classes. I was proud of her, and giddy in the surge and swell of her own excitement and satisfaction.

In 1999, when Steorling was three years old, Lash rode her in clinics and lessons, and showed her in the summer show series of the Northern Ohio Dressage Association. That summer, she and Steorling scored well and earned the NODA 2000 Adult Amateur Training Level Championship.

It wasn't until I had undergone bariatric surgery, lost a lot of weight, sold most of my horses, and Lash had been dead a while before I started riding Indy again. Then, as had Lash, I hired a professional trainer to help instruct me, to help me teach Indy and improve my riding, and as Lash and Steorling had been, Indy and I were successful. In fact, for three years, we qualified for and competed in the Regional Championships, and for three years, we won Swedish Warmblood of North America Association breed awards. In 2008, the last year I actively rode and competed, Indy was the North American Swedish Warmblood Musical Freestyle Champion at First Level. Still, years later, the championship and reserve championship medals and certificates she earned hang on display in my home.

Sometimes, I think about how much fun Lash and I could have had, showing together like we had daydreamed, having fun and doing what we'd both wanted to do for most of our lives. I like to think that she would have been gleeful and proud along with me when Indy and I earned good scores. Sometimes, especially at the year-end championships, I felt such an ache of loneliness for Lash. Leaving the arena after riding my championship test one year, I couldn't help thinking how broadly Lash would have been smiling at us. She would have ambled up to us, rubbed Indy on the neck, and grinned up at me. Look, Lash! We did it! I would have said, smiling back down at her.

But the truth was, if Lash had lived, I didn't know if I would have competed with Indy if Lash and I were riding at the same level or in the same classes. And I'm ashamed to admit that I also didn't know if I would have had the courage to tell her why.

Lash's predilection had long been to say what she thought, although I presume often only after serious consideration of what she felt and what she wanted to say. I'm sure there were times when she opted for discretion and kept silent, but from early in our relationship, I had been boggled, amazed by, and envious of her ability to take what rankled and put it out there. The first time I remember clearly was when I needed her help handling a horse for breeding; she told me she was late and needed to go. I pressured, begged, basically insisted, and she held the mare, staying at the farm for an extra fifteen minutes. I promptly forgot about it. She did not. The next time I saw her, she very calmly told me that I had been unfair to put my needs above hers, and that my assumption that her time didn't matter was hurtful.

I thought it petty and a bit selfish for her to be bothered by something so trivial, much less to say anything. Simultaneously, I admired her unwillingness to let it fester, that she took the less easy route and purged before it could evolve, combine with other trivial hurts into some malignant pain. And sharp with those ideas was the sour knowledge of my own oblivion. My own selfishness had never occurred to me.

I told her I was sorry then; I meant it in more ways than one.

Lash easily accepted my apology and moved on. If she ever thought about that conversation she didn't mention it; I don't believe we ever discussed the incident again. Yet for me, it stands as the first cogent example of the investment our relationship required. Not always taking the easy route. Giving the petty little things their due diligence. She was always better at that than I; so much bombarded me to stay silent, to be a good, quiet girl. To exercise discretion. To be stoic. To be selfless. Not to blow things out of proportion.

And fear. I recognized that later, that fear. Fear of disapproval. Fear of dismissal. Fear of rejection. It never occurred to me to question if Lash had those same fears, although I knew she did. She was as high-strung and volatile as I, as insecure and self-doubting, as susceptible to the devastation of another's critical opinion. Yet somehow, she could move beyond that. Still, a decade after her death, I wondered how she did it, how much psychic effort she invested to achieve that forthright, open honesty.

Because this was where I came from: sometimes you just needed to suck it up and deal with it. Like when I demanded Lash stay and help me breed a mare when she was already behind schedule and staying would make her late. Was that one episode so important, so life-altering, that Lash needed to bring it up again? *I* would not have. I knew that. I wouldn't have then, and perhaps would not even now. I couldn't be petty. I was above being bothered by the episode.

But the paradox was I know it would have bothered me. And I *wouldn't* have forgotten it. And the next time something insignificant and petty like that happened, I would be annoyed, exponentially. Annoyed that people didn't value my time. Annoyed that people took advantage of my generosity. Annoyed that people were so selfish. I would rehearse cutting remarks, run over the scripts in my mind I knew I'd never say, because to do so would be petty. But I'd just be waiting for the next offense. And it would come, of course it would, because people cared about themselves and what they needed and wanted, not about me and what I needed and wanted. So I nurtured a little hair trigger I didn't realize was there. And each time some petty little thing happened, my animosity built until my finger, caressing that trigger, spasmed at some insignificant provocation, and I spewed out vitriol and venom hugely out of proportion to the insignificant provocation. No aspect of any relationship involved would remain undamaged. Because one could ever tell when I might fly off the handle for no discernible reason, and I wasn't able to explain or justify my reaction, perhaps not even to myself.

And really, whose fault would my meltdown have been? If I never identified what bothered me, did not set boundaries, did not tell the people in my life if something they said or did upset me, then I was contributing as much to my meltdown as was anyone else.

I never knew how hard it was for Lash to recognize the small little hurts people put upon her; I didn't know how hard it was for her to define them, then to bring them to the attention of those causing the hurts—not when she was angry or still in the fresh sting of a hurt, but when she was calm and peaceful.

I admired and resented her capacity to do this. Admired that she saw the petty little things at face value. Resented that such petty little things carried so much weight for her. That she was so selfish. Sometimes, I thought she needed to grow a thicker skin.

Perhaps that was true. Or perhaps she was unwilling to let it chafe until it blistered. And, what did it say about me that I *was* willing to let it chafe, or that I presumed that anyone else should?

chapter seven

Adventures in Semen Collection

When I worked for two summers in the '80s at Valhalla Farm in Florida—where I met and fell in love with Johanniter—I learned a whole lot more about horse breeding. Spread over more than 500 acres, Valhalla was home to about a hundred horses, with sometimes a dozen or more foals being born each year, not a single one of them having been conceived naturally. Breeding here was exclusively by artificial insemination (AI).

There is nothing even remotely romantic about horse sex where AI is concerned. The sexually aroused stallion mounts a phantom or dummy mare, a person deflects his penis into an artificial vagina (AV), the stallion ejaculates, and the person carries the results to the lab to be processed before insemination directly into the mare. At first blush, it seems this adds a lot of superfluous and time-consuming effort for the same end result, but there are several sound reasons to employ this method. For one thing, it is a safer proposition for the stallion, because during a natural breeding puts his very valuable reproductive equipment directly in the line of fire of any mare that might suddenly decide that she isn't really in the mood after all. Plus, with AI, semen can be cooled, packaged, and shipped to mares elsewhere in the country, so that neither stallion nor mare need leave the comfort of his or her home.

I originally found out about Valhalla Farm from a horse magazine advertising the stallion services of Martini and Johanniter, and my correspondence with Jean, the farm owner, had been about breeding my mare to one of her stallions. Our relationship evolved until she asked me to come do some writing and marketing work for her–so I spent two summers during and after college at Valhalla. It was my first real introduction to the real-life application of science, this artificial insemination horse breeding, with microscopes and labs, and mathematical calculations to insure that the proper number of live, viable sperm cells made it into each recipient mare. In the college classroom, science eluded and terrified me. On the farm, it fascinated me.

I majored in English, but not because I loved literature. The fact was English was the only major with which I could graduate with just a bare minimum of math or science. Diagnosed as dyslexic early in grade school, I didn't have the brain for numbers and formulas. I also wasn't supposed to have the brain for reading or writing, and for a while, that seemed true.

I don't know who finally figured out that I couldn't read, but someone did. And eventually, by the time I was in fourth grade, I actually *could* read, more or less, but spelling tormented me, and math seemed to take pleasure in its own incomprehensibility. *I can't* became my mantra, and at some point very early on, I stopped distinguishing between *I can't* and *I won't* and ceased even trying.

I was going to spend my life working with horses, and didn't believe I needed math anyway, so in seventh grade, I read *The Lord of the Rings* then *Roots* during math class, drew horses on the back of the test papers, and on multiple choice tests, concentrated on filling in the answer sheets to make pretty patterns. Somehow, each fall when I went back to school, whining and hateful, I was one year further along.

In high school, I didn't have to take math thanks to my own recalcitrance and the wisdom of Ohio's state minimum graduation requirements. I painted and drew my school days away, or drifted through them with Huck Finn, or searched the hills with Hazel, Fiver, and Bigwig. Without anything beyond general math–without calculus or even basic algebra, I collected a high school diploma. In college, I started as an art major, but art history bored me to catatonia. I changed to psychology, but began to learn things I didn't want to know. "In a different life," I thought, "I could have been a vet, but I'm not good at the math or sciences." I finally graduated with that English degree.

At Valhalla, in the lab, under Jean's tutelage I used math every day without even realizing it–it had to do with horses and it made sense. The semen needed to be *extended* in a liquid that would nourish and buffer it during cooling and shipment. You had to know how many progressively motile sperm per milliliter there were in the extended solution, because each mare needed to be inseminated with 500 million of them. So, you had to know how many sperm cells were in any given milliliter of semen (hence the microscope and other lab equipment), and how many of those sperm were alive and going somewhere. Once you had that information, you could put the right measurement of semen in the right amount of extender, ensuring that you sent the right number of viable sperm.

I was fascinated, and I never thought about it as math. It wasn't until I'd left Valhalla, was working as a writer in the real world and had gotten involved in pre-hospital emergency medicine that I started taking my first academic windmill swings at math and the sciences. I loved running with the rescue squad; I loved being on the Hiram Volunteer Fire Department; I loved helping people, coming to the rescue, knowing what to do. But halfway through paramedic school, when we started learning about drugs and calculating dosages, and the teacher said, "It just goes back to your simple high school algebra," I suddenly felt a gulf gaping under me.

"I never *had* high school algebra," I told Scott after class, sitting in a chair in his office, staring at him wide-eyed.

He blinked back at me. "What about in college?"

I shook my head, embarrassed.

"Well, you need math here. You can't do medication calculations without it," Scott said. "How on earth did you graduate from high school and without algebra?" Scott shook his head, incredulous.

"That's a damn good question," I said, and I felt deficient in a new and unpleasant way. "Can you teach me enough that I can do this?"

Scott raised his eyebrows, tilted his head, and exhaled hard through his nose. "It's stuff you should have known before you ever got here."

He showed me formulas. They made no sense. But somewhere during our sessions, he asked me to figure out how much lidocaine I would dilute into an IV bag for a certain patient, who weighed a certain amount, and who needed to get x milligrams of lidocaine per minute. I pieced it out in my head, scribbled some calculations on a scrap of paper, and gave Scott the correct answer.

"How did you do that?"

"Ummm ... I wrote the formula like this."

He looked at it. "That makes no sense. But it works."

He blasted me with another question. I wrote my own formula, again gave him the correct answer. He looked at my formula again, and started laughing.

"That's backwards from how I ever learned, but it's giving you the right answers." And he told me one of the most important lessons of my life: If the standard formula makes no sense to you, but your own gives you the right answers, then use your own.

Now that I owned Johanniter, who conveniently came with the phantom mare, the artificial vagina, the Equitainers for cooling and shipping the semen, the microscope, even the incubator—all the essentials for modern day techno-horse sex—I planned to run my breeding program entirely via AI. I already had a booking or two to mares out of state.

Although I had experience with artificial insemination from both ends—collecting and shipping when I was a working student at Valhalla in Florida and receiving shipped semen with which to breed my own mares—when Joho arrived at the end of January, I simply stowed all of the associated breeding equipment until the spring breeding season. The phantom mare lay in pieces on the tack room floor in the barn, and the incubator, microscope, shipping containers, and the various components of the artificial vaginas were stacked against a wall in my kitchen. Wisely, very wisely it turned out, I decided I should have all of the elements of an efficient fresh cooled shipped semen operation in place and fully functional before I actually *needed* to start collecting and shipping semen.

In February, Lash and I stood in the barn aisle and debated where it would be best to set up the phantom. Logistically, this was complicated by the fact that a phantom mare is (not surprisingly) about the size of a horse, that I needed to account for the added size and enthusiasm of the stallion, and that my barn was built on a steep hill with limited level ground around it.

I pointed to a small, flat area just outside of the barn's back door. It was only a few steps away from the teasing stall, but it certainly wasn't ideal. It was not enclosed in any way. Snow swirled over the ground, piling in drifts a dozen feet or so from the door, where the ground dropped off steeply.

Lash sniffed. "You better hope he has good balance, or he'll come out the door and roll down the hill," she said, pulling her coat closer and hugging herself against the wind. I cleared my throat and looked across the fields. A cluster of Amish children marched along the road before turning up a driveway. Even if Joho didn't tumble down the hill, any interlude with the phantom would be in clear view. In the end, I opted for the site behind the barn, where I eventually installed a lattice privacy screen to shield the view from the road.

I had always prided myself in my strength, my ability to manage the physical demands of handling horses and running a farm without a man in my life, but I was also not beyond commandeering brute masculine strength when I needed to. This was a role Anton was happy to fill, especially if it involved using power equipment like chain saws or tractors. And installing the phantom was definitely a project where power equipment would be useful. First, we needed to dig the hole for the main vertical post that would support the body of the phantom; the post needed to be sunk about four feet into the ground and set in cement. After all, it needed to steadfastly support the ministrations of a 1,200 pound stallion.

With the first break in the snow, Lash, Anton, and I hacked away at the frozen ground behind the barn. Using an auger on his tractor's power take off device, Anton gleefully tore a four-foot deep hole in the ground. Steaming lumps of brown clay spewed into the snow. Two bags of cement mix accompanied the base of the steel post into the hole, and Anton and I filled and tamped the dirt and clay around the support while Lash held a level against the support, ensuring it remained plumb. Then, using the horsepower of the tractor for the main lifting and with Lash and me under the body of the phantom to align it, we put the fake horse body onto the post in the ground, adjusted it to the proper height, and bolted it to the steel support post. After an afternoon in the snow and mud, we had the phantom mare installed; it looked not dissimilar to an oversized pommel horse used in gymnastics, sans handlebars.

Sodden and chilled but triumphant, Lash, Anton, and I stood back and admired our handiwork. The late afternoon sun gleamed on the phantom as if celebrating our accomplishment, this monumental step forward in the realization of my dream. It was a thing of beauty.

"I thought you said we set that post plumb," Anton said.

"I did," Lash said. "It is plumb."

"That ain't plumb, babe." Anton tilted his head toward the phantom. Maybe it was the way the shadows from the late winter sun fell at long angles, but it was true that the post did not look perpendicular.

"It was plumb," Lash said, on the edge of angry. "I *know* what plumb is, Anton."

Anton took the level from where it was leaning against the barn wall, and hunkering down, clapped it against the support post. It was not plumb. And it was becoming unplumber as we watched. Barely perceptibly, the back end of the phantom yawed slowly toward the ground, dragging the support pipe through its freshly turned earth and unset cement.

An hour later, Lash worked on a salad in the kitchen while I threw pasta in boiling water; Anton rolled around on the living room floor with Bristol, playing tug-o-war with her and her rope toy. Outside, the last light of day faded, and the temperature plummeted. Behind the barn in the growing dark, the tractor was parked, brakes locked, right where Anton had left it, with its grill wedged against the butt-end of the phantom, shoving it back upright, its support post now plumb and level.

Several days later, Lash and I stood in the living room, looking at the phantom standing forlorn and tractor-less behind the barn. It remained up-right without the tractor help. I questioned out loud if it would stay that way. I questioned if I was kidding myself about being able to set up and operate a horse breeding operation solo. I bemoaned the fact–none-the-worse for years of having been bemoaned, that I was alone and manless. But now I was man-less at a time in my life when it seemed especially appropriate *not* to be manless, if only for a man's pragmatic brute utility. That wasn't the only reason I wanted a man, though. I *liked* men. I liked hairy men. ("Except back hair," I'd said to my college roommate. "Back hair, and it's time to break out the lawn mower.") I liked the smell of men and the look of men, and the few times I'd felt it in college, the touch of a man's hand on my skin. I liked how a man's touch made me feel feminine and sexy.

I took a deep breath, turned away from the window and the phantom, and looked up at Lash.

"Well, with Joho here, at least *someone* on this farm is gonna be having sex."

Lash rolled her eyes and shoved me in the arm.

"You could have sex if you wanted," Lash said, shaking her head.

"Yeah, right. I don't see a line of men out there ready to beat my door down to get to my fat ass."

"You're beautiful, and being big doesn't keep men from being interested in you."

I snorted and shot her a sidelong glance. Both of us fought the battle of the bulge and obsessed with it; we'd had this conversation, or iterations of it, innumerable times. It went both ways, me pointing out to her how utterly, irresistibly attractive Anton found her, her pointing out to me that my weight wasn't a deterrent to relationships. For a long time, I differentiated between alone and lonely. I had lived alone for years, did not mind being alone. In fact, I mostly liked it. And I was rarely *lonely*. By the time I was in my thirties, I tempered the sting of being manless by proclaiming myself too independent and set in my ways to share my life with anyone. "I could use a gigolo now and then," I quipped, "but I don't think I'm marriageable because I'm incorrigible."

At a deeper level, the one Lash knew, my single status was not so much a choice but a defense, one used by me as much as against me to keep me alone.

"I think you should look up Arnold," Lash said.

I scowled, shook my head. "He's married."

"I thought you said he wasn't anymore." I knew I may have told her that, but could not remember why or how I came by that bit of information, or if it was true.

"I don't know…"

"Look him up."

I glanced up at her. She leaned back on the couch, relaxed, self-assured, and looked at me as she rubbed Bristol's head.

"Lash, even if he's *not* still married, I don't know if he has any interest in me anymore."

"So, find out."

I looked away, out the window and over my fields, and thought of Arnold, the man with whom I spent one passionate summer during college, who was everything I said I ever wanted in a man but whose intensity and inclination toward alcoholism tangled with my own insecurities until I fled from the relationship and shut myself down. We kept in touch, on friendly terms, over the years, and some arrogant part of me assumed he'd wait for me forever. The day he called and told me he had married, that I probably shouldn't send him birthday cards and amiable notes anymore, was the last time I had talked to him. I had hung up the phone slightly unmoored, as if I couldn't find something important where I was sure I'd left it.

"Your history with Arnold, the way you talk about him," Lash said, quiet, looking down at Bristol and tracing her fingers over the Border Collie's markings, "reminds me of me and Anton. Of that one true love, the one that got away."

"Anton looked you up and came back," I said.

She looked up at me, keen, pointed. "And you should look Arnold up."

I gave a half laugh and shook my head, leaning back on the couch. I was acutely aware of a roll of blubber around my ribcage. My arm rested on it, and however I shifted, that roll of blubber moved with me.

In principle, AI was a simple process. Semen collected from the stallion was prepared with an extender (which had nutrients and often antibiotics) for shipping, then packaged in the Equitainer or other shipping container, and dropped off for priority overnight delivery. Mission accomplished.

In practice, it was often a bit more complicated. That first simple step, collecting the semen, depended on a lot of interrelated variables. Some stallions that have bred naturally simply didn't adjust to being collected artificially, although most did, and Joho was one of those successful converts. Then there's the issue of the appropriate stimulation. Stallions, like the males of most species, were preprogrammed to be ready at a moment's notice, but each horse was still an individual. Some stallions required the presence of a mare in heat—sometimes even standing right next to the phantom—to encourage him to mount the dummy mare. And stallions had remarkably particular preferences for the tension, heat, and lubrication of the artificial vagina (which always seemed counterintuitive to me, as I doubted one typical mare in season varied much from the next in those regards). Without the stallion's preferred "settings," he might not ejaculate, and to make matters worse, might subsequently refuse to participate in the operation altogether.

Fortunately for me, I had experience handling Joho for collection at Valhalla. There were a couple of differences from the operation I'd known in Florida, though. The phantom standing at attention behind my barn was a self-service model, meaning the artificial vagina, once prepared, actually inserted into the phantom, making an extra person to manage the AV unnecessary. Also, in theory, this was a more natural approach for the stallion, although I'd be willing to bet that most stallions weren't fooled.

Because this phantom was a self-serve phantom, the AV was different from what I'd used before, although the principle was the same. My AV was composed of a big PVC pipe, about two-and-a-half feet long and eight inches in diameter, with a nozzle welded into the middle of the shaft. A heavy latex liner covered the interior of the PVC pipe, making an envelope against the inside of the pipe (creating a semi-permanent liner, usually only removed at the end of the breeding season for winter storage). For each collection, we inserted a reusable collection liner that was also latex, but much lighter and softer, into the PVC pipe/hot water envelope. This reusable liner tapered at the far end, where we affixed a standard plastic baby bottle (fitted with a standard baby bottle liner), with a filter at the top of the bottle so only semen, and no nasty debris, flowed into the bottle.

Once I had the AV assembled with inner liner, baby bottle, and filter, I filled the envelope between the PVC pipe and the semi-permanent liner with hot water via the nozzle in the side of the pipe. Stallions were often pretty picky about how much pressure they liked and how hot they wanted it, so an instant read thermometer went into the depths of the AV, and the AV placed onto a bathroom scale. When it got to a certain weight, I knew the AV had the requisite pressure Joho preferred. When the heat and pressure parameters were all set, I slathered some sterile, non-spermicidal lubricant on the inner liner, and voila! Instant horse vagina.

Before collecting, the incubator would be steady at 101 degrees, and a batch of that commercial extender, previously prepared in 60 or 80 ml batches and frozen, was in the incubator, thawed and warmed to equine body temperature. The graduated glass cylinders and 50 ml plastic syringes used to measure and process the semen would also be at temperature in the incubator. Horse sperm took exception to sudden or sizeable shifts in temperature, often responding by promptly dying. So it was not good practice to burst into the lab with an AV full of freshly collected semen without having first ensured all was set to go.

The Equitainers used for actual transportation were specially designed to coddle the semen, cooling it a few degrees each hour until it was around forty degrees, where it pretty much stayed for a couple of days. All this helped ensure that when the vet unpacked the Equitainer at its destination he or she would inseminate sperm that was alive and well once it warmed up in the mare, or on the microscope slide.

I had the distinct advantage in this entire learning process of already knowing that at Joho's pressure preference, the AV would weigh twenty-four pounds, and that he liked it hot, between 122 and 124 degrees Fahrenheit, about twenty degrees hotter than a real live mare. Why Joho needed it that hot, I never knew. I told Lash and Anton that it in fact seemed counterintuitive.

"I don't know," Anton said. "Lash's way hotter than body temperature, you know, down there, when, ummm…"

I leveled him a baleful look, outdone only by Lash.

"Well…" said Anton, trying to look innocent.

I clapped my hands over my ears. "I don't want to know."

"What? It's true," Anton said, and grinned lecherously at his wife.

"Yeah, well, I wouldn't know about people sex," I muttered under my breath.

Lash rolled her eyes, and if Anton heard me, he didn't let on. I noticed he was busy considering the phantom, and I realized he ascertained that it stood at pelvic height for him as he turned to leer at Lash.

"Anton! Cut it out!" I yelled.

On a mid-March afternoon, with snow still blanketing any ground where the south sun hadn't found it and a cold, stiff wind still insisted it was winter, Lash and I labored in my country kitchen (which was large enough to house the incubator, the microscope, the AV, the Equitainers, and other breeding and shipping equipment), preparing for our inaugural Ohio collection with Joho. During the week after work I made a couple of dry runs installing the prepared AV in the phantom, opening the back panel, sliding the AV into place, and lining the AV up with the hole in the panel so that I felt moderately prepared for this maiden voyage with the stallion.

Lash looked over my shoulder as I explained the process to her; I balanced the AV over the sink and filled it with hot tap water (I had to turn the thermostat on the water heater up to 130 so that the tap water was hot enough to compensate for heat loss during the preparation). I felt my heart slamming and my palms sweating; the success of my breeding operation (or at least the collecting and shipping aspect of it) depended on the efficient and businesslike flow of events.

Lash had been with me at the receiving end of shipped semen in previous years, but she was new to the collection end. And my own experience at Valhalla was as a working student coming into an established program, with an established routine, and stallions familiar with that routine. Now, all of us, including Joho, had to develop and perfect a new system that worked here on Donley Farm East.

"Ideally," I said, glancing at the thermometer nestled in the shrinking recesses of the filling AV, "there should not be more than fifteen or twenty minutes from ejaculation to having the collection extended and packed in the Equitainer."

She raised her eyebrows. "Guess I never really thought about all that before."

The thermometer in the AV registered at 128 degrees. Too hot, but I didn't know how long it would take for Joho to understand what was up and shift into breeding mode; I was counting on some radiational cooling during that interlude. I lugged the AV out of the sink and balanced it on the bathroom scale. Twenty-four pounds. Perfect. A dollop of lubricant at the entrance of the AV, and we were ready to go.

We headed out the back door of the house and down the hill to the barn. The AV bumped and sloshed against my thigh with each step. Behind the barn, Lash swung open the back panel of the phantom, and I hoisted the AV into its slot, making sure the baby bottle at the end, nestled in its protective insulated mitt, didn't get knocked out of place. The panel's springs squeaked and sproinged as it clapped closed. Locked and loaded. In the barn, Mysty pressed her nose against the stall bars and watched us with idle curiosity. At the far end of the aisle, Joho stood in his stall, eating hay. All was calm and quiet. That was about to change.

I took a deep breath, glanced at Lash, and rubbed my hands on my thighs. Lash grimaced in anxious solidarity. I picked up a lead shank.

"Well, here goes nothing."

Looking back, I realize how incredibly fortunate I was that Joho was an older stallion, sensible from years of international travel and competition, seasoned in the ways of horse sex, to include artificial insemination collection, and that he was well-mannered and tolerant. I was fortunate that when I led him down the barn aisle and showed him his phantom for the first time, he was smart enough to recognize it immediately and shifted into reproduction mode, even though Mysty, my tease mare in the big stall at the end of the aisle, was not only *not* in heat but was in fact a few weeks from delivering her first foal. I was fortunate Joho knew the drill well enough that he persevered despite the lack of a receptive mare to stimulate him, that he in fact was not deterred by Mysty's violent protestations, stoically achieving an erection and promptly mounting the phantom. I was especially fortunate that even though he jerked himself off the phantom and backed off, because the AV was still much too hot, he was singularly committed, and—after readjusting the temperature in the AV to a more temperate level—was willing to risk scorching his penis and try again. And that when he found the AV too cold, or not tight enough, he pushed beyond his fatigue and frustration, repeatedly mounting the phantom until all of us—stallion, people, mares alike were exhausted, frustrated, and dirty. Really, I was fortunate he didn't lose his temper with the whole affair, with Mysty's kicking and shrieking disapproval of his presence near her stall, with the too hot or too cold AV, and that he didn't use his highly aroused half ton or so of strength to pummel me or simply go where and do whatever he wanted, including but not limited to accosting the horses pulling Amish buggies that passed regularly on the road.

As it was, after more than an hour of aborted attempts, all of the stars finally lined up, the temperature in the AV was *just so*, the pressure was *just so*, and Joho's thrusts, which previously had an understandably tentative quality, adopted a new vigor, whereupon he produced the intended results before collapsing over the phantom, exhausted but sated.

"Thank *God*. It's about time," Lash said, voicing what was clearly a universal sentiment at the moment.

Ten minutes later Lash and I stood in the kitchen with the drained AV propped in the sink, the semen poured from the baby bottle into the graduated cylinder and then transferred to the incubator, where it now sat at equine body temperature setting of 101 degrees, and I peered into the microscope at a slide full of dead sperm cells.

"Fuck!"

I stepped back and stared up at Lash. My heart was pounding and my palms were sweating again.

She glowered and bent to squint into the microscope. She moved the slide and looked again. Adjusted the focus. Shifted her weight. Pursed her lips.

"It's fucking dead," I said, stomping back and forth across the kitchen floor.

"Maybe this is just a bad sample."

Another drop from the semen in the incubator showed another plethora of dead sperm. I sifted through the analysis from the University of Florida; less than three months earlier, when Joho had provided a sample as part of his pre-purchase examination, his semen quality was fine. In fact, it had been stellar, with millions of living, vigorous sperm cells. It had been great at the time of collection. It had been great when they prepared and cooled it to simulate shipping. It had been alive and well when they had evaluated it again at twenty-four, forty-eight, and seventy-two hours. It had been a positively positive report.

"I killed it. I killed it all," I said.

"Either that or he's suddenly shooting blanks," Lash said.

"Jesus Christ."

I stood with my hand plastered to my forehead, thinking of why the stallion standing down in my barn could suddenly go from fertile to sterile. I riffled through my books on equine reproduction and stallion management, my hands shaking slightly, my palms sticky.

"A fever," I said. "If he had a fever, his elevated body temperature could kill everything for a while."

"But that would only be temporary, right?"

"Yeah," I said, reading. "It would take a couple months to get back to normal levels."

"When did he have a fever?"

I looked at her. "He didn't that I know of."

Lash looked down at me, and for a moment we stood in the kitchen in silence, the trappings of this horse breeding operation scattered and dripping all around us.

"I must have killed it," I said. "How the hell did I kill it?"

"I suppose you could do live cover..."

"Not if I'm supposed to be shipping semen to out-of-state mares."

"Maybe it'll be fine shipped," Lash said.

"I think the vets will notice if I send them a bucket-load of dead sperm, Lash." I wedged my fists against my hips and glared at her.

"You seem angry," she said, shifting into counselor mode.

"I *am* angry. I'm pissed. I got a second fucking mortgage to buy Joho, but it does me no fucking good if I kill everything."

Lash sighed, nodded slightly. Spoke with the voice of reason. "Maybe you just need to get a system down, practice more. I mean, today was all trial and error. Maybe it's just a fluke."

I nodded. "Yeah. Today was a clusterfuck for sure," I said, and that was true enough. But my substantial gut told me beginner's (bad) luck didn't have much to do with the day's failures. I felt sick in a deep, visceral way.

Over the next several days, I practiced more with Joho. I became efficient at preparing the AV—not too hot, but warm enough to remain in the temperature range he liked—and Joho learned what the sound of the back panel of the phantom closing meant, so he was bellowing and bullish by the time I led him from his stall. He towed me down the barn aisle, his neck arched, tail lashing, striking at the air with his front feet, snorting and whinnying in full stallion courtship mode, eager and willing despite the lack of a receptive mare to encourage him, impervious even to Mysty's hateful wall-kicking and teeth-gnashing. Within ten or fifteen minutes, I lugged the AV back up the hill to the house, the precious cargo protected from the sunlight and cold outdoor temperatures by a thermal sleeve over the baby bottle. With each collection, I got faster and more efficient at processing the semen, getting it into the incubator, and examining a sample under the microscope.

Those sperm cells stayed dead. They couldn't get any deader. And I didn't understand why. Breeding season was closing in, and the closer it came, the more anxious I became.

On March 26, 1999, apparently unaffected by all of the fruitless teasing and semen collection going on just outside her stall Mysty delivered her first foal, a filly by the Swedish stallion Absolut, and the first foal ever to be born at Donley Farm East. Mysty proved to be an excellent mother—doting and gentle with her filly, grizzly bear ferocious and protective. Lash helped me turn the mare and her filly out for the first time, glowed with me in the delight of this new beautiful life. And while she smiled and hovered, watching the mare and her newborn, I watched all of them, thrilled with the christening of my pastures with a precious new foal, terrified that no more would follow, at least not from Joho. So I smiled and watched them, and tried to ignore the knot growing in my chest.

The dream was so vivid I still smelled it, tasted it, felt it. Heard it all happening. At first, everything was beautiful with bucolic, gently rolling hills, my beautiful farm on a lake's shore, placid waves lapping. I stood on my porch, hands resting on the sun-warmed railing and looked out on the beauty of all I had gained. But then storm clouds rolled in, ushering a north-coast gale. The water roiled. The wind-blown waves beat on the shore, ate away little bits of it. And the water gnawed closer and closer, ate the shore, each breaker cleaved away the earth. Each lunge of the water surged closer to my farm, sitting vulnerable on the hill, trembling as the water, fierce and inexorable, devoured the earth from under it.

Frantic, I tried to think of ways to shore up the ground, to protect my farm, but I couldn't move from my porch, cold now, a crow's nest poised over the flood. I watched, my hands clutching the railing, as the first fence posts disappeared into the surf, toothpicks. The lake chewed into my dream farm, swallowing my pastures surge by surge, flowing toward my barn—my beautiful barn I'd worked so hard for, waited so long for, mortgaged myself beyond reason. I could only watch as the water ate its way to that wonderful barn, tasted it, sucked it into its gaping, roiling maw, and my barn, my dream farm, foundered, sank below the surf and was gone.

"How could I be so stupid to build my farm right on the coast?" I said, and wailed, pounding my fists against the sides of my head. I couldn't believe I'd been so naïve, so complacent. I had known the dangers of the waves, of building on the water, and yet I'd put my dream there anyway, had allowed myself to be lulled by the siren call of temptation, and I had watched it all crash beneath the waves.

"How could I be so stupid? Why did I risk it all? How could I be so stupid?"

When I woke suddenly, I felt no surge of relief. The heavy pulsing of the waves and that panicked, grieving refrain and fear did not recede with the nightmare, even though I knew as I woke it was a dream and my farm was safely thirty miles inland of Lake Erie. Even in the brightness of the daytime, I felt sick and unsettled, and kept catching myself glancing out my bedroom window, or staring out over the porch, looking for the waves advancing on my farm. Instead, I saw my mares grazing in their pastures, swishing their tails at early spring bugs trolling lazily through the sun, and Joho standing in his field, looking over his mares, and beyond all that, the wooded hills rolling where the waves had crashed and roiled in my dream.

Lash nodded, her face grim and serious when I told her about the dream, and then she gave me a sad little smile. "I know what that was all about," she said, studying the backs of her hands, spread out across her knees.

"What? Because it's freaking me out. I can't shake it."

She sniffed, pursed her lips. "I think it's your anxiety about the breeding business, and going out on a limb to buy the farm and Joho. Afraid of losing everything."

I looked at her, thinking there was a good reason she had an advanced degree in psychology, even if dream interpretation wasn't her specialty.

I gave a small laugh. "I *could* lose everything."

She nodded, and continued scrutinizing her hands. Her voice was small when she spoke. "Do you regret buying Joho? I suppose you could sell him…"

"No, I don't regret it," I interrupted, and I *didn't* regret it, and I had no intention of selling Johanniter. Besides, who would buy an old stallion that kept providing bottles full of dead sperm, even if I suspected user error and not the horse was to blame? I was in way over my head financially, and I just had to hope I'd start getting living sperm, and stay afloat, that breeding and selling would deliver me to some small sliver of solid ground.

Lash looked up, smiled in a strained sort of way, and squeezed my hand. "I'm glad you have your dream, finally, and I'm sorry it's giving you nightmares. You've worked so long and so hard for it."

I smiled back and held onto her hand. I nodded and worked against the knot in my throat. "I'm glad I have my dream too. I just hope I don't end up losing it all. At least not before you guys get a chance to build your house, so we're farmer neighbors," I added, and scratched Bristol on the head. Lash reached over and smoothed the ruffled hair over Bristol's spine. The dog was the only one grinning in the room.

"I've been reading online, and there's something else I want to try," I said, regrouping, "but I'll need your help. And Anton's." For all of his machismo, Anton squirmed at the idea of in any way being involved with artificially collecting horse semen beyond helping install the phantom.

Lash looked at me, curious. "What do you want to try?"

I cleared my throat. "Ground collection."

"Which is…?"

"Well…it's pretty hands on," I said, blushing. "Literally."

Lash blinked, her eyebrows raised. "Meaning…?"

"Meaning it's manual collection of the stallion. No phantom needed. Just a hot cloth, a plastic bag for the ejaculate. And hands."

Lash's eyebrows went up further, and she gave a quick laugh. "Hand collection?"

"Yeah. I read about it on the equine reproduction board. I guess they use it a lot in research, at universities, and with older stallions. They give specific details on how to do it."

"Which entails what?"

I blushed harder. "Well, Joho would stay in his stall, but I'll need you to hold him. And then we need Anton to hold a mare outside of his stall to get Joho aroused. Then I'm supposed to put the bag over his penis, and the hot cloth over that, and sort of apply pressure, you know, on the head… and that's supposed to give adequate stimulation that he'll ejaculate."

Lash laughed outright. "So, you're gonna jack off the stallion."

"Yeah, I guess that about sums it up," I said. "If I have the balls to actually do it."

Lash laughed harder.

"So, do you think you could talk Anton into helping?"

"Oh, he'll help," Lash said, "whether he wants to or not."

"Jeez, I can't even believe I'm considering doing this," I said then and rubbed my hands on my thighs.

"Me neither, but hey, if it works, that'll be great."

"Well, he might not go for it," I said, feeling the blush ebbing as I tried to put a scientific spin on masturbating a horse. "The vet on the board says they use it a lot for older stallions with arthritic hips or hocks because it's easier on them than mounting a phantom or a mare, but he also said some older stallions are just too set in their ways and won't adjust."

Lash laughed some more, a mischievous flash in her eyes. "Yeah, well, we're gonna help Joho give it a try even if all we get from it is torturing Anton."

As it turned out, Anton was practically apoplectic as he stood in the barn aisle holding the conveniently-in-heat Silver. Lash stood at Joho's head holding the lead shank and keeping him in one place in his stall, and I hunkered at his hind end, tried to be adept at applying the proper stimulation, but felt clumsy and decidedly out of my comfort zone. In the end, Joho was disenchanted with the experience and did not ejaculate. I was anxious to put the attempt behind me and move on.

The next day on our drive home from work, Lash told me that Anton had regaled his coworkers with the story of the unsuccessful stallion jerk off.

"They couldn't believe it," she said, guffawing. "They said they'd pay to have seen it!"

"Well shit," I said, laughing too, "maybe that'll help pay the mortgage. I should just hang out a red light in front of the barn and charge admission fees. 'Donley Farm East. Breeding and brothel of Swedish Warmblood sport horses.'"

We laughed harder, but the sting in my eyes wasn't just from hysterics but also the thought that no one had expressed any interest in sex on the farm where *I* was concerned, just sex where the horses were concerned. *The story of my life*, I thought, but I didn't say it out loud.

I scoured my breeding textbooks. I consulted my vet with questions. I talked to Jean at Valhalla Farm. I spoke with the vets at the University of Florida. No one had answers, but all agreed that it was unlikely Joho had suddenly become sterile, which was at least encouraging in that the issue probably lay with me, but it got me no closer to solving the problem. I obsessed about how I would explain the situation to the mare owners in California who were expecting to breed their mares in April.

Stubborn, desperate, I kept trying, Joho kept accommodating the demand, and I kept hoping for a different result under the microscope. I started making excuses to collect Joho at times when Lash couldn't be around to help. Somehow, I didn't want anyone, not even Lash, to witness my failure. I felt foolish and impotent, like the person who keeps pressing the already lighted elevator button, as if repeatedly doing the same thing would somehow net different results.

One day in mid-April, I stalked back up the hill to the house with the AV after yet another collection; the excitement and anticipation of that first mid-March collection had devolved to jaw-clenching frustration and resignation. Halfway to the house and the bleak picture I was sure to see under the microscope, I hoisted the AV to rebalance it, but the water inside sloshed forward. I juggled, bobbled, and the AV tipped over my forearm, decanting its load of semen into the grass before I could catch it. I stood frozen, midstride for a moment. Then I flung the entire AV onto the ground. I kicked it for good measure before I sat down next to it. I stayed there for a while, my forehead on my knees, until the April mud soaked through my jeans at my butt and my tears soaked through at my knees.

When I had composed myself sufficiently, I unscrewed the cap in the AV and let the water, now tepid, drain out onto the ground—why carry the weight up to the kitchen just to drain it in the sink?—and then I peered into the deflating innards of the AV to see what, if anything, remained of Joho's ejaculate. Halfway down the length of the AV, the inner liner stuck closed against itself; a few runnels of semen trickled around the seal it formed, finding some small open channel, and drained toward the baby bottle, hidden from my view, at the end. I frowned. I reached into the AV and poked at the liner to break the seal and let what was left of the semen flow freely to the baby bottle.

The liner stuck to itself firmly. And most of the semen stayed right where it was, right in the middle of the AV.

Right where Joho liked it at 124 degrees.

Right where it was twenty degrees too hot for sperm to survive.

I stared down the too hot AV tunnel for a moment, stunned. My heart slammed in my chest. I scrambled up and grabbed the drained AV and power walked up to the house. I removed the used inner liner and replaced it with a clean one, fitted a fresh collection bottle on the end, and refilled the AV with hot water. When it weighed the requisite twenty-four pounds, I squirted lubricant into the entrance as I always did. Then I plunged my arm into the AV. My hand carried the lube with it for a few inches. I thrust my arm elbow deep until I felt the taper of the liner, cooler, beyond the end of the hot water envelope. As I pulled my arm back, I felt the inner envelope sealing against itself as my fist retreated back up the AV. I pulled my arm all the way out, filled my palm with lubricant, and jammed it back in. Halfway down the AV, the inner liner stuck to itself. I nudged it apart and slathered it with lube until it stopped sticking. With my mouth as dry as cotton and my hands shaking, I hefted the AV out of the kitchen sink and marched back down to the barn, stuffed the newly refilled and copiously lubed AV back into the phantom, and trotted down the aisle to get the stallion.

Joho had heard me open the back panel on the phantom, and I can only describe his expression as bemused when I opened his stall door. I snapped the lead shank to his halter.

"Humor me, Joho," I said, and turned to lead him from his stall.

So he humored me. With businesslike determination he gave a repeat performance of his activity from a half hour earlier, ejaculating into the now abundantly lubricated AV. As soon as he finished, I dragged Joho back in his stall, tugged the AV out of the phantom, and unscrewed the lid to drain out the hot water as I trundled up to the house. Once in the kitchen, I stared down the center of the AV and had a clear view all the way down to the collection bottle at the end. My hands trembled as I poured Joho's latest effort into the cylinder and stuck it in the incubator. I shook one drop from the dregs left in baby bottle liner onto a slide, dropped a cover slip on it, and slid it under the microscope.

Then I stalled. I threw out the baby bottle liner. I disassembled the AV in the kitchen sink, washed and disinfected both of the inner liners, and hung them to air dry in the bathroom. I cleaned up the AV and stowed it in its slot by the incubator. I cleaned the sink and washed down the counter tops.

Finally, trying to feel casual, as if it were an afterthought, I looked in the microscope. Then I just stood there with my eye sockets jammed against the scope's eyepieces. I blinked, but my vision didn't clear. I stared at frenetic activity. My fingers shook as I moved the slide slightly, looked at a different section of the drop of semen. Watched dozens of sperm cells writhing, propelling themselves into and out of my field of vision, all of them on a frantic quest for an egg none of them would ever find. I yanked the slide off the scope, grabbed a fresh new slide, shook another drop of semen from the supply in the incubator onto it, shoved that sample under the microscope, too. Stared through the eyepiece at scores more of frenetic, ambitious cells whipping across the slide.

For the second time that day, I sat down on the spot and cried.

After I'd looked into that microscope again and again all afternoon and into the evening, watching all those sperm cells swimming madly, eventually slowing, until they had stopped moving and finally *were* dead, but only because the semen had dried out under the heat of the microscope's light, I called Lash and told her the mystery was solved.

"They were getting parboiled in the liner before they could get to the bottle."

Breathless, I told her how I figured out the liner was sealing to itself, how I'd lubed the liner all the way to the end to keep it from sticking, to let that sperm flow from the AV that Joho wanted hot, too hot, quickly to the safety of the baby bottle.

"You collected him twice in less than an hour?" Lash said, and relayed my adventure to Anton. I heard him in the background, laughing, commenting about Joho's staying power. She laughed, her voice floating over the phone, parroting Chic Anderson's call of Secretariat's historic Belmont Stakes race: "Johanniter's all alone! He's like a *tremendous* machine!"

In the barn, the tremendous machine ate his hay in the dark, resting from his day's activities and non-the-wiser of their implications, which secured that at least for where he was concerned, there would be plenty of sex on Donley Farm East.

chapter eight

Y2K

At 11:59 p.m. on December 31, 1999, Lash, Anton, and I stood in the living room at Donley Farm East in Parkman, Ohio, our champagne flutes full of sparkling cider, watching the TV screen as the ball on Times Square slowly lowered, ticking off the last seconds of the millennium. At 12:01 a.m. January 1, 2000, after the twentieth century ended and the twenty-first century began—and the lights stayed on, the clocks and computers of the world kept humming and calculating—the three of us turned to each other, cheered, toasted the new year, the new decade, new century, and new millennium. Bristol cavorted around the house in the glow of uninterrupted electricity; outside, the sodium light over the front barn door burned without the slightest flicker. The power grids of the world had met the Y2K challenge, and I thought the test of Y2K had been presented and passed.

At 12:15 or 12:20, Lash and Anton left and I went to bed. Nothing felt different than it had a half-hour earlier. I would be lying if I said in some way I hadn't expected *some*thing to change in this new millennium. Yet I crawled alone under my covers, feeling a sense of disappointment at the sameness of *then* and *now*.

When I was in grade school, our teacher told us to figure out how old we would be in the year 2000, and to think about what our lives would be like then. I remembered sitting at my wooden flip-top desk, blinking in the light of epiphany, this sudden thought of the future at a scale I had never considered. Walking on the moon was a recent novelty, Vietnam was ramping down, and Watergate was ramping up, and the turn of the century seemed ridiculously, impossibly far away. But I remembered figuring it out. I would be thirty-six years old. I envisioned a woman ringing in the year 2000 with a husband and a few kids. In that vision, she seemed old and wise, contented and settled, accomplished. I pictured the scene, these people standing in a kitchen, late at night well past the children's bedtimes. I felt the security of family. I smelled the celebration, warm like spiced cider. The Y2K Karen laughed with her family, her dark shadow of a husband, her half grown kids. Who were they? Who was *she?* I did not know, but I admired her, and that vision of my future stayed with me, offered succor over the years during bouts of childhood loneliness and angst.

Nowhere in the vision did Y2K Karen slip into cold sheets shortly after midnight on January 1, 2000, obese, alone, and childless.

The early hours of 2000 may not have hosted the vision I had seen decades earlier, but that in itself wasn't all bad, because there wasn't a farm in that vision. In the real 2000, I had a farm, with a stallion in my barn and four mares carrying the realization of my dreams. The new year had only just begun, and if the only change I had really expected was for the lights to go out and the world to shift, I was shortsighted. There were months and months yet for my world to shift on its axis.

Roanoke was due to foal first, in early March. This was her first baby, and would be the first of three Johanniter foals. Indy, herself a Johanniter daughter, was due to foal a few weeks after Roanoke. Indy was bred to Amiral, a horse famous worldwide, that had participated in two Olympic Games, and had a proven history of siring exceptional quality foals. This unborn baby had already cost thousands of dollars—the stud fee itself followed by the expense of breeding with frozen semen (Amiral stayed in Sweden, and Indy stayed in Ohio) and the close veterinary scrutiny that mandated. Aside from Joho himself, the fetus that grew and kicked in Indy represented my single largest equine investment.

After Indy, Mysty was due in early May, and last of all, Silver—Indy's mother—was due in early July with a full brother or sister to Indy.

Horses were pregnant for about eleven months, and no matter how many years I had been doing this, those eleven months never got shorter. Winter and snow always seemed to drag on infinitely as day by day, week by week, month by month, I watched mares' bellies grow and sag. I counted off the days of gestation, noted the milestones: that the heart would start to beat at around three weeks; that by day thirty-nine, endometrial cups would form in the mare's uterus, producing hormones to maintain the pregnancy until the placenta took over that role around the fifth month; that at eight months, the foal would have fine hair all over its body and would be the size of a small dog, say, a Border Collie; that at nine months, the foal should have shifted head toward its mother's tail because it would become too big to turn any later in pregnancy; that at day 299, the foal could not survive yet, but that at day 300, it changed from non-viable to extremely premature; that at day 325 and all the way to day 360, the foal was full-term. I noted when each mare needed to have increases in her concentrations of protein or dietary changes to ensure proper calcium and phosphorous balance. I administered the appropriate vaccines at the appropriate stages of gestation to ensure optimum immune response and quality antibody concentrations in the first milk for the foal.

None of this made eleven months go by faster, but it certainly built anticipation and excitement.

Lash shared in the watching and waiting for my Y2K foal crop, but her enthusiasm was for a time tempered by what was missing from the picture: Steorling's foal, conceived then lost in the spring of 1999 before it ever had a chance to develop beyond hope and dreams and a dark blob on the ultrasound screen. Although she knew well enough the uncertainties inherent in horse breeding, Lash had been practically apoplectic when Steorling had aborted her pregnancy, decrying her awful luck, pouting and bemoaning the inequities of her life. Despite her half-empty cup attitude, she still cheered as my own mares conceived, hovered with me, stared at the ultrasound screen with each pregnancy check, and by the time Y2K rolled around, her focus was on the coming months, when we would breed Steorling to Joho and when my babies would start hitting the ground.

She was as immersed as I in the anticipation, the breathless waiting and watching. She was beside me in the barn aisle and stared with me at the mares, our foreheads leaning against the stall bars, the steam of our breath collecting in droplets on the metal before freezing to a thin white film. She stood with me in the stall, me on one side of the mare, Lash on the other, our palms resting against taught, warm flanks as the mare, content, ate her hay, and Lash and I talked, then stared at each other over the mare's back, our eyes wide, smiles frozen on our faces, when we simultaneously felt the thud and bump of the mare's invisible cargo, kicking and bucking in its dark, small world.

Roanoke was due to foal in early March, carrying the first Joho baby conceived on Donley Farm East, the first foal of the millennium to be born there, and her first foal, period. Ro was a big mare, not just tall, but all over big. Big boned, big bodied, and from all appearances, she carried a big baby too. As her belly grew and extended earthward, and her udders expanded, indicating she was getting ready for the big event, Lash and I grew more excited. So did my mother, who actually owned Ro (although this first baby would be mine), and

Amy, my student worker, a neurobiology student at Hiram College who was getting good practical experience helping out around the farm.

Most mares foaled at night—a survival mechanism built in so that they have some cover from predators—and their deliveries were fast, at most a half an hour from the time the mare's water breaks until the foal was completely delivered. And that foal will be on its feet within an hour or so of its birth, ready to run with its mother. These safeguards helped ensure survival of the mare and foal during a normal delivery. They also gave virtually no margin for error; small problems could become catastrophic within minutes. Which was why it was so important for someone to attend the birth—to watch that all went normally, to intervene when appropriate, to know when to call the vet. Being there was complicated by the fact it was the mare's instinct to foal alone and undisturbed, that labor was fast and explosive, and that the mare could interrupt early labor if she wasn't relaxed in her setting.

I spent many years sleeping in barns in the spring because once I witnessed a mare foaling when I was thirteen years old, I was determined to attend every foaling I possibly could. How could I explain it? At one moment, there was a pregnant mare quietly eating her hay, and a half an hour later, she was lying flat on her side in the throes of labor, and this new life emerging from her, diving from the womb to the world, its two front feet first, its nose extended over its shins, and with each push, more of this miracle came forth. You saw, even through the white, translucent amnion covering the foal, its color, its markings, the shape of its face. You watched its eyes blink open, looking at its new world while its back half was still gripped within its mother. You watched it slip, steaming, onto the straw, lift its head, shake the amnion off, listen to it sputter its first breaths. You smelled the heat of the mare, the amniotic fluid dampening straw, a tang of blood, manure. Then the mare rolled up onto her chest, straw and sawdust clinging in her mane, and she looked around behind her, at what she had just done, and even a mare that had never had a baby before sniffed, ears up, and whickered a greeting. When she lurched to her feet a few minutes later, breaking the umbilical cord as she turned to nuzzle and inspect her foal, her baby was already flailing, responding to some primal urge to stand, eat, run, *now*. The half-ton mother orbited her new mission in life, answered to new instincts pummeling her, poured milk from her udders, and met people or horses she knew and welcomed an hour earlier with impressive hostility.

A foaling was one of the most life-affirming events, and made me grateful and jubilant at the wonder and beauty of it. When it all went well. When it didn't go well, someone being there to recognize and correct the problem, to call the vet, could make the difference between live and dead horses.

In all the years I was involved with horse breeding, spending my springs setting up camp in the barn and sleeping outside mares' stalls, I witnessed as dozens of beautiful new lives came into the world and only experienced a small handful of problems. I gladly played the role of equine midwife for friends' mares when I wasn't babysitting a mare of my own, and over the years, I learned to judge what seemed normal and what did not. I became a pretty accurate prognosticator as to what night a mare was likely to foal, and what night she was less likely to foal. Even so, I was not comfortable enough with mares' predictability to risk missing it, so spent many, many nights camped in the barn, sleeping on hay bales outside mares' stalls, waiting. Lash spent many of those nights with me, as did Nettie, waiting out the mares, determined to be there. When we were young and restless, it was an annual spring adventure, and sometimes we spent weeks sleeping in the barn.

By the time Roanoke showed all the signs that she was nearing the end of her pregnancy, the novelty of sleeping in the barn had worn off me years earlier, and the barn especially was not inviting in early March in Ohio, when snow was common still and sub-zero temperatures not unheard of. Inhospitable weather for camping, and not the best weather for foals, either. Of course, a big advantage of living on the farm instead of driving between my apartment in Hiram and where I had boarded was that I was able to get up all night long and trudged down to the barn in my bathrobe. In fact, from my bed, I was able to look out the bedroom window and watched the mare in her stall if I had the barn windows open.

As far as Lash was concerned, another advantage of my living on the farm with my mares was I could call her at any point in the middle of the night if I thought the mare was getting ready, she stayed warm and snug in bed with Anton and waited for the phone to ring.

As it turned out, Roanoke started her labor on the evening of March 6, when Lash had evening appointments and couldn't be there. She left the farm in the late afternoon after extracting promises from me to call her with updates. So it was my mother and me, with Amy video-recording, who watched Ro's labor progress, watched as her water broke, watched as the huge mare eased her bulk down into the straw. I went quietly into the stall and knelt behind the mare. Donning a sterile obstetrical sleeve, I slipped my hand into Ro's vulva, and immediately a hoof thrust into my palm; I took a mental note: *good, active baby. Moving a lot.* I cupped the hoof, *big, big foot, big baby*, then slid my hand in further, felt the foal's ankle, and the other hoof just next to it. *Good. One leg slightly advanced—the way it's supposed to be so those shoulders fit through the pelvis.* I groped my way deeper, against the push of the mare's body, past the foal's second ankle, my hand and arm clamped in the vice of the mare's birth canal, until my fingers bumped into the wedge of the foal's nose, resting atop its shins, exactly where it belonged. *Good. Two feet and a muzzle. This was a big baby.* I slid my hand back down, brought my arm from the dark warmth of Ro into the cold air, and the first hoof followed my hand out.

Feeling a foal in its mother, feeling it positioned correctly, feeling it move was exciting, but seeing the first glimpse of a new baby always hit me; those were the moments that stayed with me. I saw the first rim of hair at the top of the hoof and knew what color the baby was, something that was determined at the moment of conception, had been true all along the eleven months of pregnancy, but that I didn't get to know till now. Or, if I saw white hair, I knew there was a marking on that foot. When the next foot appeared, I got to find out if that leg had a sock or other marking. As the nose, then face, then forehead appeared, I got to see what facial markings, if any, the baby had. It was like Christmas or a birthday, the wrapping fell away to reveal the treasure it had been hiding.

The hoof that followed my hand out of Ro's vulva and into the cold March air was topped by black hair. A bay, or possibly dark bay. Not a chestnut. No marking on this first foot. And it was big, as big as it felt, and even though all was progressing normally, I felt a thrill of anxiety. *Such a big baby for a first time mother.* But Ro herself is a big mare. Big mare, big baby.

The next hoof peeked out, slipped back in, then slid out to the ankle with Ro's next push. Another black ankle, no markings.

With both of the foal's feet now clear of the mare, the next to appear would be the nose, and as the baby's forehead cleared the mare's vulva, its shoulders—the widest part of the foal—would be passing through her pelvis. Usually, even if the delivery itself seemed slow, there was measurable progress. Each push the mare gave yielded another inch or two of foal.

And that was how it started with Ro, but before the foal's nose emerged, her progress seemed to halt. Ro, lying flat on her side—a position in which the mare's own weight and a horizontal plane for the foal to travel aided the mare's expulsive efforts—pushed and strained. With each push, the foal's legs protruded, and I saw Ro's rectum bulge as the baby's nose, wedged atop its shins, strained at the tissue veiling it from the outside world. When Ro's contraction eased, so did the bulge, and the legs would be no further out. I waited for a few minutes of Ro pushing like this; sometimes with a first time mother, it took a while for the tissues to relax and stretch. But when the nose stayed hidden from view, I grasped the foal's ankles, and pulled when Ro pushed, just a little help to move the baby along.

Still, the nose did not emerge. The rectal bulge increased, and I stared wide-eyed at the bulge. *Jean's mare prolapsed her rectum and died just last week*, I thought, and I swallowed. I had never seen a mare with a prolapsed rectum, but I knew it could happen. The mare could push and push and if something kept the foal from moving, then from the force of her contractions, the mare could push her intestines out. *Get this baby out before she prolapses*, I thought, but I wasn't panicked. I pulled, and told my mother to come in to help pull. And the legs seemed to emerge more, but the bulge at Ro's rectum emerged too.

I wracked my brain, tried to understand what was happening and what to do, when Ro pushed once more, and the foal's nose tore through the bulging tissue and stabbed into the world through the mare's rectum, and I understood.

"Shit! Stop pulling," I said. I turned to my mother. "Call the vet. Tell them we have a recto-vaginal fistula," and I turned back to Ro even before my mother rose from the straw. I cupped my hand over the foal's nose and pushed it back inside the rectum, back through the hole it had rent and held it there, while I reached in Ro's vulva with my other hand, and groping up, felt for, then found the baby's chin. I grabbed its lower jaw, pulled its chin and pushed its nose down, and redirected it until suddenly, the muzzle popped out of Ro's vulva, right on top of the shins where it belonged, and the baby began emerged just as it should have to begin with.

But the damage to Ro was done, and it was my fault. I knew something wasn't right, but hadn't figured it out when I should have, hadn't prevented preventable damage.

For as huge as the foal was, Ro delivered her first baby fast and efficiently once I corrected its position. And if I didn't know Ro had a muzzle-sized hole in her rectum, I would have delighted, as I always did, at how lively the foal was, at how smitten Ro was, looking over at what she had just done. Instead, I was on the phone with the vet, sick to my stomach with guilt, explaining yes, the foal was out, yes, he seemed fine, and yes, the mare was in trouble. By the time the vet arrived, just before 10 p.m., Roanoke had gotten to her feet and was nuzzling her colt, himself wobbling precariously on his own tenuous stilts. She had massive swelling, but the vet's exam showed she wasn't actively hemorrhaging. We needed to give her antibiotics and pain killers plus keep her as comfortable as possible. After the swelling went down and she had some time to recover from foaling, she would need surgery to repair the damage. She was not as badly injured as she might have been—often when a foal was as badly positioned like this colt had been, it would tear its way out through the rectum and all of the surrounding perineal tissues.

"You saved her," Amy said, almost breathless.

I shook my head. "I failed her," and even though I knew that correcting the foal's position had prevented the muzzle-sized hole from becoming a gaping chasm, I also should have recognized what was happening and corrected it before there was any hole at all. But I had not. I had simply stared at it and watched it happen. I looked at the camcorder hanging around Amy's neck, and felt a twist in my stomach. She had filmed the entire scene, and now that evidence of my failure lurked there in digital detail. I had failed Roanoke by not protecting her, and I had failed my mother by not taking care of her horse. No one else needed to blame me or point a finger.

I named Ro's colt Sandusky, and in every way he was impressive: huge, with beautiful conformation, and an intelligent, sensible nature evident in his first early hours. And even injured as she was, Ro proved an excellent mother. She doted on her colt, stood rock still for him to nurse, and importantly, she was sensible with people being around him and with her in the stall. Some mares, like Mysty, were especially nervous and protective during their babies' first few days. Although Ro was appropriately maternal, she was nevertheless manageable and easy to handle, which was good, because she needed regular treatment for her injury. But she was very uncomfortable, and spent a lot of time lying down. Sandusky sometimes lay down right in front of her, which looked adorable, but made me nervous because I was afraid Ro would accidentally step on him when she stretched her front legs out to get back to her feet.

The next afternoon, the vet stopped by to check on Ro and Sandusky. The colt was the picture of health, and Ro was doing as well as could be expected. With the vet's approval, Lash and I let Ro and Sandusky out in the pasture late in the afternoon, as the March sun was rolling westward in the sky and the shadows lengthened. Ro seemed happy to be out, and moved off across the field, whickering to Sandusky, who bounced along by her side like a dinghy. It was a beautiful sight, this first Johanniter baby on Donley Farm East, out testing his impossibly long legs, taking in the huge new world with his mother.

Lash and I followed the pair around the pasture, laughed as Sandusky tried to imitate his mother eating grass, gasped when he stumbled, and heaved a sigh when he trotted off unharmed. Even Ro, sore and damaged as she was, seemed buoyed by the time in the sun, grazing at the first suggestions of spring grass. Sandusky roved around her, sniffed at the air, swiveled his head and blinked at the world. He trotted next to Ro, and suddenly one of his hind feet disappeared below the surface of the winter-matted grass, his tiny hoof finally hitting solid footing when it seemed the ground had swallowed half his leg. Lash and I gasped simultaneously, a reflex, but Sandusky kept moving, his momentum carrying him forward, lifting his leg out of whatever deep foot print or cleft had claimed it, and he continued on, unperturbed, sound and whole. Lash and I shrieked on our exhale, leaning against each other, clutching and laughing at the sudden horror and instant relief we'd just experienced. I had never owned a horse with a broken leg, or even seen one, and I didn't ever want to.

Lash and I watched Ro with her new baby for a few hours that afternoon, the colt robust and hale, spending his new life nursing and breathing and soaking in the world; and Ro doted on him, smitten yet sensible, posing as the epitome of the ideal broodmare. Yet when we brought the mare and her new foal back in to the barn at dusk, her grotesquely swollen perineum, draining blood and bits of manure, sobered my mood. When she got back into her stall, she ate her dinner, then lay down, clearly uncomfortable. Sandusky cavorted around her before settling himself into the straw as well.

After Lash left that evening, I tried to watch the video of Ro's foaling, but pressed stop as the footage neared the calamity. I felt my skin prickle and I stared into space for a while, my heart thudding, horrified at what had happened, shamed that the video captured it in graphic detail, so clearly testimonial to my incompetence and guilt. After a moment, I pressed record, and videoed the living room floor for several minutes, as if recording over the history of what had happened the night before would somehow also erase my culpability. Then I stood alone on my back porch in the dark, staring into the night sky awash with stars. A blaze of light startled me, and for several seconds, I watched the most vibrant shooting star I had ever seen course across the aborigine canvas before it sparked and flared out.

A sign, surely.

So I prayed. *God, please help Roanoke. Please let her heal and be all right.*

I watched the mare and foal on the closed circuit TV in my bedroom. Watched in black and white as Sandusky capered around the mare, watched him nurse, watched him investigating the wooden walls and straw floor of his vast new world. I watched Ro loving on her colt, mothering him, the consummate doting mother. I watched as her pain frequently distracted her, so she'd curl a hind leg toward her belly, or lie down only to get up in a moment or two, then lie down again. Sandusky stood over the mare when she lay down and mouthed at her mane, or cantered in a circle around her. When she'd stretch out her fore-legs in front of her to rise again, she seemed to take up the whole stall, and the colt bucked and bounced around her. For a long time, I stood and watched the TV, watched this enormous, vibrant, healthy colt, my first Johanniter foal born on my farm, and he was the embodiment of the quality, temperament, size—everything I hoped to produce with my breeding operation. I should have been flushed with pride, this colt validating my plans and efforts. But every time Ro lay down again, my guilt surged against my pride.

Late in the evening, when Ro was lying in her stall with Sandusky curled asleep in the straw in front of her, I walked back down to the barn. As I ap-proached, I heard the mare hoist herself up again, and I couldn't help cringing at the sound of her scrambling and bashing the stall walls. I entered the dark barn; at the far end, the single light in the foaling stall cast shadows on the barn aisle floor. The straw rustled as the mare and foal moved in the big stall, a bright sound I'd long ago associated with the joy and excitement of new babies; and even despite my guilt, a little thrill jabbed my tummy, so when I got to the stall front and leaned my forehead against the bars, I was smiling at the mare and foal inside. I stood for a moment outside the stall, looking in at the pair, breathing the distinct odors of babies, straw and milk, and maybe a little tang of sweat and blood.

Ro stood over Sandusky, who was sprawled across the straw. He scram-bled to rise, but still hadn't quite mastered coordination of his long, long legs. I went into the stall and when he tried again, I supported and steadied him. Then he stood there, his butt wedged against my thigh. Something about the way he moved, or rather didn't move, and how Ro circled him, hovering, bothered me. Ro swung her head around me and nuzzled Sandusky's back. I shifted my weight so he no longer leaned on me. The colt stood still. When I reached out and stroked his neck, he looked at me and took a tiny hop, not putting any weight on his left front leg.

My own legs felt like lead. I squatted next to the colt and ran my hands down his limb, my palms gliding over his solid forearm, grazing over his knob-by knee, stopping at the scuff mark on the middle of his shin, right over the mid-shaft of that long, vulnerable cannon bone that flopped like a broken branch under my palms.

I stood back up, my mouth dry as cotton, my heart slamming, and with the colt leaning against me again, I looked through the window up to my house and knew a visceral urge to go back there, into the warm light and safety and benign black and white closed circuit TV, to leave this scene that was so wrong, and come back down in a few minutes, when surely it would be different, not this accident, this incongruity. For an instant, I breathed that urgency and it sizzled through me. Then I turned from Sandusky and Ro, hurried from the stall and into the tack room, where I gathered bandages and two heavy tree stakes.

When I returned to the stall, I had already left an emergency page for the vet. In paramedic mode, I busied myself treating the emergency in front of me. I hunkered down next to Sandusky, wrapped quilts and bandages around the colt's leg, using the tree stakes as splints. Ro stood behind me, hovering, sometimes touching her muzzle to my back, sometimes reaching over my shoulder and pressing her nose against her baby's neck. He stood on three legs in the middle of the big stall and did not move as I wrapped a quilt around his cannon bone, then placed one tree stake at the front of his leg, one at the back, secured it all with a polo bandage. His leg was immobilized from the ground to his elbow when I stood back up.

Then, with bile stinging my tongue, I stood in the cold March night and waited for the vet, Sandusky standing crippled in front of me and Ro standing damaged at my back.

An hour later, the vet sat on the stall floor, Sandusky's broken leg resting across his lap, my bandages and splints removed and lying in the straw next to them. "That's a good splint," the vet had said as he removed the bandages to examine the colt. A good splint. Not that it mattered. The baby's cannon bone was snapped in half, a fatal and preventable injury. If I had prevented Ro's birth trauma, she would not have been so uncomfortable that she was constantly lying down and getting up. She would have stayed standing guard over her newborn as he lay sleeping; she would not have been lying down, Sandusky curled into the straw in front of her, and she would not have stretched her own front legs in front of her, one of her huge hooves landing on and pinning her colt's leg to the stall floor, shattering his bones as she rose to her feet again. And Sandusky would not be lying dead now in the same stall into which he'd been born a day earlier.

Ro, tranquilized into a stupor, stood over her dead baby and she wasn't aware of it when we lifted Sandusky's body and carried him from the stall. We wrapped the colt in a blanket, hoisted him into the bed of my truck, and took him to my Amish hay-man Danny's house, where the next morning, Danny buried the first Johanniter foal born at Donley Farm East.

In all the years I had been around horses, I'd never lost a baby, and I'd never seen a broken leg. But suddenly, the night of March 7, 2000, I had both, and within hours of praying on a shooting star for Ro's recovery. Had I prayed wrong, or my request been audacious? Had I asked for too much, I who already had so much, begging for reparations of damage, which should never have occurred, because I should have foreseen and prevented it? So Ro suffered, and for a little while, Sandusky suffered too, bone-shatter suffering. But when his bright, quick life ended and his suffering was finished, Ro's was compounded for a time, her baby disappeared, her body still torn.

Lash helped hold me together in the next few weeks as Indy's foaling date approached. I was terrified for Indy, and asked Lash, more than once, what had I done to my favorite mare? I had bred Indy, and now she carried her first foal, just as Ro had a few weeks earlier. Now Ro was seriously injured and her colt was dead. I could not undo Indy's pregnancy, or Mysty's, or Silver's. The long winter wait of impatience morphed to anxiety. What had I done?

I spent the nights as Indy neared her foaling hunkered down in the hay in her stall, lying against the wall as she nibbled the hay out from under me, determined to protect her, only a little worried that she might step on me, and feeling it would be some kind of karma by-proxy and well-deserved if she did. But she didn't, and I had long night hours to fret and love her desperately.

Lash didn't reassure me with platitudes, but held my hand, literally, and together, we reviewed foaling text books, including all the sections on dystocia, abnormal foaling, so I could feel as prepared as possible. And in the evening of March 25, 2000, when I felt pretty confident that Indy was gearing up to deliver at any moment, Lash stuck to my side like a remora. She was calm and pragmatic. When Indy's water broke, she made note of the time. She kept track of how long each phase of the delivery took, and quietly relayed that information to me, telling me in that way that everything was proceeding normally. She heaved a sigh of relief just as I did when Indy's foal's nose followed its legs into the world without doing any damage to the mare. And when Indy strained to push the big foal's shoulders through her pelvis, Lash stood grasping the stall bars, intoning in a hushed voice, "Push Indy, push! That's a good girl! Push!"

Just after midnight on March 26, Indy rolled onto her chest, reached her head around, and nickered a greeting to Mackinac, a big, strapping, entirely healthy, entirely whole colt. Indy had a textbook delivery, Mack was textbook perfect, and Lash took me into her arms, hugging and rocking me, both of us toggling between laughing and sobbing.

A day went by with no disasters, then a week, then a month, and I bred Indy back to a local Swedish Warmblood stallion. I had a breeding farm, and that meant I needed to swallow my fear and breed horses.

About the same time the vet confirmed Indy in foal again, Mysty delivered the second Johanniter baby at Donley Farm East. Mysty's delivery was efficient and trouble-free, and her filly Savannah was tall and healthy and elegant and beautiful. The only incident occurred when Lash was helping me disinfect Savannah's umbilical stump and Mysty, a nervous and protective mother, bit Lash's shoulder. But even as she was writhing in pain, Lash was blaming herself for being careless, for not paying enough attention to Mysty's anxiety over her baby. That afternoon, she had mocked up a placard and plastered it on Mysty's stall door: *KEEP OUT!! Hostile horse!* And Lash had impressive bruising on her shoulder for weeks to prove it.

We bred Mysty back to Johanniter on her first heat cycle, two weeks after Savannah's birth, and two and a half weeks after that, the ultrasound revealed a little black blob to match the little black blob of Indy's ultrasound. And Lash's own Steorling was safely in foal to Johanniter, too, and showed no signs of early pregnancy loss as she had the previous year. Now 2001 was promising to have an active nursery, too. My grief and agitation over Roanoke and Sandusky's disastrous birth didn't disappear, but two healthy mares and foals, and successful breedings afterward helped ease it.

Silver, Indy's own mother, was due to deliver the fourth and final foal on Donley Farm East in early July; it would be my third Johanniter baby, and a full brother or sister to Indy. And because Silver had had an easy delivery with Indy and had been a good mother, I settled back into feeling competent and professional. But sometimes, sitting on my back porch at night, listening to the sound of the mares and foals in the darkness, grazing and moving around their pasture, I thought of Sandusky, and how he should be there with them, and how Ro should not have a hole between her rectum and vagina, waiting to be surgically repaired. The thoughts, deep and oppressive like the June night, kept a little seed of anxiety twisting and poking in my gut. Those were the times I sat in the dark, alone, and cried, and sometimes wondered if I was a fool, thinking I could do this; and the fact that I was sitting there alone in the dark seemed to confirm my foolishness.

chapter nine

The Thaw

In retrospect, I don't think it was chance that in 2000 I began the slow thaw from my decade long self-imposed romance exile. I think some things are set in motion according to a bigger plan. But at the time, I just thought I was tired of being alone in my bed all the time, and the Internet provided a vehicle by which I could dabble tentatively in the treacherous waters of romance with some degree of safety. For one thing, I could peruse with an anonymity that deflected or at least eased the sting of rejection.

At first, it was just a game Lash and I played one afternoon, cruising an online dating site, and cheerfully appreciating or cruelly rejecting my potential bedmates. It was fun, and somehow empowering to feel I had a choice, that I could inquire into a variety of men, throw the bait out and see what was biting. And because I did that with an online persona, I didn't risk putting *myself* out there, yet. It offered the kind of baby steps I needed to even consider the journey.

The first time I sent a message to someone online, I sat at the computer for a long, long time, my palms sweating, before I worked up the nerve to click send. Then, I dreaded a response, then fretted and glowered when no message came back to me within a half an hour. When the reply did come—*hi, thanks for your message, wow, you sound busy! I like horses too*—my stomach flipped and I literally paced the room in the dark, getting a feel for this strange new inroad I was exploring. When I breathlessly admitted to Lash what I had done, a grin spread over her face as if she'd just been invited on a cruise, and pretty soon, my email filled up with links she sent with the profiles of men she thought I should pursue. We had disagreements about how aggressive I should be. I refused to contact anyone who noted in his profile that he sought a thin or athletic or fit woman. Why set myself up for failure, I reasoned. Lash argued that I shouldn't judge my attractiveness to a man for him. I countered that he had already judged me unattractive because he wanted thin or fit. I simply wasn't willing to try and convince someone that I met his physical criteria when I did not.

I was pleasantly surprised when I actually developed ongoing dialogue with a few men, even though they knew I was a bigger woman. I even met one or two for coffee or lunch in public places, and although no sparks flew, somehow being able to say I was *dating* battered at some psychological barrier I had imposed. Even if I never left the coffee shop with a man, *dating* let me move from the realm of unwanted old maid spinster, a fat woman who sat alone and unattached for years, to the realm of the bigger woman who had a choice in matters of romance.

Having started was enough for the moment; I hadn't yet found anyone I wanted to introduce to my life on the farm. Lash again encouraged me to hunt down Arnold, but I just rolled my eyes at her and sent messages to strangers online.

In early July, in the small hours of the morning, Silver efficiently delivered her second foal, a full brother to Indy. Nettie and I were alone with Silver in the barn to welcome that last foal of 2000, and once again returned to delight in the beauty and surprise of birth. This colt was chestnut to his mother's dark bay, and he had a star, stripe, and snip on his face. He and Silver were healthy and vibrant, and I named him Cyprus. If he had been a filly, I would have named him Venice. These names were especially fun to choose, because I played with a Shakespearian theme. Silver's registered name was Iago's Quicksilver. Her mother's name was Othello's Treasure, and Treasure's father's name was Modern Iago. And because Cyprus and Venice were the settings of *Othello*, I was especially pleased at having thought of them for names.

For the first few days of Cyprus's life, I turned Silver and him out in a separate pasture adjoining the pasture that the other mares and foals were in. This way, they could all see each other and get used to the new baby before I put Silver back with the herd. It was always a balancing act, deciding when to turn a mare with her new foal back in with their herd; horses are herd animals, and don't want to be separated. But the new mother is protective and jealous at the same time that her herd mates want to investigate the new arrival.

The Sunday after he was born, I decided Cyprus and Silver could go back with the herd. The other horses ignored them in their adjoining pasture, and

Silver paced the fence line, pining to be back with her friends. So, Nettie and I opened the gate between the two pastures, and Silver led her new baby out of solitary confinement and into company. It was a beautiful sight. Purple summer blossoms flecked the clover, and the glossy mares and foals coasted over the turf in the afternoon sun. My farm. My mares. My foals. My stallion stood in the next pasture, watching over his children. I stood in the back of my barn leaning on the gate, with the summer breeze drifting over me, and watched the embodiment of my dream, all that I had worked so hard for.

We were getting ready to go out and gather up Silver and Cyprus and bring them in when the mares and foals headed toward the barn on their own. I watched them move along the fence-line, saw Savannah stretch her neck toward Cyprus, curious, investigating. Cyprus stopped to meet his sister, and they touched noses. Savannah squealed, playful, but at that sound from her baby, Mysty leaped toward the two babies, herself squealing and kicking protectively. Silver swooped into the fray and shuttled Cyprus away and toward the barn.

Cyprus cantered with his mother, his legs so long he moved giraffe-like, and I watched as he ran toward the barn on four legs, then suddenly on three legs. Each time his left hind foot touched the ground, his hoof splayed out to the side, the bones in his ankle shattered, slicing through his skin with each step.

Nettie swallowed a shriek, corralled him in her arms, and between the two of us, we half-carried the crippled colt back to the barn, Silver glued to us like a remora. Cyprus's mangled leg flopped against my own legs as Nettie and I shuttled the baby down the aisle; his blood smeared my shins. We got the pair into their stall, and I lifted the colt and laid him down on the floor; he fell immediately into an exhausted sleep, his head on Nettie's lap, his blood-spattered legs sprawled across the straw. Silver stood guard, her head hanging low over her colt.

As if ensnared in some kind of recurring nightmare, I repeated my actions from a few months earlier. I put in an emergency after-hours page to the vet because I had a baby horse with a broken leg; while I waited for the vet to arrive, I treated the emergency in front of me. I put another splint on another broken leg of another of my Johanniter foals. I decided, sometime during the wait for the vet, I would be proactive and send the colt for surgery, spend whatever it cost—even though I didn't have the money, even though my credit cards were already maxed out—to give Cyprus a chance.

"That's a good splint," the vet had said as he removed the bandages, just as he'd said months earlier when he unwrapped Sandusky's leg. It didn't matter this time, either. He examined Cyprus's leg, his face grim.

"There's nothing we can do, Karen," he said, and told me what I already assumed but had hoped I was wrong, that both the pastern bones below the colt's ankle were shattered, irreparable even if the wound weren't open, horribly contaminated, shards of bone lodged every which-way through the flesh.

"But I was going to take him to surgery," I repeated, as if that would somehow influence the injury's character.

"There's nothing we can do," the vet said in a thick voice, shook his head and slumped back against the stall wall. "Even if this were Secretariat, they'd put him to sleep."

Twenty minutes later, the vet stood leaning at the back gate of the barn, looking out over the pastures. Then he put his head down on his arms, and kicked at the dirt with his foot. Nettie and I sat in the stall with Cyprus's lifeless body, and I stroked his silky brown coat, and told him over and over again how sorry I was, told Silver I was so sorry I hadn't protected her baby better, so sorry I'd let him die.

Again, I called Lash and told her my new foal was dead, his leg broken, and again, Lash held my head above water as I floundered. She'd been by my side before when I had to euthanize horses. She'd stood with me by Cassie's side as the mare sank to the ground by her grave and I wept farewell to the mother of my first Johanniter baby. Two years later, Lash held me in her arms as the vet gave Kalinka a lethal dose of barbiturates. And she rocked me and let my keening roll over her when Lilly went from this world in the driveway in front of the barn at Donley Farm East, an old mare claiming the dubious distinction of being the first horse to die on that farm.

Amid the birth and death at the farm, Lash absorbed my horror and anger and grief when my uncle committed suicide. It was she I called late at night, immediately after hanging up with my mother, and wept out the words, "Dick committed suicide," and I felt stunned and stymied by the irrevocability of the past tense in "committed." When my mother whispered into the phone, barely able to say the words, that her youngest brother had killed himself, my brain kept screaming *wait, wait, wait*, but that past tense word meant there was no undoing the bullet from having smashed through his brain.

And bookending Dick's suicide, these two broken legs and my two dead foals, and there seemed some exclusive agony that belonged to the ending of an infant's life. These two babies should not have died. They'd been born perfect, I should have been able to keep them that way, but I had failed them, failed their mothers. Silver, who was uninjured as Ro hadn't been, didn't respond to the heavy sedation the vet administered, but whirled frantically around the stall, screaming for her baby, calling him again and again all day, into and through the night, until I thought she'd settled when I couldn't hear her the next morning, then realized only that she'd lost her voice. Still she called and called, her mouth open, her body shuddering with each mute whinny she belted out. Milk sprayed from her udders, and when we turned her out with Indy and Mysty and their two foals, Silver paid those babies no attention, but paced the pastures, searching for Cyprus, smelling, I was sure, where he'd been. For days, Silver searched for him, and even when we bred her back to Joho on her foal heat, ten days after Cyprus's birth, still she dripped milk from her udders.

Somewhere in my gut, doubt and grief and fear and anger and guilt wrapped around each other until they'd knotted into a tight, dense poisonous core, some kind of seed of despair and doubt that didn't die, but took root and burrowed into my farm dream and my confidence. And for all of Lash's support and quiet presence, the knowledge that effort and desire and good intentions could be irrelevant was born and wouldn't die.

I tried to be pragmatic and reason through my angst, telling myself and others I knew horse breeding was uncertain and shit happened, and perhaps I was due, because I'd been mostly shitless and lucky over the years. So I plowed forward with my breeding plans, because I wouldn't have a horse breeding business if I didn't breed horses. When Silver was confirmed in foal again a few weeks after Cyprus died, I had a barn full of pregnant mares again, but the excitement was tempered now, despite even the soundest logic and reason. It was like a crack in glass, a flaw you couldn't erase, damage that was done, and crept and grew like a fault, destroying the integrity of the something once clear and strong and brilliant.

Sometimes, even with the ground tremulous under me, with anxiety and doubt planing everything into knife edges and sharp turns, exquisite moments found me, surprised me, and buffered some of those knife edges with an honest simplicity. In those moments, the horses and the dream shone through my tension and doubt, like sun burning the dew off the grass, and I could breathe. That these lovely moments were ushered in by fear of disaster, of losing a horse, seemed at once requisite and apologetic. Almost soothing. As if something sought to give me some gentle token of solace, show me glimpses of beauty at a time when I was losing sight of it.

Several times that summer, Joho's screams would wake me, and I sat bolt upright in bed, my heart adrenaline-slamming. If I could hear him with my windows closed and the air conditioner running, I knew my Amish neighbors could hear him. His screaming followed the sound of his hooves, pounding the ground along his fence line, from the barn at the top of the hill, down into the dip, thundering back to the high crest of the next hill.

I looked out the window next to my bed. I couldn't see him, or any of the other horses, in the darkness, but I knew what set him off, got him running and bellowing in the small hours when the civil world was sleeping. In the deep summer, fog nestled like bolsters on the ground between the hills. The mares had grazed their way into the fog, disappeared from the stallion's view, left him alone and apoplectic on his side of the fence.

I threw my covers aside and hurried through the dark house in my night-shirt, not bothering with clothes or even a robe. My heart was coming down from its adrenaline full throttle, but I was still anxious and hurried. Aside from the stallion waking the entire community and souring my current good neigh-borly relations, I was afraid he'd hurt himself in his frenzy. Or would run him-self into an early grave. That had seemed to be my luck with horses this year; niggling paranoia made me wonder if some keen cruelty would create a spring with two dead foals and follow that with a summer and a dead stallion. He was an old horse, and I intensely wanted him to continue getting older. He scared me when he did this.

In the mudroom, I stuffed my feet into a pair of muck boots, opened the door, and stepped into the steamy wall of the night. I couldn't see the road, so no one on the road could see me; in the rural countryside, I was nearly invisible, so I could walk in the wide open spaces in my all-together, and not concern my-self with critical glances. The moon, riding high in the sky, was bright enough to cast shadows. I followed my own shadow, wide and squat, toward the barn. My moon shadow was not so far from my body's truth, but it seemed particu-larly harsh for even the moon to point it out.

I hurried down the drive to the barn, looking to my right over the pastures and catching my breath at the loveliness of the fog, piled like meringue in the valleys. All around, fireflies flickered. I wanted to stop and soak in the beauty of this nightscape, but I couldn't, not yet. Joho did not appreciate the beauty. He galloped his fence-line, screaming for his mares to return. I wondered if his heart was about to explode, or if he'd battered his feet and legs to smithereens.

I hustled through the barn without turning on the lights, found a lead shank on a stall front, and slipped through the sliding door into the mares' pas-ture. The stallion heard the door, knew then that I was there, and he thundered back along the fence-line, sliding to a stop and spraying me with bits of dirt and pebbles. I could not calm him, only his mares could do that, but he knew I was there to retrieve them because we'd done this before. I hoped that knowledge quelled his anxiety. He stood next to me for a moment, just the fence between us; the heat poured off him and rolled over me like a wave, heavy and humid. I heard and felt the slam of his heart in his massive chest; the air vibrated with it. *Please don't kill yourself, Old Man*, I thought, maybe even muttered it out loud as he blew and quivered next to me in the dark. My own heart rate ramped up a bit, so I tried to exude calm and quiet, hoping low-key vibes would calm him, help him relax and settle. I didn't know if I could bear it if something happened to him. Emotions aside, I had mortgaged my farm to buy him. I was barely placating the bank now as it was; I could not afford for this horse to die—couldn't afford it emotionally, couldn't afford it financially.

"Don't worry old man," I said, "There's no fog phantom stallion out there steeling your mares. I'll go get them for you." I turned and started toward the wall of mist, and Joho twisted and bolted down his fence-line again, his bellow starting somewhere deep within him, gathering in volume and rumbling out as he galloped. He seemed less frenetic, but I knew he wouldn't fully settle until he saw his mares again.

The moon illuminated the fields, and I followed one of the trails the mares had made over the summer. I walked down the hill and into the fog; it enveloped me. Taller weeds, bowing with dew over the trail, brushed my bare legs, left droplets and seeds. I saw nothing but the fog, which somehow still seemed to glow white even in the middle of the night.

I walked blind for a while, hearing my breath and the tread of my own feet and somewhere, as if filtering through from above, other quiet night noises. I stopped to listen. Behind me, muffled by the mists but distinct, came the sound of the old stallion, still running the fence. I strained to hear the mares—a sigh, a tail swish, a mouthful of grass being ripped, telling me their direction and distance, but they were still lost to me in the mists.

"You girls are probably all standing at the back fence hushing each other and giggling at Joho," I said and laughed. I wondered how far my voice carried in the mist, if the mares heard me, wherever they were in the six acres of this field. Next to me, clinging to the top of a tall stem of orchard grass, a firefly blinked in a steady rhythm. But its light seemed stymied. How many more fireflies occupied this cloud on the ground, were in there blinking away, even though the fog swallowed up every flicker? I looked at my firefly, watched it send its light out, a light that died only inches into the fog, but the firefly didn't stop flashing. I wasn't sure if it was a stoic little bug or just naïve, following the basest of bug instincts.

I walked on, and must have been three-quarters the way to the back of the pasture when I stopped next. I stood again, silent, listening. Joho thundered some distance behind me now, almost a background noise. At least he'd stopped his screaming. From the woods beyond the pasture fence I heard an owl, then another. The hem of my nightshirt was damp and clung to my thighs. In a few hours, I'd be sitting at my desk in work clothes. I doubted very much any of my coworkers besides Lash could picture me as I was, standing half naked in the middle of a pasture in the middle of the night, trying to round up a group of mares gone AWOL. It struck me how atypical my nighttime activities were. When I left my bed in the wee hours to roam my pastures, no husband or boyfriend waited for me to slide back under the covers with him. No one would become concerned if I did not return.

Perhaps I should have been frightened out there, groping my way through the dark and fog, alone and vulnerable. But I was not frightened, whether or not I should have been. I felt no fear of what lay in the dark or hidden by the fog, but rather a ripple of exhilaration that this was my here and now. This time and place was mine. It didn't matter that I was fat. Even the bank couldn't see me here, couldn't reach out to take it away from me.

I focused my attention. Soon I heard what I had been listening for, a little ahead of me in the fog: a contented, nostril-rattling horse sigh.

"All right girls, time to stop playing games with the poor old man," I said to the mares ahead of me, and walked fog-blind through the dew-wet grass toward the sound of a sigh, or thump of a hoof, listening for more evidence of them. I walked until the horse sounds and smells were all around me, and a darker form took horse shape in the fog. I recognized Indy, and she lifted her head to greet me; I reached out and stroked her forehead, felt under my palm the cool damp of the dew on her hair and then, rising beneath, the heat of her. I ran my fingers through her forelock, and she nuzzled my nightshirt with her prehensile lips. Mack materialized from the fog and stuck his wet muzzle in my face, snuffling and lipping until I pushed him away. He turned then, bumping against his mother, and I heard the smack and slurp as he nursed. Indy's scent was just another current in the air, mingling with the scents of dirt and chewed grass and milk and nighttime, and I could have been content to simply stand there, sequestered in the misty night, with my hand on her forehead.

But her sire's mania still rumbled through the ground and fog to me, so I looped the cotton lead rope around the mare's neck. "C'mon, Indy, let's go back up before your old man has a heart attack."

I turned and headed back the way I'd come, following my own tracks I could just see in the grass; Indy ambled by my side, placid and content; her foal fell in behind me, sometimes butting my back with his nose. I heard and felt the other horses shifting in the dark and fog, moving with us, although I could not see any of them. Ahead of us, the sounds of the old stallion's snorting and running came to me through the mist.

As we neared the fence and moved uphill a bit, I heard the mares flanking us pick up the pace, heard their four-beat walks accelerate into two-beat trots, heard the foals cantering, and they all passed us by, even Indy's colt, running ahead with them. When Indy and I walked out of the fog, as if we were emerging through a door in a wall, I saw several of the mares already by the fence with the stallion. He stood tall, his huge neck arched, striking at the ground with his front feet, lashing his tail, nickering and squealing his greetings and reprimands. I let the lead shank slip from Indy's neck as she too meandered toward the fence.

I climbed the hill to the barn and lugged a bale of hay out to the mares. They didn't need it, but it would encourage them to stay near the stallion. Chaff stuck to my sweaty skin as I spread flakes of hay around in piles for the mares, and tossed a flake over the fence for the old stallion. Then I shimmied through the fence and ran my hands over his chest and neck; he was still hot but the sweat was already drying. He swung his massive head around me long enough to let me scratch his forehead, then turned his attention back to his mares and his hay.

Back in the barn, I latched the door to the mares' pasture. In just a couple hours, in the gray predawn light, I'd be back down here, dressed in my grubby barn clothes, bringing the horses in through that door to feed them in their stalls, where they'd snooze the day away, out of the sun and bugs while I was at work, trying to finance this whole farm folly.

I put the lead shank back on the stall door, and trudged up the hill to my dark house. On the back porch, I stopped and looked over the barn and pastures. My moon-shadow was slightly taller now, but no less pudgy. The moon rode westward, and under its pewter light I saw the hills, the white shock of fog in the valley, the faint pale ribbons of the fence lines, and fireflies scattered like glitter across it all; but the dark had swallowed the horses again. Owl calls floated from the woods with the murmurs of some other woodland creatures, prowling through their night lives. Closer, horses chewed hay, sighing, content.

I stood for a moment on the porch before I kicked off the muck boots. I brushed the chaff and bits of grass and seeds off my legs. I stripped off my damp nightshirt, used it to wipe my face and blot the sweat gathering in runnels in my cleavage. For a moment, I stood naked on my back porch, looking out over my pastures, clutching my damp, balled-up nightshirt to my chest. The buzzing white noise of ill fortune, of broken legs and my obesity and my debt seemed not to find me here. I felt I could breathe. Here was the silent flash and fade of fireflies, wending their way through the air of my farm, floating among my horses, drifting around my home, lighting their tiny territories, igniting their miniscule fires again and again, gentle, resolute flickers.

In November, my mother and I loaded Roanoke into the trailer and took her south to Columbus, where she had surgery at Ohio State University to repair the damage done at Sandusky's birth. Lash and Anton took care of the farm while we were gone. When we got home, and Ro went back into her stall to convalesce, I thought the changes Y2K brought must surely be finished, but I was wrong about that too.

During the late fall, I met with one of my online dating acquaintances enough in coffee shops and restaurants that we had exchanged home phone numbers, emails, and addresses. He was intelligent, kind, and seemed genuinely interested in me and my life. I invited him to the farm for dinner; then we watched his favorite movie, *Moonstruck*, and had a pleasant evening.

And that was all. If feelings were burgeoning in either of us, I was not aware of them.

That night, as I stood in my driveway in the dark and watched this perfectly nice man drive away, the thought *I miss Arnold* hit me unexpectedly, but with such force I had already decided what I was going to do before I got back in the house. I did something Lash had pushed me for years to do. I reached out to Arnold. I sent him a Christmas card.

I told Lash the next day.

"I don't know if he's still married," I cautioned her, and probably myself as well. "But I figured a Christmas card was benign enough that even if he *is* still married, no one can really object."

"Did you leave your contact information?"

"Of course."

"Like what?"

"Phone, address, email. You know."

"You should call him."

"No! Jeez. Cut me some slack. Besides, I don't have his phone number," I said on a sigh, exaggerated, rolled my eyes, and felt a giddy surge of excitement. "If he's available and wants to get back in touch, he will." I fully believed that was exactly what would happen.

I didn't start anticipating until a few days after I'd sent the card, and I waited with the assured impatience you felt when you waited for the first leaves in the spring. But Arnold didn't call or write, and as the days turned into weeks, I slumped, resigned and dejected.

"Must still be married," I said.

"I think you should call him," Lash said.

"No."

Lash and I both worked for Penske Logistics, but as with many employees of that large company, our desks were in different buildings; much of the communication between coworkers was via instant messenger or email. Because of an impressive firewall, not too many spam emails got through. So I resisted my immediate impulse to delete what I assumed was spam from an address I didn't recognize and with a subject line reading, *Imagine my surprise.*

Instead, I opened it.

Imagine my surprise when I went to my mailbox and found a Christmas card from Karen Louise Donley...

I was pounding out an instant message to Lash before I had even finished reading the email.

I got an email from Arnold!!!!!!!

In a flash she responded. *OMG!!!*

I know!

Is he married?

I don't think so.

Are you going to call?

I think so. Maybe tomorrow.

What's wrong with now?

Indeed. I picked up the phone and dialed the number Arnold had included in his message. I heard a grouchy voice, harried. I would not have recognized it. How many years since we had talked? I felt a little smile. "Is this Arnold Hayes?"

"Yeah. Who's this?"

"This is Karen Louise Donley."

And suddenly, such a change in that voice. "Karen Louise Donley, how the hell are ya?"

We spent the next half hour on the phone, telling each other how the hell we were, and by the end of the conversation, had set a time to meet on the campus of Hiram College, our alma mater.

Arnold says he never knew I was scoping him out that first date when we finally met in person again; he didn't even know it *was* a date. I joked that I had to be sure, to see him again, before I let him in on that little fact. But we did meet at Hiram; we went to lunch, we stopped by the farm, and back on Hiram's campus, visited our old haunts. By the end of that first afternoon, I'd told Arnold I missed him, and we'd agreed to give our romance another try.

Two days later, I invited him to come to the farm for dinner and our first *real* date. In the fifteen-plus years since our short, hot college fling, he'd been married and divorced, and I'd been almost entirely relationshipless. But in February of 2001, when he came to my farm in Parkman for that second date, we both knew we were where we were supposed to be, and he never left.

I sometimes wonder why I waited until that traumatic year to end my man drought, after so many years by myself, after I had accepted grudgingly my lot was to be alone, a year dominated by such tumult that toying around with online dating or forging new relationships should have been superfluous or trivial. Why that year? Why then for Arnold to be available, to come back into my life, slide in so completely and fully?

I didn't really believe God killed my foals, and I didn't believe God planted the seed of cancer that was already germinating in Lash when I sent the Christmas card to Arnold.

But I can't help thinking something more than chance was at work to set in motion the resurrection of Arnold's and my relationship; maybe it's all part of the bigger *something* I believe in when I say I think something good results from something bad. Maybe that something bigger was at work to bring Arnold and me together again right at that time, to shore each other's lives up, give to each other love and security. And to give me solace and hope over the next two years when the center of my world was crashing.

Arnold and I had been back together only three months when the lump swelled in Lash's breast and nothing was ever the same again.

chapter ten

Fat, Fat the Water Rat

A few weeks before she died, I told Lash that I was toying with the idea of bariatric surgery.

In fact, I was beyond toying and was actively lumbering toward the first hoops the insurance company insisted I jump through before they'd consider paying for it. And yet, with Lash sitting there in her hospital bed, dying in front of me, I felt petty and selfish confessing I was investigating drastic surgical measures to achieve weight loss and improved health, something I felt I should have been able to do without going under the knife. Still, if she had not been sitting there, wasting away and I ballooning, I might never have even considered this route at all. Her illness, in part, spurred me out of complacency. Now I was to undergo a sleep study as part of the pre-surgical work-up.

"It's just preliminary testing. I might not do it, you know," I told Lash.

Lash sat in her bed, picking at the sheet covering her edematous legs. She shot me a quick look, not lifting her head. "You'll do it," she said, quiet, and we both knew that she was right. If insurance cleared me, I would have bariatric surgery. But by then, Lash would be dead. We both knew that too.

Lash and I had been compatriots in the battle of the bulge from our adolescent years. In the '70s, when role models for girls were Twiggy or Farrah Fawcett or Nadia Comaneci, we suffered with our physical aberrations, in our size twelves or fourteens, Lash with her six-foot plus frame, me with hips and breasts of shame. We had not lissome bodies, and we collaborated in decades-long flirtations with thin, with lithe, with beautiful, with *good enough*. We made friends with some foods, temporary alliances, and shunned others. That's when we were *good* girls. Even when we were thin—and each of us did achieve thinness at times—we were never thin enough. For Lash especially, who during a longer thin spell dabbled with some modeling, she could not get too thin. Even when I thought she looked gaunt, she was too big because models had to fit into stock sizes off the rack, and at six foot one with a thirty-six inch inseam, Lash had simply outgrown a modeling career.

I was never model quality; even during my episodes of thinness I was too big. If I had been born with testicles instead of ovaries I could have been a linebacker. My shoulders were too broad, my hips too wide. Big feet, big head. And my breasts: sagging disappointments. The girls headed south as soon as they sprouted, never pausing at perky or even pert, nor were they in agreement as to size or expression (Marty Feldman eyes for nipples). In front of the mirror, I assessed my mammary aberrations. I nudged and pulled, wondering if tape or staples or magic exercises could gather the skin on one so that the nipple stopped looking at my knees, would gaze out more toward the world like her sister (who herself was moderately downcast by nature).

Trying on clothes, Lash and I bemoaned our personal physical shortcomings. I had ordered a bathing suit that looked nice in the catalog—conservative in cut and design, but still this side of a muumuu. When I squirmed my way into the thing, I was horrified by the reflection I saw: rolls of fat and cellulite even the heavier fabric didn't hide. My pale skin looked translucent and blue as the belly of a dead fish. My sagging breasts just added insult to injury, hanging in that suit like melons dropped into a pair of tube socks.

I lifted them one at a time shoulder-ward, tried shifting and rearranging, but it was useless. Gravity had them. I slumped (which did nothing to counteract the rising puff pastry effect), and in disgust, rolled the suit off and tossed it aside. I reached for the cover of my over-sized clothes.

"I'm never going swimming again," I sniffed. "Someone will think I'm a manatee that swam too far north and beached its fat ass."

I puffed my cheeks out and wobbled side to side.

Lash snorted. "Me too. We can lie around on the beach. When Greenpeace tries to save us, we'll tell them we're an evolved species. We're *land* manatees."

Lash puffed her cheeks again and turned her concentration on assessing her own bathing suit selection. Reviewing her own reflection, she took considerably more time assessing and targeting all of her areas of imperfection. Unlike the utilitarian one piece I had tried to make friends with, Lash's suit was a two-piece—a bikini top and a small tutu-like bottom. I thought it was cute, and Lash did know how to dress to play off her assets and minimize her liabilities. However, creative attire could not hide the fact Lash had an impressive butt and thighs, her self-proclaimed nemeses. She hated her butt and thighs, even during her thin modeling days. They inspired her to create new nomenclature: *burbleage*. n. the pillows of flesh that bulge from beneath and around the constriction of clothing, particularly extraneous flesh on the butt and/or thighs; sometimes called *muffin-top* in contemporary vernacular when referencing fleshy protrusion over the waistband. Two elective surgeries Lash said she seriously wanted were liposuction and Lasik. I thought she would have done the lipo first, given the financial opportunity.

Looking over her shoulder at the reflection of her backside, she pulled the elastic on the tutu away and let it snap back. A ripple ran down her thigh. She turned and looked at me before bugging her eyes, gaping her mouth, and poking at the back of her throat with her finger.

Lash and I both had ample thigh and butt burbleage; I also had abdominal, back, and boob burbleage—that bubble bulging at the top of the bra.

"At least you *have* boobs," Lash said, pouting.

"Your breasts are beautiful," I said, and I meant it. Shapely, symmetrical, pert. I thought they looked like breasts were supposed to look.

"Plus, you have a waist," I said. Or rather, no waist at all. Tiny. Enviable. Even at her heaviest, Lash's waist disappeared under belts or wraparound sashes; classy, designer clothes hugged Lash's curves, showing off the beautiful workmanship of the clothing and quality while showing off their wearer. Designers could have looked at Lash and quivered with the possibility, with how this tall, wasp-waisted woman could have donned their designs. There was a valid reason Lash modeled during her thinner runs. I thought she should have, could easily have, modeled forever, thin or no.

Me, I was thick. Thick legs, thick arms, thick head. My waist, while not huge relative to my hips and bust line, was not small. Even during sit-up ridden fitness frenzies, my waist was thick. No washboard abs, no reason for a belt except to accentuate what wasn't there. I tended to wear clothes that floated over me or at least did not cling. It wasn't until I was closer to menopause than menarche that I learned the benefits of full support bras, those garments that lifted and separated, and sculpted my bust-line into something I occasionally appreciated.

Lash and I partnered through fasts and breaking of fasts, we cheered each other's successes and commiserated with pints of premium brand ice cream when we failed. After trips to the store to pick out our pints—Chubby Hubby her favorite, Coffee Toffee Bar Crunch mine—we'd curl up on the couch to watch a movie or a horse race, holding our pints with potholders to keep our hands from freezing, eating the entire things, loving it, then groaning, hands to bellies, loathing our poor self-control, and thinking about what flavors we'd get next time.

I envied her waist, she envied my breasts, and neither of us was ever contented with all aspects of our individual bodies at once. We both hated the bathroom scale, which inevitably declared our inadequacies, derision spinning in black and white or blinking in digital judgment. Lash's waist could get as tiny as Scarlett O'Hara's, my legs as strong and supple as Lucy Lawless', and the blind verdict from that scale snuffed out any sense of victory. When I was a freshman in college, and the number on the scale rolled toward 175, I silently vowed I would have to kill myself if I ate my way to 200 pounds. I didn't tell anyone (not even Lash), so I was the only one shamed when I passed that mark, failing not only to control my eating but even to keep my private vow.

When Lash and I regained weight after losing it, and we always did because we were classic yo-yo dieters, our respective skinny jeans shifted to the backs of the closets or the bottom of the dresser drawers. Beyond that similarity, our wardrobes differed. I was never particularly comfortable, psychologically, dressing in a way I thought called attention to myself. I preferred T-shirts and jeans, or better yet sweats; for work, I chose loose slacks or sweaters, trying to hide my size and not draw any attention to my body. And while Lash hated gaining weight, hated being heavy, that did nothing to change the fact she appreciated, sought out, invested in a quality wardrobe: silk suits, lined woolen slacks, velvet bodice dresses, and fine linen blouses. She carried a high end designer purse or clutch. She adored, and proudly wore whenever the occasion called for it and sometimes even when it didn't, classic, elegant evening wear. She was one of those rare women who could wear a hat, and made it all look beautiful.

Even at the barn with the horses, Lash wanted quality: quality riding apparel, quality tack. For dirty barn jobs like cleaning stalls or putting up hay, she turned out in sweats or T-shirts, but it was only a ruse. Anton said once, in amazement and appreciation, that Lash was the only person he knew who came home from the barn, sweaty and dirty, hay and mud in her hair and under her nails, and emerged from the house an hour later, resplendent in a forest green satin gown, lovely and stunning in every way, to attend some high society event.

Regardless of how lean or heavy she was, Lash's waist seemed to barely change. She gained in her hips and thighs, after a while in her face, and at the heights of her weight gains, she eventually also gained in her breasts—the only plus, she said, to being plus size.

One day in early 2001, Lash and I stood in the parking lot of a Chinese restaurant, waiting for cross traffic to pass while a brisk wind sucked any warmth the sun cast off, and both of us had left the office without jackets. Chilled and impatient, Lash stood hugging herself, and rocked up and down on her feet, waiting for the slow-moving cars. I leaned out, looking around her at the elderly driver who was barely moving but in front of whom we dared not cross, when Lash started laughing.

"What?" I asked.

Her face beamed, her eyes sparkled and a blush jumped into her cheeks. She kept rocking and hopping, but she wasn't watching the traffic anymore. She was gazing down at her own chest, pointing with both hands.

"Look! They bounce!" she said and hopped to illustrate. A distinct jiggle rippled through her sweater, and she looked back up at me, an awed grin on her face.

I laughed with her, because her delight was contagious, but for me, bouncing breasts were no novelty. If I jumped up and down like that without a bra, I'd get a black eye.

Eventually, the centurion driver idled past us, and we scuttled across the drive and into the restaurant, but Lash had a new spring to her step and remained in an especially bright mood.

Later, sitting snug in our booths concentrating on our General Tso's chicken and orange beef, we talked about the various diets or weight loss programs we'd tried or were planning on trying or wouldn't consider trying (that was a very brief part of the conversation). Both Lash and I had participated in Weight Watchers, both with moderate success until life got in the way and we stopped going to meetings. My most successful diets as an adult involved restricting fat intake or ruthlessly slashing calories. Lash said she was preparing to embark on the Atkin's Diet, her *farewell* lunch before she said goodbye to carbohydrates. I told her if it worked for her, I might try it before I totally looked like Jabba the Hutt; we laughed and shoveled more food into our faces.

Lash pointed out that as loathsome as we found ourselves, as much as we were genuinely overweight or obese (not to mention deviating from svelte, trim bodies society mandated), still, "If we went to a doctor and said, 'hey, I want my stomach stapled,' they'd laugh us out of the room."

We were fat. Just not fat enough.

Lash lost fifty pounds on the Atkins Diet, which I pledged to try but never quite got to. The only thing Lash was moderately rueful to see shrink were her breasts.

"Last to come, first to go," she said.

Maybe that shrinkage made it possible to feel the lump before she otherwise would have, but would it have mattered if she lost the weight six months earlier, never lost it, or had never gained it in the first place? I believed some black little seed sowed itself, grew, was thoroughly ensconced, spewing bits of itself, before the early April day when Lash came into the barn with a frown. She frowned not infrequently, annoyed with something at work, or something at home, or something about herself. I was in a good mood and wanted to stay that way, so I was prepared to be annoyed with Lash until she said, quiet, almost stunned, "Anton found a lump in my breast last night."

For a moment, we stood there in the barn aisle, the breeze rolling past us, staring at each other, forgetting the mares and foals all around us in the barn, beautiful new life we'd been kooky about for the last several days. Lash's eyes, wide and unblinking in her pale face, bore a frightened look but with a hard edge.

"Can you feel it too?" I asked.

She nodded.

"Do you want me to look at it?" I finally asked, and she nodded again. I looked around the barn, its main doors open, and we shuffled around the corner into the tack room, out of view of passers-by on the road. The mare and foal in the stall opposite could have seen us, but I have no idea if they looked.

"It's here, on the left," Lash said, pointing with her chin.

In my days as a paramedic, I had touched, handled, and moved more breasts than I could count, gently shifting them out of the way for EKG leads or to listen with my stethoscope to patients' chests. It was simply part of taking care of the human body, and that was my approach now—the medical professional—standing in my tack room, sliding my hand under Lash's sweatshirt, across the heat of her skin.

For all we did together, including appraising and talking about our respective breasts, I had never felt Lash's breasts, nor she mine. But now, both of us wanted me to feel her breast. I thought of the impassive, thoughtful expression my own OB/GYN wore, the way he moved his fingers, how he breathed, concentrating, when he examined my breasts each year. I tried to embody that concentration and competence. I didn't look at Lash but gazed at the frame of the window. I did not expect to feel anything abnormal, not even really knowing how abnormal might feel. I expected to palpate as a medical professional, to feel nothing but soft skin and the soft fat below, perhaps the nipple, to walk my finger pads slow and purposeful medially, then down, feel the inframammary fold holding its bit of moisture, then keep walking, feel the subtle prickle of a shaved axilla, that after a moment or two of feeling nothing abnormal, I'd remove my hand and say, calm but appropriately concerned, *I don't feel anything, babe, but it would make sense to get it checked out by a doc.*

That's what I was thinking as I felt soft skin, the soft fat underneath, walked the pads of my fingers, gently probing, across the skin of Lash's breast, and all was smooth until—until my fingers padded onto it, an abrupt, hard shelf, as if someone had slid a shelled pecan just beneath her skin. My fingers stopped. I inhaled. I exhaled. I looked at the wall, seeing out the window the view across the field and up the hill but not seeing it at all. Then I looked up to Lash, to her dark wide eyes, and we stared at each other, breathing in the tackroom, my fingers still resting around the lump in her breast.

The next few days were a flurry of activity; by the end of the week, Lash had undergone a needle biopsy and was waiting on the results. We were at work, sitting at our desks in different buildings, talking via instant messaging, when she spoke with the doctor on the phone.

On phone now with doc, Lash typed.

What's he say? I typed.

Reading the report now.

And ????

Cancer… malignant… lymph nodes… staging…

I remembered those letters flowing from left to right across my computer screen, Lash transcribing her fate as she heard it from the physician, and I remembered my eyes clouding and something like panic clutching at my heart, making it hard to breathe and think. I don't remember what I typed in response.

Those anomalous cells banded together and formed a mass and flourished so rapidly that by the time surgeons cut in and removed it, snipping slivers for biopsy, the cancer had already immigrated beyond its homeland. Lash demanded a copy of the pathology report; she researched her cancer and insisted on a sentinel node biopsy when she entered the hospital for her lumpectomy, because she understood that to be one of the best ways to determine the pathways the restless cancer cells may have taken from that primary tumor. This biopsy required radioactive dye be injected around the tumor, so the physicians could track the radiation on its travels. On the way to the surgical suite, Anton walked next to the gurney, held his wife's hand, and said he would get her a superhero outfit emblazoned *Glowing Boob Girl.* The three of us laughed like hyenas; the surgical staff eyed us warily.

Lash came home with a dent in her breast, which sported a blue-green bordered grimace clamped around a drainage tube like wizened lips around a pipe; dried Betadine and surgical tape and surgeons' ink marks took anything lovely or graceful or sexy away from that which once bounced.

Lash's first round of treatment included chemotherapy, steroids, and medication to keep her bones from aching, to help her nausea, and to boost her blood counts and so on ad nauseam. Lash's oncologist—Anton dubbed him Dr. Spiffy because of his ever-present bowtie—wrote her a prescription for a wig; we laughed when we read the script: *total cranial prosthesis for chemotherapy-induced alopecia.* Why not just say *bald?*

Lash indeed lost her hair. When it started coming out in handfuls, she had Anton shave her head. Her eyebrows disappeared, then her eyelashes. She wore her wigs to work but otherwise went bareheaded. If people stared or were shocked, their reaction was less bothersome to her than the discomfort of a wig or hat or scarf. Often, out in public, she started out with the wig, only to remove it. That's what she did some months into her treatment, as we stood at the bathroom sinks at a movie theater. We were making a stop before settling in for three hours to see *The Fellowship of the Ring*, the first of the *Lord of the Rings* trilogy. The theater was also showing the first of the *Harry Potter* movies, and children (and teenagers and adults) roamed the building dressed up as hobbits and elves, witches and wizards. Two Hermiones skittered from the bathroom, their wands clattered on the doors, and their excited chatter disappeared down the hall. The atmosphere was frivolous and fun. Lash looked at me, smiled, swiped the wig off her head and stuffed it in her pocket.

"Hope it's not too scary for the little kids," she said and grinned as she turned on the water and lathered up her hands.

I laughed. "You have the right head to go bald, anyway. It's pretty," I said.

Lash sang happy birthday twice because that's how long they'd told her she should wash her hands to ensure effective massacre of any viruses or bacteria, and her expression took on a wry twist. She looked at me sidelong, grinning. "Yes, I lost my hair. *All* of my hair." She paused for effect. "Anton asked if there was some way to keep specific anatomical portions of it from growing back."

I gave her a withering look.

"I told him no," she said, rolled her eyes, and dried her hands.

We went up into the theater, settled into our stadium seating with our buckets of heavily buttered popcorn and soft drinks, and for three hours we lived in Middle Earth and forgot about cancer and wigs.

chapter eleven

Three's Not a Crowd

When Lash finished her chemotherapy, she got tattoos on her breast: landmarks to ensure precise aim of radiation treatments. When she was finally finished with her chemo treatments in the fall of 2001, a half year after she'd first found the lump, she was fifty pounds heavier than when she started.

"How can she have gained so much weight when she was on chemo?" people asked. They usually whispered it, and they didn't ask her because they asked me.

"It's the chemo drugs," I said. "I think some are steroids. They cause weight gain." I did not know if there were steroids in Lash's chemo cocktail, or if they would have caused the weight gain or not. But that's what I said, and it seemed to placate the inquisitors. I also gained a lot of weight during Lash's illness, but nobody asked me why I was getting fatter.

My weight did not bother Arnold, a fact I had a hard time understanding yet no trouble believing. Although I had been thinner in college when we'd first dated, I was never *thin*, and it had not mattered to him then either. In the years I had embarked on my horse-breeding business, I had virtually stopped riding. I said I simply didn't have time to ride, which was not untrue. I started each day around 5 a.m., managed a barn-full of horses, commuted sixty miles to my fulltime technical writing job at Penske, and spent time after work doing barn chores, yard work or something farm-related. Just not riding. I could have carved out time to ride, made that a priority, but privately, I felt almost cruel swinging my leg over a horse's back.

Most horses can comfortably carry twenty percent of their own body weight according to sources in magazines and books. By that standard, I should have stopped riding the average half-ton horse when I myself topped 200 pounds. I didn't keep my vow to myself to commit suicide when I reached 200 pounds, but I do think 200 pounds marked a decline in my time in the saddle; as my weight increased, my riding decreased. I felt self-conscious and borderline abusive. And there was a new element to the omnipresent fear-factor. Obesity impeded my balance and agility; I was afraid of falling, of inertia, and gravity commandeering any slight loss in balance. So it was easy to be too busy to ride much, then to ride at all, so by the time Arnold and I got back together, I hadn't ridden in three years.

I told Arnold, before we even saw each other again, that I'd gained a lot of weight; he said he didn't care. Even though I didn't understand how he didn't care, I believed him. On our first date that went beyond hand-holding and chaste platitudes, he had skimmed his hand over my shoulder, across my chest, over my hip, and said, "You've filled out nicely."

Arnold was a breast man, which suited me fine. In his company was the first time I appreciated my breasts and thought I might actually learn to like the girls. I liked Arnold's enthusiasm, reveled in his touch, and was just as happy to look at the top of his head buried in my cleavage as I was to kiss him long and soulfully. Lash had said once Anton always hurried to her breasts, and it annoyed her, as if the physicality of sex enticed him more than the beauty of her face, or the sensuality of the *fact* of their togetherness. For a long time, I had a hard time understanding, and it always left me boggled and a little saddened that she could think that way. It seemed glaringly obvious to me Anton was smitten with *Lash*, and her physical body was all part of the beauty he saw in her. Anton thought everything about her was sexy, breasts included, and wasn't that a *good* thing?

One day, early in the course of Lash's illness, when Arnold kissed my saggy, ponderous, healthy breasts and nuzzled my nipples, I looked down on his head, watched his enjoyment, delighted in it myself, and found myself surprised to see, perhaps for the first time, my breasts as sexual things, and I wondered at that. I wondered that I hadn't really known that before, wondered at my own naïveté, and thought maybe I saw a glimpse into Lash's way of thinking. Something suddenly felt small and mean in me, and even as I felt my skin flush with pleasure, I gazed down at Arnold and asked, "What would you do if I got breast cancer and lost these?"

He looked up at me, startled, perhaps a bit hurt. "I would not feel any differently about you."

I kissed him then, hugged him back to my chest, feeling a sting of guilt that I had asked such a question at such a time, and maybe also a sting of guilt it was not I whose breasts were betraying her.

Although we'd purchased our land at the same time and I almost immediately put a modular home on my farm, Lash wanted a real house, which meant considerably more time before she and Anton actually were able to come up with the funds to build and live on the land. When she'd first found the cancer and was diving from one test and exam to the next, she sat next to me in my truck as we left the physician's office; she'd read aloud her mammogram report: *suspicious mass, right breast, clinical correlation required.*

"*Right* breast?" I said, surprised. I distinctly remembered feeling the mass in her left breast.

"Wrong boob, you boobs," Lash had yelled, shaking the papers toward the medical building as we drove away.

"Make sure they get that right before they operate," I said on a laugh.

Lash snorted a laugh without smiling. "Yeah," she said, looking down at the papers. "Right breast," she said again, shaking her head, and gave me a sidelong glance with just the shade of a smile. "Well, *that* woulda paid for my farm."

The surgeons operated on the correct breast, and Lash and Anton financed building their dream farm via non-medical-malpractice lawsuit means. As it was, I had lived on my farm a few years before Lash and Anton finally moved into their dream house, which was built to their exacting specifications in the spring of 2002. Lash had been through chemotherapy and radiation therapy, and spent the winter recovering, her hair growing back, her life settling back on track for her future. Finally, after decades of fantasizing about it, we sat in our houses on our hills, looking toward each other across our horses in our pastures.

That's in fact what I was doing—standing with the phone to my ear, looking out my living room window, over the pastures and into the woods on the hill, where the May leaves hadn't come out enough yet to totally obscure my view of Lash and Anton's new house—while Lash stood now on the other end of the phone line, her voice tumbling out of the receiver.

"My tumor markers are over 400 for ovarian."

My palm, wrapped around the phone, became suddenly slick. Outside, wasps danced on the back deck railing, warmed by May sunshine. In the pasture, my mares and new foals grazed, tails swishing at flies.

"What does that mean?" My voice sounded calm in my own ears, the paramedic taking over, unflappable and fact-seeking. Lash said they told her she needed to get an ultrasound of her ovaries and an abdominal CT scan. I would go with her, I told her, if she wanted.

Two days later, I sat with Lash and Anton in the radiology waiting room at Hillcrest Hospital in Mayfield. I hated this place. Ambient light from a bank of windows poured into the room but never seemed to illuminate the place. And it stank. It reeked of disease and anxiety and the unknown. You didn't come here and sit in these chairs because you had found a friendly, welcoming place. You came here because of suspicion or brutal knowledge. You sat down and maybe flipped through a dog-eared magazine, and you waited for someone to escort you into the bowels of the place where the machinery would look inside and regurgitate the specifics of your innards for the doctors to ruminate on. Two years earlier, Lash sat in this very room with me as I prepared, at age thirty-five, for my maiden voyage into annual mammograms. I was high risk, sort of, a family history that put me in the suspicious category. Lash came with me for moral support and to hold my hand. The jaws of the machine gnawed my breasts, chewing and considering, then spewed information on my content. My mammogram report served an ample helping of medical terminology and had one word under conclusion: "Negative."

One year later, Lash's and my roles were reversed. I went with her to hold her hand and for moral support. She was here because of brutal knowledge: an obvious lump. Her mammogram report served an ample helping of medical terminology, then under conclusion: "Suspicious for malignancy. Clinical correlation required."

Shitloads of clinical correlation, chemotherapy, and radiation later, it was supposed to all be behind us, yet now we were in this stinking room again. From one corner, up on the wall, Oprah tried to drown out the hum of machinery lurking behind the closed doors. A soap opera ran through its throes from the opposite wall.

"Ashley?" A tech stood in the doorway of the gullet leading to the machines; she held a thick folder against her scrubs as the three of us got up and walked toward her. Behind her, the pale linoleum floor and pale yellow walls stretched into corridors and passages.

Lash hooked her thumb over her shoulder to Anton and me; "This is my husband, Anton, and my best friend, Karen," she said. The tech smiled and turned to escort us. I held Lash's hand. It was cold. Anton walked behind us, his massive hand cupped around the back of Lash's neck, his thumb working on the cords running from her shoulders. The tech glanced back at us, slowed her purposeful gait, then stopped. We stopped too.

"You're all coming?" she said, waggling her hand toward Anton and me.

"Yes," the three of us replied in stereo.

The tech furrowed her brow, sucked her cheek for an instant, and shifted the folder against her chest. She lowered her chin, looked up at us, with a serious expression to make a point. "You do know what the test is, right? A trans*vaginal* ultrasound," she asked, her eyebrows disappearing into her bangs.

"We know," Lash said. "It's OK. I want them with me."

The tech slowly retracted her eyebrows, and for a heartbeat she looked like a deer in the headlights. Then she nodded, turned back down the yellow corridor, and motioned with her head for us to follow. "OK. We don't get that very often."

"I'll bet not," Lash said, and the four of us forced chuckles.

The tech led us to a room, closed the door on the yellow corridor, and pointed to a paper gown on the exam table.

"Please strip from the waist down," she said. "You can use the gown on your lap."

The tech excused herself and flitted out the door. Lash stripped from the waist down, sat down on the table, and put the paper gown over her lap. The tech returned, fumbled with the machinery, and turned off the already dim lights. Lash lay on her back, knees bent; Anton sat at her head, rubbing her shoulders and neck and running his fingers through her short growth of straight dark hair. I stood by her left knee, letting her lean it in to me. Only the glow of the ultrasound monitor illuminated the theater.

"OK, you ready?" the tech asked, self-assured now in the dark familiarity of the exam room. Lash nodded, the paper on the table crinkling under her head. From a drawer, the tech extracted the ultrasound probe and a curled, half-empty tube of lubricant. With the ease of long practice, she prepared the equipment, slipping a thin rubber cover over the probe and squeezing a dollop of jelly onto it. Regardless of my cloistered sexual history, I felt certain the probe was enveloped in a condom, never mind the fact that I'd never actually seen one up close and personal. I narrowed my eyes, assessing the probe and its prophylactic covering, glowing in the spotlight of the monitor screen.

Anton had apparently noticed as well, and he cleared his throat. "Is that what I think it is?"

The tech shrugged and smiled; she may have blushed. "I don't know who came up with the idea. But it works."

"How romantic," Lash said, deadpan, and we all snickered.

The tech went to work. With one hand between Lash's legs, and the other typing codes and notes on the monitor's keyboard, the tech performed the exam. I held Lash's knee and watched the ultrasound screen and was not enlightened. After many minutes, the tech announced that she was going to bring in the radiologist, and she left the room. She returned almost immediately with the radiologist, whose white overcoat billowed behind her.

The doctor stopped dead in the open door and stared at the three of us, one hand on the doorknob, the yellow glow of the corridor backlighting her. Her overcoat caught up with her. Her face did not move, her mouth a thin straight line.

"Hello," Lash said.

"She wanted them here," the tech said from the shadows.

The radiologist sniffed, raised her eyebrows, and closed the door without a word; she sat next to Lash. The doctor looked intently at the monitor, scrolling through various readings. The tech prepared a fresh probe with a fresh condom and fresh gel. She was pulling the condom over the probe when, with a whispering rip, it disintegrated and slipped useless to the bottom of the probe, its shredded remains falling open like petals of a past-prime rose. The radiologist looked around over her shoulder, frowning, her hand poised mid-scroll at the keyboard. For a heartbeat, there was dead silence.

"Oops," Anton said.

"Good thing that wasn't being used for its intended purpose," I said.

The tech looked at me and blinked. The radiologist's frown deepened into a scowl.

Then Lash tittered. At her head, Anton chuckled. Lash tittered harder, her knee shook in my grasp, bounced against my belly, and I snickered. The tech twitched and started to giggle. The radiologist glared at us like a raptor. I tried to stop snickering and snorted instead. Mortified, I slapped a hand over my mouth, snorted louder, and Lash and Anton exploded in laughter. And suddenly the radiologist reared back in her chair, erupting with a belly-guffaw; she slapped her thighs and clapped her hands, rocking through the revelry, wheezing with each gasp.

Eventually, the tech recovered, removed the failed condom gingerly with her thumb and forefinger, pinky extended, and deposited it unceremoniously into the garbage. She took out a fresh condom, applied it without incident to the probe. She then handed the probe and its accoutrements with exaggerated fanfare to the doctor, who, amid the dying embers of our hysterics, performed her own perfunctory exam.

As it turned out, Lash's ovaries were fine, but her liver was fucked. So were her lungs. Tumors everywhere.

Five months after Lash finished her radiation therapy, those wanderlust cells had wormed their way into her liver and her lungs. We again sat in the office with the oncologist, who was explaining the options for therapy. Unlike the previous spring, he did not mention five-year survival anymore, or cure, only slowing the onslaught.

"I don't want the fat chemo this time," Lash said.

Dr. Spiffy looked at her, perplexed, suddenly unsure of his footing.

"The last chemo made me fat," Lash said. "I want skinny chemo this time."

Dr. Spiffy frowned and gave a curt nod. "This treatment is not known to cause weight gain."

"Good."

Later, in the parking lot of the drug store, Lash said at least she wouldn't be fat in her coffin. I shoved her in the arm.

"Promise me something," she said.

"What's that?"

"I want to look good in my coffin."

I didn't say anything but walked beside her toward the pharmacy doors.

"If I don't look good, at least as good as a dead person can look, close the coffin, OK?"

I looped my arm through hers, and for a few strides neither of us said anything. Then I nodded. "OK."

When people asked me how I was doing, how I was handling my best friend dying, I replied, deadpan, that I was self-medicating with chocolate and once it was over I was going to have my stomach stapled. Everyone laughed, I laughed, and added (still laughing), "You think I'm joking." Everyone laughed harder.

I was not joking. I had been only half joking when I whined to my doctor, during an appointment when she said my blood pressure was consistently too high, that it was too bad insurance didn't pay for weight loss surgery. When she replied that insurance *did* pay for it when it was medically necessary, I wasn't joking at all when I asked if I might qualify. And I was stone cold sober when I left her office with the contact information for the Cleveland Center for Bariatric Surgery.

Arnold was the first person to whom I mentioned my weight loss surgery idea. He wasn't opposed, but he was concerned with how much pain would be involved. Perhaps he wondered why I would subject myself to more pain in the midst of all the turmoil of Lash dying, but if he ever wondered that, he didn't say. His acceptance and support—and the fact that my weight wasn't an issue in my appeal to him—bolstered me when I told my parents I was looking into surgery. Each time I mentioned the idea, it morphed a little more away from frivolous extremism to a reasonable, albeit drastic, measure to manage my future health. When I finally met with the bariatric surgeon himself, I had spent enough time researching bariatric surgery that I knew I wanted to have the surgery if I qualified.

So it was that I was going to be spending the night in the sleep lab at Hillcrest Hospital in early October 2002, two floors below where Lash withered in the oncology wing. I hadn't told her about any of this, even though I had been clandestinely making my bariatric surgeon appointments while she had her appointments with oncologic surgeons. I snuck around, feeling furtive and guilty as if I were pilfering out of a collection pot, and the more serious I got about it, the longer I said nothing to Lash, the harder my secrecy became.

When I was going to be staying overnight at Hillcrest for the sleep study, I worked up the courage to tell her what I was doing. I said I'd stop in to see her in the morning, before I went to work, knowing this—stopping in the morning before work—would pique her curiosity. She cocked her head, crinkled her forehead in question.

"I'm having a sleep study downstairs."

"Is everything alright?"

I hesitated, played a little air piano on the arm of the chair, and flicked my hand dismissively. "I'm looking into bariatric surgery, and this is part of the pre-surgical testing they require."

Lash looked at me for a drawn-out moment, and gave a long sigh. She smoothed and folded sheets over her sausage-swollen knees. I looked at her, shifted in my chair, suggested it was all preliminary testing, that I might not do it, regardless. "You'll do it," she said, and focused on her linen origami.

I swallowed. "Are you mad at me?"

She smiled a little, shook her head, and sighed again. When she looked up, her eyes were bright and sad. "All these years, we've lost and gained weight together, and now you're going to do this without me."

I moved from my chair onto the bed with her, and we hugged and cried for a while.

"You're a rack of bones now, and I'm fat and getting fatter," I said, sniffed, swiped my nose. "And nothing personal, but I'd rather lose weight this way than your way."

Lash laughed, one of those bitter chuffs that acknowledged the humor in a shitty situation. "Yeah," she said. "I really can't recommend my way."

chapter twelve

Buying The Farm

PART B

In late September 2002, Lash had just turned thirty-six and had just told me that her grandparents weren't sure any longer where Paula, her birth mother, was buried. Paula had died of cancer when Lash was four; Lash still visited her maternal grandparents in Texas on a regular basis.

"We went to visit her grave when I was in Amarillo a couple years ago," Lash said, "and they couldn't find her. They didn't remember where she was anymore."

Her mouth twisted; she clamped her eyes down, tears seeping through her long, dark lashes, newly regrown after that first round of chemo. "I don't want to be alone and forgotten."

How could you argue against that, tell her you would never forget her? She'd seen it happen—her grandparents didn't remember where they'd buried their own daughter. It was irrelevant that they were older, that their memories were failing in general. It made no difference, because it did not change the fact that they *didn't remember* where Paula was. They say there's nothing worse than burying your own child. So, how could you ever forget where the grave was?

Lash, not drifting from her granite position in her marriage, had already mandated Anton was not to commit himself to a grave next to her. She told me this as we sat in her living room, alone except for two Abyssinian cats, the fall sunshine, and Lash's cancer. The cats scaled the couch and scuttled over Lash, unperturbed by her yellow skin or her bulging liver or that her legs had lost their definition.

"As much as my selfish romantic self in a way wants Anton to pine over me forever," she said, giving a half laugh and swallowing hard, "that really isn't what I want for him. He is such a wonderful person. He'll have a whole life after I die, and he shouldn't obligate himself to being buried next to me. That's not fair to him, or whoever he's with after I die."

"I'll never forget where you are," I said quietly. "I'll be buried next to you, if you want."

I looked past Lash and her cats, out the living room window at the trees just starting to cast off their leaves for the year. Beyond the hushing rattle of cat purrs, the only other sound was the discourse of the woods, floating in through the windows. The air carried a thin cashmere warmth and the tang of fall.

By the time Lash and I came searching at Fairview Cemetery in Hiram, all the good spots were taken, long ago occupied. The shaded and sun-speckled lawns and stones overshadowed by gnarled and hoary rhododendrons; the rising hill crowned with mammoth trees and tilting stones so worn by time they stared blind and mute, tired monuments to Civil War combatants lying under them. The subtle and sober slope south of the hill, younger land but still resting in the shade of the hilltop canopy—all this land belonged to others.

We followed the drive out of the tree-and-sun dapples, beyond the foot of the hill, where the lawn slid down a casual grade toward the woods; here, near the edge with a paucity of stones to navigate, the field had been mown by a tractor and brush hog, leaving stark yellow stalks prickling and stiff. A smattering of lone headstones stood blinking in the afternoon sun; they seemed self-conscious, left out in the elements, as if they wanted to diminish in size or scooch up the hill into better company. Lash leaned her head against the truck window, looking out over the stubbly grass, then looked back down at the plot map in her hands; she turned it sideways, frowned, tilted her head. When she looked up again, she pointed with the plot map toward the edge of the field.

"There are a few left over there," she said. "And some in the middle here." She tapped the window with the paper.

"You want the middle or the edge?"

She shrugged with one shoulder.

I took a deep breath. "Well, let's see what we got." We climbed from the truck.

Ahead and to the left, the ground sloped down, steeper. A little footbridge arched over what was probably a stream in wetter weather. Beyond that, trees and brush marched uphill steeply to the backyard of a house.

"What about over there?" I asked.

Lash shook her head. "Too wet." She looked down at the plot map, and continued without looking up again. "I don't want to be pushing up mushrooms any more than I need to." Lash hated mushrooms. "Besides, I don't think it's in the cemetery."

I pelted out a laugh. "Bet the neighbors would like *that*. 'Dammit, they buried dead people on our land again.'" Lash sniggered, her eyes flashing in her gaunt face.

We shifted to drier ground, where the threat of mushrooms was less, and along the eastern edge of the cemetery property, honed in on a stretch of unclaimed plots. Lash reasoned that here, on the property line, no one would crowd our feet when the cemetery eventually filled up.

We settled on three plots along the drive; Lash would be in the middle, and I would be just to her right. The plot to her left might just remain empty forever. ("That way, I won't have to be next to someone I don't know," she'd said, only half joking, not knowing that sometime later, her parents arranged that some of their ashes would find their way to that third plot.) We looked at the plots, then sat on the ground there. Lash propped against me, and we considered the view we would have, looking east over our feet: disheveled thickets and woods—not the mature hardwoods from atop the hill behind us, where the good grave sites were. This whole section of the cemetery seemed like an afterthought, an addition that didn't mesh with the rest of the place, like an in-law suite tacked on to a century home.

I sometimes wondered what it looked like, what you would have thought if you'd seen us at the cemetery, on that wan early October afternoon—a day in which the chill in the air argued with the tepid sunlight over whether or not summer was over. Would you have seen my unease, my ungainly dance with grief and necessity? Would you have been able to see why we women, not even middle-aged yet, were here, or known I was here at this time only because Lash was *out* of time? Would you have looked at her, standing as she had, hands on hips, appraising the ground, and known how fast she was dying, how soon she knew she'd be buried here?

Sometimes, I thought Lash had a list: *Things to do before I die:*

- Build our house and move to the farm. Check.

- Get a horse that's really big enough for me. Check.

- Get a blue Abyssinian kitten. Check.

- Take the cruise of European capitals with Anton. Check (even though it nearly killed her slightly before her time).

- Pick out grave. Check.

I thought of the things on that list not checked:

- Be Karen's matron of honor.

- Have a baby.

- Live.

It had only been a few years ago that we'd purchased our adjoining pieces of farmland. We had planned on spending our lives living on our horse farms right next door to each other. We had planned how we would walk out our doors any time we wanted and saunter down to our barns, perhaps hack through the woods or down the country roads or to each other's front porches just for the hell of it.

In March, Lash and Anton moved into the house they had finally built on their land a few years after I'd built my farm on my own land, and for a summer, Lash and Anton and Arnold and I lived on our horse farms next to each other.

In October, Lash and I were buying real estate again.

So we sat on the ground, right on top of the graves we'd selected, and we leaned against each other. We looked at the diagram of the cemetery, all of the plots marked and numbered, and Lash started to chuckle.

"Look," she said, tapping the map with her pale finger. "Our plots are numbered 61, 62, and 63. Not bad dressage scores." She glanced up at me, that competitive, mischievous sparkle there still, even with her face shrink-wrapping around her skull. "I want the higher score."

We marked our plots on the map, got up off the ground, and left the cemetery.

Three weeks later, we were back. The cold in the air had overruled the epilogue of summer. Wind blasted sleet under my coat collar. We carried Lash, all six foot one of her, laid out straight-legged in the plain Amish coffin she had custom-made, to her final real estate.

We carried her coffin to her graveside, stood by for the service, and few of us left when the time came to lower the box. The staff paused, shuffled, and someone explained that lowering the casket wasn't like it showed on TV, that it could be awkward, but we didn't care. So they proceeded, and I don't recall it being awkward, just that there was something so viscerally *wrong* with the *fact* of lowering Lash in her coffin into the ground. When it settled at the bottom, the staff stood back and Lash's entourage filed by, and one by one, dropped a handful of sleet-slicked earth onto her coffin. The dirt landed with small, hollow thuds. I took a handful, too, dropped it onto her coffin just as we all had, even though it felt pathetically cliché, a useless gesture entirely devoid of catharsis.

I blinked at the sleet pellets pinging on the dirt, turning it to frosty, clumped mud. *You're not supposed to be here.* I wanted to grab handfuls of mud, fling them as hard as I could anywhere I could. But I just stood there, inert, until the cemetery staff shoed us away, so they could fire up the backhoe and, with clouds of diesel smoke puffing into the November weather, shove the rest of the half-frozen pile of earth into Lash's grave and cover her up.

I visited Lash over the winter, sometimes putting the truck in four-wheel-drive to Baja through the snow to our plots, and I visited during the following spring, then the summer, the fall, the winter and spring and summer and fall and winter and every time I visited, I clamped my jaw and stood on my own grave. I was angry. I'm not sure at what. Not God. Not Lash. Not me. Not Anton or Lash's parents or the horses or cats or anything tangible. Perhaps I was angry with inequity. Or impotence. Or the irrelevance of sheer desire to live and force of will.

Anger is tricky when you can't pin it on anything.

Johanniter was already an old horse when I bought him at the end of 1998. At twenty-one years old, he'd already outlived many breeding stallions, and although he was in perfect health and still very fertile when I bought him, there was no guarantee on how many more foal crops he'd live to produce. There was no guarantee that he'd live to see his first breeding season on Donley Farm East, to sire even one foal crop for me, to even begin to earn back the investment I'd made, the risks I'd taken, in buying him. But then, there are no guarantees on how long *any* horse would live.

As it turned out, Joho did not disappoint me; he was hale and hearty and virile his first breeding season with me in 1999. He thrived in 2000 and 2001 and into the 2002 breeding season. And even though he'd lost weight during the winter of 2001-2002, and the vets and I couldn't figure out why, he nonetheless retained a healthy appetite and enthusiasm—in the breeding shed as well as where the feed bucket was concerned. Joho turned twenty-five in the spring of 2002, and it seemed his age was catching up to him, taking over and draining away his strength and vitality. Feeding time and breeding time brought flares of enthusiasm, but aside from that, Joho seemed to live that summer in a slow rising tide of apathy. His stall opened onto his pasture, where for years, he'd spent his days and nights standing on his hilltop watching over his herd of mares, or chasing Amish buggies on the road as they passed along his fence-line.

But this summer, he barely left his stall, standing with his head in a corner. His body seemed to sag with fatigue as well, and regardless of his hearty appetite, special feed blends, supplements, and veterinary attention, by fall the old stallion's hips jutted out and his ribs became more and more prominent; even the flesh over his withers and shoulder blades melted down around his bones. He looked like a neglected, starved old horse; but it was his change in attitude, his listlessness and fatigue, that told me more, that told me his hearty years were behind him and gone, even if I didn't talk about it a lot, or obsess about it, I knew I was watching his end approaching. And I knew I had the responsibility to mandate that end when it seemed living for Joho was harder, more painful and exhausting, than I had a right to demand. When that point came, I knew I owed it to him to ensure a peaceful and easy end.

So I waited and watched all summer and fall, trying to define and weigh the old stallion's *quality* of life relative to his *quantity* of life. The obvious fact that his decline coincided with Lash's did not occur to me until several years later.

In early December, when it became obvious to us Joho's natural death was not far off, Arnold and the vet and I made the decision to ease his exit. Six weeks after we buried Lash at Fairview Cemetery in Hiram, Joho settled into his own grave at the top of the hill in his pasture, overlooking the farm fields and pastures. His mares stood just the other side of the fence, watching him, saying goodbye in their own way, I couldn't help feeling. Roanoke, eight months pregnant with Joho's last baby, stood tallest and longest, ears up, and she did not turn and leave the hilltop until the cold clumps of mud had nearly filled Joho's grave. It was a bitter December day, the end of a bitter year, the end of much of my life's directive forces. So much gone into the ground. So much buried.

The evening of Joho's death, as Arnold and I sat down to dinner, a vision flashed through my mind, so vivid I relayed it to Arnold as I saw it. I saw Joho standing on the hill by his grave; he bowed his head, blowing softly through his nostrils as if bewildered and uncertain, as if he'd suddenly woken and found himself in unfamiliar territory. And as he stood there on the edge of uncertainty, I saw Lash. She walked up the hill to the old stallion, holding her hand out to him as she came up to him. He reached his muzzle out to her, recognized her, and his body seemed to relax as he rested his nose in her palm and she stroked his forehead.

"Come on, Joho," she said then, turning and moving away down the hill. "You'll like it here." Joho sighed, content, and lowering his head, he walked with her down the hill. I watched them walk away together, side by side, before the vision ended.

After that, I felt as if I could suddenly breathe easier.

Over the years, our stark section of the cemetery has started to fill out a little bit. Slowly, others have planted themselves, bringing with them trees and eclectic shrubberies, so the field looks less like an accessory. In the early spring, sometimes even before the snow has completely forsaken the ground, a smattering of crocuses grows over Lash's grave, popping out of the cold and sodden mud right where Laura and Roger scattered them the spring after we buried Lash. A hydrangea tree, chosen and planted by Bill and Janeen, does its slow work at the foot of her grave. Janeen said the tree is their way of being there by Lash now, before they get there permanently. One fall, wide swaths of its bark disappeared, gone onto some young buck's velvet antlers, and I wondered if the tree would survive the injury. But in the spring, the little tree tossed out leaves and flowers, and the buck rub seemed smaller.

Every time I come here, I stand on my own grave and look at the ground, my face taut; or I prune dead branches off the hydrangea tree, or slip off its dried and finished flowers at the end of the year. Sometimes, I sit on the marble bench that is Lash's headstone—"best friend" is inscribed on it—and just look at our two little plots of land, side-by-side.

Maybe I'll plant a magnolia tree at the foot of my grave to rub shoulders with the hydrangea, to share in buck rubs and sisterhood.

chapter thirteen

Taboo

L ash handled the finances and bill paying in their household. She couldn't
abide Anton's lackadaisical management style, so did not relinquish control of that until late fall, 2002, about a week before she died. In fact, she
delayed, deferred, put off this task of organizing it for Anton, grew weaker,
until her dwindling energy magnified the chore to near monolithic. Sometimes
I believe Lash procrastinated on this because each month she paid the bills
and organized the finances was one month more she wasn't dead, one month
longer she'd lived past her thirty-sixth birthday. When she finally sat in the
study, preparing a list of what bills were due when, which were paid through
automatic withdrawals, from what accounts, to what creditors, it seemed like
some grudging concession. The process was exhausting. Finally, Lash slumped
over the desk, putting her head down on her arms. I rubbed her back. Her ribs
and vertebrae jutted through the fabric of her t-shirt.

"I don't want to do this," she said, quiet, without raising her head.

I looked at the bills scattered around the room, then at the back of Lash's
head. Her dark hair had regrown a few inches from the first round of chemo,
but it couldn't hide the contour of her skull or how thin her neck had become.
On my lap, I held the pack that supplied the intrathecal pump feeding narcotics
into the fluid in Lash's spinal canal.

"By 'this,' do you mean organizing the bills for Anton? Or dying?"

She didn't lift her head for a moment. When she did, she looked fatigued
beyond illness.

"Dying."

One evening in early 2001, we cleared the dinner dishes and set up my dining room table for Taboo, a board game Lash swore we would love. Actually, *she* loved it, in no small part because she and Anton were really good at it. In Taboo, you get a card with a word or phrase you need to get your partner to utter, along with a list a taboo words you can't use as clues. An opposing team member gets to look over your shoulder at the card and slap a buzzer if you say something taboo. Imagine Charades on steroids. Married for almost ten years at this point, Lash and Anton knew each other so well, and had so many little experiences from which they could draw clues, that Arnold and I, having only been back together for a couple of months, were at a decided disadvantage.

I frowned over Anton's shoulder, looking at his card as he pondered how to clue his wife. I leaned in, hovering, my hand hovering over the buzzer. He wasn't allowed to use the words *fruit, flightless, bird, New Zealand* ...

"Good luck with this one," I said, and smirked.

Anton ignored me. He squinted at the card, tapped it against the table for a couple seconds, inhaled deeply through his nose, and leveled his blue-eyed gaze at Lash. "It's what you call our cats' assholes," he said.

Arnold and I looked at each other pop-eyed, but Lash never missed a beat. "Kiwi," she said.

Anton gave a quick nod and slapped the card down on the table. Arnold and I erupted into hysterics.

"What the hell is that? Your cats' asses are fruit?"

Lash simply raised her eyebrows and grinned.

"Well, look at 'em," Anton said, making little circles with his fingertip. "All those little cling-ons are the seeds. Little ass holes in the middle. Kiwi."

Arnold literally fell out of his chair and lay on the floor spread-eagled, guffawing. Bristol bounded to him, her tongue lolling and tail wagging, and she ricocheted around the room as only a Border Collie could. A couple cats scattered and disappeared into the dark recesses of the house. I doubled over and wrapped my arms around my sides, tried to breathe and not pee my pants. Lash was gasping too, undulating in her chair, periodically snorting. The snorting was nearly more than my bladder could bear. I launched out of my chair and only barely made it to the bathroom in time. I didn't think I would ever be able to eat kiwi fruit again.

By the time I reemerged, relative calm had returned, and we continued the game. Lash and Anton were soundly trouncing us, so when Lash slipped and uttered a taboo word, Arnold pounced. With the glee of a five-year-old, he slammed the buzzer. Lash frowned and glared at him.

"Illegal word," he said, and stuck his tongue out.

"Fuck you, you fucking fuck," Lash said.

Arnold blinked and gaped. So did I. Lash looked from him to me.

"Dennis Hopper. *Blue Velvet?*" she said as if this explained everything.

I shook my head, shrugged. "Never saw it." Lash rolled her eyes.

Arnold and I stumbled through our ensuing turn without scoring any points, and as soon as the hourglass's sand ended our turn, Anton picked up a next card with his word on it. Neither he nor Lash had reservations about routing us.

I looked over his shoulder, my hand poised over the buzzer. He wasn't allowed to use the words *flower, yellow, margarine.* He looked at the card and pursed his lips; he cocked his head, paused about two seconds, and said to his wife, "This is the chick in your favorite girlie movie."

As one, Arnold's and my heads swiveled over to Lash.

"Buttercup!" she said without the slightest hesitation. Her expression was serious, all business, intent and competitive. It didn't hurt that we'd all just watched *The Princess Bride* – and at least I knew who Buttercup was now. But Lash would have gotten it anyway. *The Princess Bride* was one of her favorite movies.

Arnold and I had been back together only a couple of months when Lash found the lump in April of 2001, so he really never got to know her outside the context of her illness or independent of my own lens. When he and I had our short, intense relationship while we were students at Hiram College in the mid-'80s, Lash was attending the Agricultural and Technical Institute of Ohio State University then Miami University, and he never met her.

"I wonder if we would have liked each other if she had lived," Arnold wondered recently. Sometimes I've wondered the same thing. Would they have loved or even liked each other just because I loved them both?

I had tried not to like Anton when he came back into Lash's life. Maybe I was suspicious of him for having left Ohio and broken Lash's heart back in high school. Over the years, she'd mentioned him with a *the-one-that-got-away* wistfulness, especially in the wakes of other tumultuous relationships. I had not met Anton back then, having at that time been out-of-state at school, but Lash had regaled me with stories of the tall, dark, handsome man. She talked about how he stood a full head taller than she, about his thick black hair and his gray-blue eyes, and about his flirtation with drugs and alcohol and subsequent sobriety. She told me of his family's royal history in Austria and Romania, and their flight into exile decades earlier, escaping with only their lives and the clothes they were wearing. How his grandmother, Princess Ileana, had stowed in the folds of her dress a tiara, which she'd sold in her exile to support her young children and their new lives in America.

Lash seemed to think him admirable and noble; I thought she was infatuated with his physical attributes, his family history, his choice of a sober life. To me, Anton Habsburg had sounded a little dangerous, and the fact that he'd left had done nothing to convince me otherwise. So when he'd returned years later and I'd finally met him, I was dubious. He and Lash certainly did make an attractive couple, and at six foot seven, he still topped Lash by half a foot. He seemed intelligent, generous, quick to laugh, and showed no signs of bolting from Lash again. And both he and Lash appeared deliriously smitten with each other.

Still, he hadn't truly won me over until he rescued a kitten from a Dumpster. He'd heard it crying, and had climbed into the garbage bin to find and save it. *That kind of caring is an attractive quality*, I told Lash later.

Lash had never needed to share *me* before, although I suspect she would have shared me with Arnold well enough. She pestered me for years to find and reconnect with him, and I guess she would have derived pleasure from my pleasure, even if ultimately all she and Arnold had in common was being left-handed. Only a few months after her diagnosis she was already predicting our nuptials, long before either Arnold or I discussed marriage. We didn't marry until a year and a half after Lash had died.

"I'm going to be your matron of honor when you get married," Lash had informed me, and certainly her presence infused our wedding, not the least because without her influence, we never would have asked our pastor to evoke *The Princess Bride* tone of lightheartedness. The concept delighted him, and he played the part flawlessly.

"Maaay-wedge," he said, in perfect drawn-out intonation, opening the ceremony with a line from the movie and to an explosion of laughter.

"Maaay-wedge is what bwwwwings us togeeeeaver.... tooo-daaaay."

On the altar, we set an eight-by-ten portrait of Lash and a vase of periwinkle irises, her favorite flowers that she'd carried at her own nuptials. That was as close as she got to standing next to me in my wedding, as I had stood next to her fifteen years earlier. As it was, Laura, whom I'd met through Lash, was my matron of honor. Perhaps Laura and I grew close, our friendship born of a common loss, where we may otherwise have remained simple acquaintances. For some few years we had known each other, but to me she had always been "Lash's friend Laura." In the course of Lash's illness, that evolved to "Lash's and my friend Laura."

Lash saw our embryonic friendship, recognized it enough to tease me when I suggested, a few weeks before Lash died, that Laura should apply to work at Penske. Lash had leveled her best imperious gaze at me then.

"You only want Laura to work at Penske so you have someone to eat lunch with after I die."

We had all laughed at that, Lash included, but I flinched internally, as if I were chastised for already starting to backfill the voids Lash's death would leave in my life, without even doing her the courtesy of letting her die first.

Laura didn't apply to work at Penske, but as my matron of honor, she did fill a role that was Lash's. And yet, I did not feel having Laura at my side that day was settling, nor do I believe Laura felt that way. Rather, I think we both felt an inclusion of Lash in Arnold's and my wedding that Lash's portrait alone as it stood propped on the altar could not have engendered.

Lash surely would have enjoyed the frivolity, would have loved incorporating *The Princess Bride* line; she would have loved being in our wedding. She would have thrown herself into the role, would have relished the details of my day, would have enjoyed making an impression. She *did* make an impression, whether she was with us in the flesh or not. The wind kept knocking over her portrait as it sat smiling in the May sunshine. Someone would right the picture, but it would dance in the wind again until finally, it toppled, taking with it the vase and irises with a resounding crash.

We all looked at each other, pausing for an instant; and even on the video of the ceremony, you can hear Janeen laughing.

"Well, she's here," she said, a smile clear in her voice.

I nodded then; I'm still nodding.

All Lash's actions for months spoke to how much she did not want to die, but also that if she had to die, she would mandate what parameters she could. She wouldn't go passively, and the fact that our society historically shuns death and dying did not impel her to slip quietly from view to die unobtrusively out of sight and out of mind. She was forthright in not only letting us help her die, but in letting us help her live to her fullest in the time she had.

Sometimes, despite Lash's candor, her coworkers and friends needed guidance. At work, people would ask me, in hushed tones, how Lash was doing, even when Lash was there in the office. *Ask her*, I would reply, and if that suggestion induced recoil—even if it didn't—I would add, *She'll help you. She's fine talking about it.* What was remarkable to me was how much this was true— how her friends and coworkers surged against their discomfort and fear and approached Lash directly, and how she welcomed them, helped them be with her, acknowledging her cancer instead of dancing around the subject.

Contemporary society doesn't teach us how to go about dying. Perhaps one of the most remarkable aspects of Lash's illness was how she lived it as openly as she lived the rest of her life, so those near to her could not avoid it. The Nathers had remained close with Lash throughout her illness, and they didn't slack off when her cancer metastasized, rushing her toward death before any of us were ready. Tom and Nancy brought their daughter Sarah to Parkman every week, and while Sarah helped Lash in the barn, grooming Rainier or building stalls or working on the pastures, Tom helped there and wherever Lash or Anton might need him, and Nancy stayed in the house, cleaning and cooking meals for the week ahead.

Tom had hired Lash at Penkse, and shortly after she started there, she made me aware of a writing position with the company, which is how the three of us came to all work together. When I first met Tom, Sarah was only a portrait on his desk, but Tom was quick to point out the ten-year-old girl in the portrait was a "horse nut," and because Lash and I were "horse nuts," we surely had wisdom to impart for his daughter. Where Sarah came by her horse nutness no one knows. Neither Tom nor Nancy are horse people, but to Sarah, this peculiar form of insanity was inherent. Just as it was for both Lash and me.

We laughed and told Tom he and Nancy should not buy a horse for Sarah until after she reached puberty, a time during which many a *horse nut* girl loses interest in horses in favor of boys—an expensive proposition if one has already invested in a horse. Tom dismissed that possibility. I suspected at the time his dismissal was more protectiveness of his daughter than intuition about her innate horse-attraction. And while I still believe my impression was right on the former, Tom was right about Sarah's horse nutness. She had horses in her heart and soul and would never relinquish that love for boys. When she was old enough, she had room enough in her heart for horses *and* boys.

While Lash had many coworkers with whom she was friends, she did not often extend that contact after hours; I think she chose to devote her energy in her family, her few very close friends, and her horses. And perhaps it was the latter that changed the dynamic this time; Sarah was the catalyst that took Lash and Tom's relationship out of the office. Something in Sarah attracted Lash, perhaps something synergistic about Tom's fierce love and protectiveness for his only child, his stories about her horse-craziness, which he seemed to adore even though neither he nor his wife Nancy were horse people. Something impelled Lash to invest herself more into this relationship. Casual office conversations evolved into serious discussions; it seemed the more Lash learned about Sarah, the more she wanted to know.

I don't remember exactly what circumstance surrounded Lash and Sarah's first meeting; perhaps it was as simple as Tom and Nancy bringing Sarah to meet Tom's *coworker's* horse. Or maybe Lash went first to them, to watch Sarah ride at a stable on Cleveland's west side where she was taking lessons. Soon though, the relationship had blossomed, the visits and forays increased, and if Lash took Sarah under her wing, Sarah nestled in there with equal and reciprocal adoration. Even as Lash became weaker, the Nathers kept coming, and Sarah remained unflagging in her exuberance.

One early fall afternoon, Nancy and I were alone in the house chopping vegetables and cooking meals for the coming week. Lash, Anton, Tom, and Sarah were in the barn. A few days earlier, Lash had told me to take anything I wanted from the barn after she died. "Then I want Sarah to have whatever she wants."

I mentioned this to Nancy as we stood in the kitchen.

Nancy paused in her chopping and frowned at me. "That's a little pessimistic, isn't it?"

I looked at her closely as we stood there in the kitchen, bright fall sunlight pouring in the windows around us. I recall asking her, carefully, if Tom had not told them Lash's cancer was terminal. Nancy stood there, her eyes glittering, and shook her head.

"I don't think he knows that," she said.

"Lash told him," I replied, feeling almost defensive.

"How soon?"

Now I shook my head. "I don't know. Soon."

Nancy stood, hands splayed on the countertop, looking at me, tears spilling now.

A few minutes later, in the barn, I found Lash sitting on the bench watching the others. Tom and Sarah laughed as they groomed Rainier. The horse fidgeted.

"Brush him within an inch of his life," Lash said, and Sarah's laughter bubbled around her.

I sat next to Lash, smiled with her as she watched them. I leaned against her, whispered in her ear, recounted my conversation with Nancy.

"I *told* him," she said quietly, looking at me, surprised.

"Nancy didn't know. And certainly Sarah doesn't."

"Oh, Tom," Lash said on a sigh, and let her forehead plop into her hand. "Thank God I didn't tell Sarah to start putting labels on what she wants when I'm dead." We were both laughing a little bit now, in that black humor sort of way you do when you realize a crappy situation could have suddenly been a whole lot crappier. I went back to the house, and before they left the barn, Lash had another conversation with Tom.

I don't know how Tom and Nancy told Sarah, but they did not let the new knowledge hinder them; all of them, Sarah included, plunged ahead with us. And the beauty of it was, grief and fear and anxiety did not quell their enthusiasm or commitment. Sarah didn't shrink from this reality but kept bright with love and enthusiasm just as she had been, and that young *horse nut* girl's laughter floated through that fall, resonant. I thought for Lash, it was like a tonic.

Lash solicited support to help her experience, in the time she had left, some of the living she wanted to do. Less than two months before she died, she and Anton embarked on a two-week cruise of the European capitals. "I have always wanted to do this," she said. "It's now or never."

We set up a collection box in the office at Penkse to help fund the trip; Lash's coworkers' generosity helped make the cruise a reality. And she immersed herself in the cruise experience, letting Anton shuttle her through airports in a wheelchair, rallying her physical and emotional resources to attend a formal dinner gala on the ship; she looked stunning, vibrant, in the portrait they had taken at that event.

"I made sure we were turned at an angle so my port wouldn't show," Lash told me later, laughing a little over her insistence that the small box surgically implanted under the skin just below her clavicle not be visible. But it worked. She did not look like a woman six weeks from her grave in that photo, even though she was so ill she entered the hospital the day of their return to the States and didn't come home for a week.

From her first diagnosis, Lash was very open first about her illness, then about the fact that she was going to die. "Don't use any tidy euphemisms," she'd said, even mandated. "Don't say, 'she passed away,' or 'God took her home.' Say, 'she died.' Tell it like it is." Not only was this true to her character, it also gave her and others some measure of control over how she lived her death. I felt it enabled those involved in her life and her death to walk into its shadow and acknowledge it.

Peter, a senior vice president for whom Lash worked at Penske, registered on this; he knew Lash well enough to want to visit her at home when she was no longer able to come to the office. We arranged that one day he followed me home from Penske, and I led him straight to the house. I thought he was a little anxious; it was easier to *not* visit a dying friend and employee than it was to leave the security of the office and walk into her house, to come to her as she was dying. But Lash and Peter genuinely liked and respected each other.

For herself, Lash looked forward to the visit. She sat on the couch in the living room, her face yellow and gaunt; she was tired but engaged. And she helped Peter in the visit, I thought, not only in dealing with the immediate circumstance of an employee dying, but with facing death in general, of walking up to it, sitting down with it, living through it instead of simply waiting for it to happen and be done with. Peter's own mother had died recently, and he'd spent some time with his family in England afterward, but somehow, even for that recent experience, for all his corporate worldliness, for his vast travels and cultural knowledge, I think in this farm house in Parkman, Ohio, Peter stepped into a new and different board room, unfamiliar and foreign. Lash welcomed him and led him through there.

She asked Peter how things were at the office, how some of her pet projects were unfolding. They *talked shop* for a while. I sat on an ottoman and listened. Anton drove in about fifteen minutes after Peter and I arrived at the house; he came in, tossed his keys on the kitchen counter, and stood behind his wife, his hand draped over her head. He didn't say anything, listening to and enjoying her camaraderie with Peter. He ran his fingers through her short, dark hair, massaging her scalp.

She tilted her head back and gazed up at him. "How's my box look?" she asked.

Anton nodded, took a deep breath. "It's good," he said.

"Is it long enough?"

Anton nodded again. "Yep."

"Good. Thanks, Pookie."

Anton gave her a little smile.

Lash lowered her chin and looked at Peter. "I'm being buried in a simple wooden Amish-made coffin," she said. "Most Amish folks aren't all that tall. So Anton just went to the coffin-maker's place and checked my coffin to be sure it's long enough. I don't want to spend eternity with my knees bent."

When I walked with Peter back to his car, he didn't hurry to leave the macabre scene and get back to the comforts of the corporate world. We stood for a moment by his car; he seemed reluctant to leave just yet, as if he wanted to say or do something but didn't know what. He expressed amazement at Lash's openness, how she faced her impending death and allowed others to face it (perhaps insisted they did), too, in her company and on her terms.

Peter stood by his car for a while longer, looking around him at the woods, and he seemed a little rudderless. I gave him a hug, thanked him for coming, telling him that I know it meant a lot to Lash, and he seemed relieved to be able to stand there talking for a little while longer. I felt the man who drove off that afternoon was somehow fundamentally changed from the man who had driven in an hour earlier. Perhaps I simply projected on others my own emotions about the impact Lash's death had, or perhaps more accurately, the impact of *how* she lived her death. But I didn't think so.

Earlier in the summer, Lash and I sat in her living room talking about work and Rainier and the Swedish inspection at the end of August—plain and mundane things, the stuff that makes up daily living. Lash looked down at her hands—smooth hands, and that tanzanite stone partnered with the big honking diamond Anton had gotten her for their tenth anniversary ("I want a big honking diamond for our tenth anniversary," Lash had told him over the years). Her fingers were refined and her fingernails, especially on her index fingers, curled over when they got longer.

"Will you be my durable power of attorney for medical care?" Lash was still considering the backs of her hands.

"I'd be honored to be."

"I don't want Anton to have to decide to do *nothing*," Lash explained, answering my question before I asked. Her face was pale. Part of her beauty had always been her porcelain skin and black hair and dark saucer eyes. Audrey Hepburn and Lash could have been sisters. "I want to be sure no one goes to heroic measures," she made finger quotes and rolled her eyes. "I'm not sure that Anton or my dad could do that." Or *not* do that, more like, was what she was saying.

"OK," I said. I could hear cicadas outside in the trees, but something in my head seemed to match their buzzing.

"Can you do that?" She looked at me intensely; I nodded slowly.

I could do that—by *that*, do nothing. My medical background gave me a platform of impartiality, some ground that was pragmatic and analytical from which I could watch and assess and ask the questions our emotions throttled and elbowed and bulldozed into the background. It was a platform that enabled me to be a strong patient advocate for Lash; it was also a platform that would enable me to do nothing at all when the time came. For the year Lash had been fighting this cancer, I felt good being able to bring something strong and supportive to the fray, and I believe it helped all of us. I also thought it helped me sometimes to not *feel* at all, or at least let some impersonal, clinical mode take over where emotion seemed too dangerous. But the emotion was always there, pulsing just under that pragmatic façade, twisting my stomach, slicking my palms, rushing cicada buzz into my brain.

"Do Anton and your dad know about this?"

Lash nodded.

"They're OK with it?"

Lash cocked her head, nodded. "Anton wanted to, but he understands."

"OK," I said quietly.

She glanced at me, tweaked a little smile. "Thanks," she said.

"Man, this fucking sucks," I said, but it didn't sound as deadpan as I intended, because the claw clenching my stomach had moved to my throat.

"Yes," Lash agreed. "Yes, it surely does."

I slouched against the arm of the couch, and Lash leaned against me; I massaged her head and neck; I couldn't take her cancer away or do anything magic to make her live, but at least I could do this little thing to make her more comfortable.

"I'm not afraid to die," Lash said eventually, leaning back against me and looking up at the ceiling, "but that doesn't mean I *want* to die."

"I'd do it for you, if I could," I said.

Lash leaned her head back and looked at me, smiling. "Nah, you have too much to live for."

I snorted. "What, and you don't?"

"No, it's just that now you have the farm, and your breeding program going, and Arnold's back in your life. It wouldn't make any sense for you to die instead of me."

"I don't have more to live for than you," I argued. "You waited your whole life for this house and farm. You have a job you love and they love you. You and Anton could have a baby now…"

"So much for the baby stuff," Lash said, sardonic.

I sighed, and rubbed the cords in Lash's neck. She leaned into it.

"My point is," I said, "if we look at the life potential, yours carries more weight than mine. So from a completely practical standpoint, trading places would make sense."

I suppose I believed this; I remembered feeling strongly about it. But I can ask now, even if I couldn't then, how much of that was true conviction and how much rhetoric, however heart-felt. I imagine I considered, even if obliquely, what elements of our respective lives should tip the scale in her favor: marriage, beauty, education, intelligence, career success, her status as an only child, mine as one of three. Or maybe it was that I was single, even with Arnold freshly returned to my life, or that I was fatter than Lash, or a few years older than she so had already lived longer.

And what weight did desire to live carry, anyway? People in Lash's family, it seemed, died young and unwilling. People in my family killed themselves, or tried to. My mother had tried but failed because my father had shouldered his way through the door on time. But my mother's youngest brother had not failed. Nor had my cousin, hanging in a closet at Christmas, or her daughter, two years later overdosing herself out of this life. What of my other family members who had attempted though not succeeded in killing themselves? And what about me? I had thought about suicide off and on for years. What weight did *intent* to die carry? Shouldn't that weigh on the scales, tip them in favor of the one who shunned death? Surely here was measurable inequity, the weight of suicidal intent in me and my family on one side, the weight of desire to live in Lash and her family on the other. Shouldn't that simply have lightened her off the scale, slide me into her place, where perhaps I belonged more than she?

Maybe I really believed if we *could* trade places, we *would*, that I'd do it willingly, perhaps with regret but no hesitation. As much as I wanted to believe my own words, believe I would give my life for Lash's if I could, I think Lash did us both a favor by calling me on the subject. She turned her head slightly so she could level her gaze at me; she frowned, but cracked a smile, too.

"You are so full of shit."

I glowered, opened my mouth to defend my position, and stopped. The absurdity of our conversation smacked me, not just that we were arguing over whose life had more merit but that we were debating it as if we could do a damned thing about it.

We stared at each other. Lash cocked an eyebrow. I started to snicker. Leaning against me, Lash jounced with my laughter and pretty soon, we were both gasping and snorting in hysterics.

"Thanks for being willing to trade places," she said finally, catching her breath.

"You're welcome, sweetie. You know I would, too, if I could," I said, whether or not it was true.

"I know."

I didn't try to stifle what throbbed out of my chest then. "I'm going to miss you so much."

"I'm going to miss you, too," Lash whispered back.

"What am I going to do without you?"

Lash didn't answer, but leaned deeper into me, resting her head on my shoulder, her tears soaking my shirt. I wrapped my arms around her, cradling her life against me, my cheek against her hair, and we rocked for a while in silence, until eventually, we fell asleep there, nestled together on the couch.

chapter fourteen

The End and Forever After

Lash sat stiff in the wheelchair, hands clasped on her lap, elbows stiffly hugging her sides. She refused to have a hospital bed brought in to the home, and she refused to make a *sick room* downstairs. She wanted to die in her own bed in her own bedroom. Which is why, now that she no longer had the strength to climb the stairs, Anton and I carried her up in her chair.

All those years I saved the world as a paramedic, plucking lives back from the brink, but it was the practical experience I brought that mattered: moving someone who could not move herself. I orchestrated it: With the wheelchair's back to the stairs, Anton hunkered on the first step behind the chair, his bear-paw hands wrapped around the handles; I stooped at Lash's feet, grasping the chair's frame. Chair wheels locked.

"Ready?" I asked Lash. She nodded. Anton climbed the first stair, and we lifted the chair and Lash up. Held it steady on that stair, shuffled up to the next, and lifted. The chair's rubber wheels grabbed the wood on the stairs. Up a step, lift; up a step, lift. I was starting to breathe hard. Anton laughed; it tumbled over Lash at me, and I scowled up at him, glancing quickly past Lash's eyes, huge and dark, staring straight at me. "Heave," Anton ordered, exaggerating his voice. I heaved the chair. Lash sat motionless and silent, face set and pinched. Lift, pause, step, lift, maybe ten or twelve steps to the landing.

On the landing, with only a few more steps to go, Anton and I straightened up to take a breather. I leaned against the wall; it looked pale yellow, reflecting the light from the upstairs hallway. But it wasn't yellow. Or white. It was ecru.

"What the hell color is ecru?" I asked months earlier when Lash told me what color they'd chosen for the walls of the new house.

"It's sort of an off-white."

"Why not just call it white, then?"

"Because it's not white. It's ecru. It has just a hint of color to it—it's *nuanced*."

I shifted off the ecru wall. Anton and I bent, looked at each other over Lash's head, regrouped, and stutter-stepped Lash and her chair up the last few steps, moving from the wood stairs to the carpeted hallway. The carpet was light gray; I'm sure the color had its own name.

I tried not to breathe too heavily—I didn't want Lash to feel guiltier than she already did—but I was too fat, and even though Lash was shrink-wrapping around her skeleton, hauling her and the chair up the stairs was a workout. I stood next to her, unlocked the wheels, and tried to breathe normally. Lash unclasped her hands.

"I'll go get the bed ready," Anton said, and as he moved past Lash, she turned her chin up to look up at him, that intense, unflinching gaze. He returned it, their own mute and eloquent discourse. He laid his huge hand on her hair, and it draped over her head like a bonnet. She gave him a small smile as his hand slipped off her hair, and he disappeared into the bedroom.

Lash turned to me. "I get the feeling everyone thinks I'm going to die tonight."

An hour earlier, she had convinced her parents that they did not need to spend the night. She'd been adamant they should go home. Just this afternoon the hospice nurses confirmed what we already suspected.

"I think they're afraid it's soon," I said.

"What do you think?"

I paused. I was afraid it was soon, too, and afraid it wasn't and would never come. This morning, even before hospice nurses visited and given their verdict, after we'd carried her downstairs and helped her to the couch, Lash had asked Janeen if Anton had a radio on. "No, why?" Janeen said.

"I hear voices," Lash said, and Janeen asked if she could hear what they were saying. No, Lash replied, just the voices. Somewhere, in the hospice literature probably, we'd read that the patient may see or talk to deceased loved ones, and this is normal as death approaches.

"I think it's soon," I said.

She nodded slowly, twisted her lips slightly. She looked down at her lap. Her belly bulged.

"What do *you* think?" I asked quietly. Hospice literature also said the patient would know when death was imminent. I was breathing a little more easily now, but there was nothing easy about this conversation. Few of our conversations had been easy of late.

Lash nodded again, considering; she looked up at me, her eyes clear. "It's closer than I thought," she said. "But I'm not quite ready yet."

I held her hand, met her eyes.

"I want to live just a little while longer," she said.

"OK," I smiled and squeezed her hand.

And then Anton was back. Once we got Lash on her feet, she was able to shuffle to the bathroom, to her bed. She made one reluctant concession at a time. A week ago it had been climbing the stairs. Two days ago, getting up from her chair. Now, at the top of the stairs outside their bedroom door, Anton stood in front of Lash, facing her, and leaned over. She hooked her hands behind his neck, and when he straightened, pulling her up, I lifted, my hands on her sides, then grasping her hips until she was upright. Once standing, she shambled the rest of the way into the bedroom, around the bed, and into the adjoining bathroom. I carried the pack that fed narcotics into the catheter surgically implanted in her spinal fluid.

She stood at the sink and moved through her evening routine, slow and methodical. She took out her contacts. She brushed her teeth. She sat on the toilet. Anton helped her stand upright again, and she moved into the bedroom, sat down on the bed. Anton bent and lifted her legs onto the mattress; those long, elegant thirty-six-inch-inseam legs she'd always been reluctantly pleased with, too swollen for her to manage on her own.

I stroked her hair, looked at her, and we cried for a while. Eventually, I said goodnight. "Call me if you need anything."

"I'll see you in the morning," Lash said.

I left. I went home to my farm next door, and before I crawled into bed with Arnold, I laid out my clothes for rapid-fire dressing. But no summons came during the night, and before the sun rose, I fed my horses, turned them out, cleaned, and set up for evening feed. Up on the hill, Lash and Anton's house stayed dark until a light flickered on at the normal time.

I called my boss and told him I was "out for the duration." I had told him the day before that I thought the time was nearing. I feared making a judgment that the time was near for the same reason Lash had procrastinated on filing permanent disability, fear that she would outlive the allocated vacation or disability time for which we had benefits. Then what?

The waiting and that open-endedness was excruciating. And how can one even admit fear of that open-endedness, almost as terrifying as that fear of the end itself? But it was there, like some ugly gargoyle, *don't die but don't wait too long to die,* leering fantastical and real.

Not too many days before, Anton had written an email to a relative describing Lash's illness and decline, what her treatments consisted of; he'd cc'd Lash on the email as was his habit. Unfortunately, in this particular correspondence, he'd expressed that Lash was very hard on him; or maybe it was Lash's illness was very hard on him. I didn't know for sure, and I never saw the email. All I know was there was a different tenor in the sick house that afternoon when I arrived, a tension so palpable I asked Janeen as soon as I walked in the door what was wrong. She told me about the email. That Lash had read it. That she was crushed.

I went to the couch and sat down next to Lash; she wouldn't look at me for a while. She concentrated on the backs of her hands, on smoothing the sweatpants stretched over her edematous legs. When Anton got home, she looked up at him with such an expression of pain and guilt and…betrayal almost … that both of them started crying before either said a word. Anton sat in a chair next to Lash, who remained next to me on the couch; Bill and Janeen moved from chair to ottoman to couch to doorway or hovered near the fireplace. Anton laid his head against Lash's, and whispered he hadn't written what he meant in the email.

"Well, what did you mean?" Lash said, sputtering through her tears and throwing a harsh sidelong glance at her husband. He just shook his head, closed his eyes, and said he didn't know.

Bill and Janeen discreetly moved from the living room into the study; I watched Janeen's back disappear, felt alarmed, and decidedly out of my comfort zone.

"I get the feeling everyone wishes I would just hurry up and die so you all can get back to your normal lives," Lash said, pelted it out on the force of grief and anger. Anton covered his face with his massive hand and keened. "I'm sorry I'm such an inconvenience for you," she said.

"That's not fair," I said, trying to force a voice of reason. And even as I said it and Lash cast her tear-shot glare at me, the thought *none of this shit is fair* ran through my mind. Where did I have the authority to tell Lash if her behavior was fair or not? And yet, she *wasn't* being fair, was hurting those who loved her most, and some stubborn or diplomatic part of me couldn't let it go unanswered.

"I'm sorry," Anton kept saying, "I'm sorry."

Lash asked if her illness, her decline, if the time and commitment I made to her was disrupting my life, making it difficult. She asked in a tone so injured I wanted to lie, to tell her no, it was no problem, I wouldn't want to be anywhere else. Instead, I told her the truth. I reminded her that I was in therapy to treat my depression and to help me deal with my best friend dying. She squeezed her eyes shut and her shoulders shook silently. Anton wrapped his arm around her, leaned his head against hers, and wept with her rhythm. And while Lash grieved, I admitted to her the waiting was hard. I even felt the edges of anger, or bitter sarcasm coming into my words, anchoring me in this flood, this cataract of emotion. "Of course it's hard," I said. "It should be hard. How would you feel if we all had no problem dealing with this?" *Now who's not being fair?* I thought and felt a knot in my stomach.

Lash looked up at me, her face a smear of tears and plastered strands of hair. She smiled then frowned then shrugged, and planted her face back in her hands, saying through them she didn't want to make our lives harder, that she was sorry. Anton and I cajoled; we loved her, and our own pain in the face of her death was the price we paid for that. In ebbs and flows, we talked, cried, reasoned, but still I felt there was some pocket of poison we hadn't purged yet, I didn't know what it was, and I felt overfaced and out of my league. Why had the psychologist left the room when she could be moderating this discussion so much more effectively than I? But Janeen didn't reemerge from the study, and somehow, I couldn't bring myself to retreat for her aid. So we kept talking and crying, and eventually, I don't remember what prompted it, I asked Lash what in her life she had control over right now.

She looked at her feet and shook her head; her eyes glistened again. "Nothing," she said. Then she clenched her teeth and balled her fists. "Nothing, nothing, nothing!" Each time she said the word it was louder, harsher, and she began pounding her fists on her thighs until Anton grabbed her wrists, so she pounded him, shrieking and wailing, *"NOTHING! NOTHING! NOTHING!"* When she'd exhausted herself, the three of us slumped against each other in a sodden, shell-shocked heap. But somehow, her apoplexy purged that poisonous seed. It did not make our lives dealing with Lash's dying easier—or maybe it did because that putrid irony that the person dying was not the only person suffering terribly from her illness had been exposed. If we'd felt the impulse before to conceal the difficulty, we felt it less so now.

And truly, while there was no easy way of acknowledging that her illness made my life difficult, acknowledging it was better than feeding her some platitude, because she knew anyway. We had worked so hard for so many years to speak honestly with each other, even when that seemed harder than silence.

And when would she die? And that I privately worried that she would linger and linger and not die and not die for days and weeks and months; did that worry reflect more concern for her pain and suffering or for mine? Does hoping your best friend dies a rapid death define something small and selfish and evil in you? Or was it small and selfish to want her to never die, even though she suffered?

That question about when without a definitive answer and no right answer anyway grew from whatever seed it came from on whatever day it was born. If a question could have belligerence, gall, temerity—WHEN? When, when, *when?*—has all that and more. And no answers. Yet I danced with the truth a couple of weeks earlier, as we sat in Dr. Spiffy's office, just the two of us. Now that oncology was finished with her, Lash said she wanted to live until Christmas, and asked did I think that was possible. I held her hand and said, "I don't know." I did not say what I thought: *No, not until Christmas.* But I didn't *know*, so that's what I said. Did I fear she might live that long? Perhaps. Regardless, the gargoyle was there, because even though this hell was supposed to be all about Lash, also it was selfish and about me. How long could I stay off work before they got tired of it and fired me? How long could I just go on waiting?

Lash's birth mother, Paula, had lain comatose for weeks before she died. Lash was four years old. She told me she remembered asking where her mother was and crying. Lash never saw her mother dead. When she was still very young, she accompanied Janeen to a speech by Elizabeth Kübler-Ross, the Swiss-born psychiatrist who wrote *On Death and Dying,* and Lash spoke to Kübler-Ross after the speech. "I wonder what my mother looked like in her coffin," she'd said. She was six years old. Janeen recounted Kübler-Ross's advice, how Janeen and Bill then could help their daughter; Bill told Lash what Paula was wearing in her coffin and drew a picture of her. And Lash took it and seemed satisfied, perhaps some of her questions answered.

Paula was thirty when she died; probably she already had the cancer while she was pregnant with Lash. Lash had feared thirty as if her sickness were prophesied, but thirty came and went and she was alive and seemed unscathed. It wasn't until she was almost thirty-five that she found the lump. She had just turned thirty-six, and we all knew she would be long dead before her thirty-seventh birthday.

Once, when she first knew the cancer was back, running rampant before her hair had even had the chance to grow back an inch after the first round of chemotherapy, I feared she would ask me to help her die so she would not have to suffer the coming pain. I did not know if I could kill her in some Kevorkian way, and I dreaded her request.

The dread flared then fizzled quickly in the face of how much she just wanted to live. That dread morphed into a squirming desperation as her pain mushroomed and her narcotic patches and oral medications were abandoned for an implanted patient-controlled anesthesia device. The maximum dosages kept growing on that, too, but her pain outgrew it, and enveloped everything. One day she lay thrashing in some alcove in the hospital because she was no longer an oncology patient; the pain clinic had not registered her yet and they didn't know what to do with her. We all waited while Lash writhed on the gurney. I asked if she wanted me to keep pressing the button on her PCA pump; her eyes clenched, she nodded. So I kept her dosed to the maximum the pump allowed. Even drugged into semi-consciousness she was still in agony until Anton and Bill left and, storming the halls, hunted down the pain clinic doctor who finally throttled her pain by feeding narcotics directly into her spinal canal.

That day, I would have killed her if she'd asked.

The sun rose, I cleaned up from the barn and drove up the hill. I parked, let myself in the house, called out my arrival, and headed upstairs.

Lash sat on her bed, head bowed, eyes closed. She opened them and looked up when I came in, offered a wan smile. Anton stood next to her by the bed.

"Do you want to stay here today or go downstairs?"

She paused just for a moment. "I'd like to go downstairs."

So Anton and I helped to lift her from the bed to her feet, steadied her on her slow trek from her bed to the toilet, then back to her bed, where she sat while we helped her dress, slowly, exhaustingly. Anton doled out her contact lens case, her solution, received each back as she "put in her eyes." He doled out her morning heap of drugs, held the bottles and glass for her while she put each pill in her mouth, tilted her head back, swallowed. Then we rested—Lash sat slumped on the side of the bed, her edematous legs hanging over the edge, her eyes closed again. Anton and I sat next to her, waiting in silence as pale gold sunlight fell through the bedroom's south-facing windows and warmed a square of carpet. Addis, their cat, stretched herself out in the sun spot, languorous, drowsy, and around us in the silence the house made its slow morning house-noises, a clock ticked somewhere, the furnace kicked on then off, and the sun spot slowly slid over and away from Addis until the cat opened her eyes, stretched again, and pulled herself back into the shock of light, her tail flicking as she looked up through half-closed eyes at where the three of us still sat on the edge of the bed.

"Are we going downstairs?" Lash asked, not raising her head.

Anton and I looked at each other. "We were waiting for you to say you were ready."

Lash looked up then, cracked a smile. "I was waiting for one of you to do something."

A flurry of activity then, stutter-stepping Lash down the stairs in her wheelchair and leaving behind Addis who was snoozing in her sun spot on the bedroom floor.

At the foot of the stairs, we set the brakes, helped Lash stand up, and accompanied her on the slow journey to the couch where she slumped down in her usual spot. Anton put on his jacket and went out to take care of their horses. I got a Diet Coke and asked Lash from the kitchen if she wanted anything.

"Juice," she said. I returned with our drinks, sat down next to her, and handed her the glass. She took it but sat with her chin down and eyes closed as if dozing. Eventually, she opened her eyes and for a while gazed at the glass in her hand before slowly lifting it toward her mouth. Then she paused and looked up at me, her eyes as large and deep and clear as ever, a shadow of a smile on her lips.

"I'll drink this," she said, "because it's good for me."

I don't remember most of that day, really, just Anton and Bill and Janeen and my moving around, Lash sitting on her couch, mostly sleeping, not moving. For hours, I sat next to her and watched and waited. Her feet and ankles, so swollen now for weeks, were colored with blue and purple splotches of pooling blood along the bottom edges of both feet; this typically happens when the heart stops beating, and the blood stops circulating, eventually draining and collecting in the lowest parts of the body. What appears like massive bruising is not a sign of trauma but of death. It is, in fact, one of the very few reasons not to provide CPR. I had seen dependent lividity many times, but never in a living person. I didn't know it was even possible in someone still alive.

I asked Lash if she were cold, or if she wanted a blanket. Did she want me to put her feet up to make her more comfortable?

She shook her head. "I'm still here," she said.

I looked at that dependent lividity all day, looked from it to her face, watched her breathe, listened to her mumble in her sleep, and gave her a wrap or put a blanket around her shoulders even though she'd said she was not chilly. And several times she told me, "I'm still here."

In the late afternoon, as Bill and Janeen prepared supper and Anton busied himself in the barn taking care of their horses, I went down the hill to my own farm to care for my own small herd and have dinner with Arnold. He had slowly stopped coming with me to see Lash over the last weeks. He told me months later he didn't want to see her so sick, and that he wanted to remember her as she had been, when she was still some semblance physically of the woman he'd first met a year and a half earlier.

I would go back up the hill around nine o'clock., when we would begin Lash's evening journey from the couch back upstairs to her bed. I don't remember going home. I don't remember taking care of Joho and the mares, or letting Bristol out, or having dinner with Arnold and talking to him. I don't remember the call a little after six o'clock, Janeen telling me that Lash wanted me to come back *now*, that she needed to go to bed *now*. I don't remember hugging Arnold, holding onto him, kissing him, telling him I didn't know when I'd be back, and then leaving. I don't remember any of that, though I know all those things happened.

I vaguely remember Anton and Bill and me carrying Lash in her wheelchair up the stairs, and Anton and me helping her to the toilet and back to her bed. I clearly remember standing next to Lash where she sat on her bed, swaying, gasping, near panic, saying again and again, "I need to sit down, I need to sit down." I kept telling her she *was* sitting. When I realized that made no difference, I glanced at Anton and wrapped my arms around her, held her against my body, and said into her hair, "We have you, we won't let you fall. We have you. We won't let you fall, we have you." We kept saying this, nearly chanted it, and slowly, Lash's gasping moderated to normal breathing, and her grip on my arm loosened, and when I slowly unwrapped my arms and asked her if she was OK, she nodded.

"That was scary," she said.

We helped her undress, helped her ease herself back against the wedge pillow she had so she could sleep semi-sitting. I helped her pull the duvet up over her bare breasts, and I sat with her for some time while she dozed. Outside, night fell, lights came on in the house, and in some kind of spontaneous tide, Anton, Bill, Janeen, and I moved into and out of her room, never leaving her alone; time ticked by. Anton mostly sat in a chair he'd pulled to Lash's bedside. He said at one point she woke from her doze, sat up, looked at him and said brightly, "OK, let's go."

Much of that day is a haze in my memory. But the evening, the night, I remember. "Karen," I thought I heard Janeen call from upstairs. Bill and I sat in the living room; the TV was on, but I don't know if either of us was watching it. I looked at Bill. He looked at me, and I got up and started toward the staircase, but before I got there, Janeen called again, urgent. "Karen!"

I ran then, my bare feet slapping up the wood stairs, and then padding on the carpet of the hallway. I heard Lash gasping before I came through the doorway to the bedroom. I can still hear it. I came into the bedroom; Lash sat in her bed, lurching with each gasp; Anton had pivoted from his chair, was reaching for the oxygen. Lash turned her head and looked up at me, her brown eyes wide and acutely aware. She reached out to me. I see that look still today, wide eyes, reaching hand, and I can still feel when I took her hand and settled on the bed next to her; she grabbed my hand tightly. Still heaving gasps, she turned her glance back toward Janeen standing at the foot of the bed and to Anton sitting again in a chair next to her, leaning toward her, oxygen tank and tubing dangling in his hands.

Her bright gaze clouded; she gasped, and stopped; gasped again. Stopped. She seemed to shrink, a slow slouch, but she didn't loosen her grip on my hand. I stroked her hair with my free hand, felt my heartbeat and the knot in my chest grow and twist, but I watched and analyzed and considered as the paramedic in me had been trained to do.

Lash gasped again, and stopped again. I looked down at her, watching, waiting. The small lamp on the night table cast a soft glow across the covers, pale across Lash's chest. It was bony and yellow and still. I watched, breathed, waited for her chest to move again. Lash's head was tilted forward, her chin resting against her gaunt collarbone. Small dark curls of hair dropped over her forehead and framed her brow. I looked at Lash's still chest, felt her hand clutching mine. I looked at her face, her eyes half open, dim, her mouth open, lips pale. I raised my eyes to meet Janeen's. She stood at the foot of the bed, leaning in, her own eyes wide and dark.

"Would you get Bill?" I said.

Janeen breezed out of the room, called her husband from the top of the stairs, and breezed back in. The duvet had shifted down Lash's chest; her breast peeked out, looking benign and harmless. She did not move. I pulled up the duvet. Bill came into the room, and he and Janeen stood propping each other up at the foot of the bed, looking down at their daughter. Anton leaned over her, reaching out to her.

Lash gasped again—two, three, gasps, agonal. I held her hand holding mine, felt my heart beating out the time. I watched her not breathe again, and

I *did nothing* as I had promised. I breathed, ran my fingers through her hair, and shuddered at the fist around my heart; tears gushed hot and blurred the room.

"It's OK to go," I said, the words sounding strangled in my ears. *They* said you should tell the patient it's all right to go, but it felt like a lie. But that's what you were supposed to say.

"We love you, Ashley. You can go, sweetheart," Janeen said. "We love you. It's OK to go, it's all right."

"It's all right, Byrd," Bill's voice now, cracked and choking.

"Thank you for sharing your life with us," I said, and *that* felt true enough, and so that's what I kept crying to her, and all of our cries mingled in that room and floated around, and Lash lay in her bed and didn't move again.

Anton sat next to his wife, reaching toward her, calling her name, his face glistening. Her chin rested on her chest, her eyes half closed, a dull glint, her mouth slack.

Anton looked up at me. "Is she still with us?"

She wasn't, and I knew that, I knew, but I couldn't say anything, so I just shook my head.

Anton's face contorted. He snapped back in his chair, and then launched out of it and stormed the room, punching the air, crying Lash's name. I sat on the bed with her, holding her dead hand, and lowered my head, blinking through my own tears. She didn't move. She didn't seem at peace, nor did she look angelic or joyful. She looked dead.

She still clutched my hand. When I finally got up, pulled myself away from her and moved off her bed, still Lash grasped my hand, as if she had held on to life as hard and tight as she could, and even lying there now dead, was reluctant to let go. I unwrapped her fingers one by one, pulled my hand away, and lay her open, empty palm back on the covers.

Eventually, I went home to Arnold, and when I crawled into bed with him, he wrapped his arms around me while I sobbed. I had never felt so rudderless.

After Lash had finished her chemotherapy and radiation treatments, before we knew that her cancer was spreading, Bill and Janeen had given her a silver bracelet inscribed, *And Lo, I am with you always.* On the inside of the band in small cursive lettering, "Love, Mom & Dad, January, 2002." Lash wore it every day.

Sometime the night Lash died, after they'd come and taken her body but while we were still milling aimlessly around that house, Janeen and I stood alone in the empty bedroom. Without a word, Janeen opened Lash's jewelry box and slipped the silver bracelet into my hand.

And Lo, I am with you always.

chapter fifteen

Altered States

One evening, when Lash was just a few weeks this side of her grave, someone suggested that surely she would recover if only she would focus on praying right.

Lash was no pagan. She had been raised Episcopalian, although the family later joined the nondenominational church in Aurora because of, Janeen explained to me some years later, "our priest's stand on issues with which we did not agree." Lash and her parents were all involved in Stephen Ministries—lay ministers trained to be caring listeners for people in crisis. Already with a PhD and JD, Bill earned his MDiv in theology, and after he retired from his fulltime service as the public defender in Portage County, Ohio, he ministered fulltime. Janeen added an MA in divinity to her MSed and PhD in psychology, and Lash earned her MA in pastoral counseling. Lash and Anton remained members of The Church in Aurora even after Bill was ordained to the ministry in the United Church of Christ.

So it's fair to say, I thought, that Lash's feet were on a solid and comfortable path, well-mapped and surveyed. But apparently, she didn't know how to pray right for her own life.

Three simple statements, years apart, have helped inform my personal spirituality. One of these simple statements came from a good Catholic boy I went to college with. Another came from Lash. The third came from an Amish man sitting on a tractor in a field.

First: In my senior year of college, I confided to my Catholic friend that, although I'd been raised in a Christian household and to all appearances was a card-carrying Christian, I was, in fact, not an official member of any religion.

142

While my older brother was baptized, neither I nor my younger brother Ted had been, and although Ted eventually partook of the necessary classes in his early teens and was baptized, he subsequently reversed gears and declared he was an atheist. I believe in time he upgraded to agnostic or maybe even beyond, but we haven't really talked about it in decades. I try not to talk about religion much. I respect religion, and I respect other people's choice of religions. I just don't want it in my house.

I should make it clear now, I think, that I'm a deeply spiritual person. And also that I make a clear distinction between religious and spiritual; a person's spirituality is intensely personal, grows in and on one, and may be profound even in the absence of organized religion. And I believe that a person can wallow in religion and yet remain parched spiritually.

Part of my point being, religion can be ugly, in many different ways and on many different levels. I rarely disclose my unbaptized status, not out of shame or embarrassment, but because I don't like the hungry look that seems to come over some folks, as if they've learned I am some unholy pagan. As if they have a mission, or an obligation, to snag me and reel me in to their fold.

Even so, years ago when I was in college, before I became comfortable with and settled in spirituality vs. religion, I wondered out loud to my Catholic friend if I should take the requisite classes in a church, follow the lesson plan, and earn that dip in the water that was supposed to make me a card-carrying member in God's fold, complete with all associated benefits, like eternal life. Except I didn't know that I believed much of what the churches would tell me I needed to believe, or at least that I needed to say I believed. So I was ambivalent.

And this good Catholic boy asked a very simple question:

"Would the hypocrisy be worth the *security* of being baptized?"

My immediate and equivocal answer was no. And for whatever reason, his question, its wisdom and insight, and the surety of my answer, seemed to give me permission to have my own beliefs, give me permission to not conform. Such a simple moment. Pivotal. I have never since then considered joining any organized church, although I have been known to gesture to a pasture full of horses, or a sun-dappled woods, even the snow floating in the air, and say, "this is my church."

Second: Over the years of being overweight and alone, regardless of how hard or fervently I prayed for strength in dieting or wisdom and guidance in love, I nonetheless remained a failure in my dieting and a failure in finding love. For some time, I felt my prayers had been answered negatively, but I gradually came to the profoundly lonely conclusion that God was simply unaware of me. I believed there was a God, or some kind of higher power, but not that God knew I was here.

It was safe to talk to Lash about religion and spirituality because she'd known me forever and had no conversion agenda. And I told her this deepest of my secrets without worrying that she had some ulterior motive in listening to me. She was my best friend, my soul mate, and if I couldn't tell something like this to her, I couldn't tell it to anyone.

"I think prayer is the cruelest lottery," I said.

She looked at me quizzically. I explained I thought there was a supply and demand problem, like God was sitting at some ethereal switchboard in the sky, plugging into prayers as they floated His way. But with more than six billion people down there throwing prayers of all shapes and forms His way, it didn't seem possible that He could plug into each and every one of them. So some slipped through and were lost. It was only by random chance that a prayer connected. But we, spewing forth our prayers, could never know if any specific prayer, as we prayed it, would be connected or float past His switchboard and be gone. The prayer of a child to receive Butterfingers while trick-or-treating had as much chance of connecting as did the prayer of a parent for a sick child's life.

So, that's why I felt prayer was the cruelest lottery.

I told this to Lash in a hushed voice, the first time I had ever spoken my suspicion to anyone, and feeling blasphemous—pagan or no—saying it. But Lash nodded gravely as I confessed my belief.

"The only problem with that concept," she said, "is that you're assigning your own limitations to God."

"What do you mean?"

She shook her head and considered for a moment before she continued. "I think God is more than we have the capacity to understand," she said. Seeing prayer as the cruelest lottery was ascribing my limitations to God. But if God worked beyond my capacity to comprehend, I did not need to understand it. Indeed, I couldn't.

Such a simple statement. Pivotal.

And did God know I was here? Lash did not need to try to answer that one. God did.

The accident happened on a beautiful sunny September day, some time—years perhaps—after I'd shared my "prayer as the cruelest lottery" theory with Lash.

Regardless, I wasn't thinking about God at all that day. I was thinking about the long road trip my partner and I had, taking a patient from the Cleveland Clinic to a rehabilitation facility in West Virginia. It was the best kind of road trip—a beautiful, sunny September day, with only one patient who was stable and in my care for my entire shift. But it was a day that would change everything for a lot of people, because several hours into our trip, we happened upon an accident that had just occurred, involving four people. But the baby changed everything.

I didn't even know she was there at first. I was preoccupied with caring for three people I did know where there: one critical, one serious but stable, one in remarkably good condition considering there was nothing left of the car. The driver—she was the critical one—was lying on her back on the pavement, the shoulder strap of her seatbelt still around her. That's how demolished the car was. I was working on her, starting an IV, getting vital signs, when someone said, "There's a baby in the back."

A baby? A man, his face pinched, pointed off to the right. A baby? In the median? How had I missed that? I was getting up from my squat by the driver, and looked past the guy pointing toward what had been the back of the car. A baby ejected? And good God, how had I not assessed the scene well enough to see a baby in the median? I stepped around the back of the car, each step weighted, the median coming more into view with each step, step, step, but there was no baby in the median. All this stepping and looking took maybe four or five seconds.

Just to the left of my leg rested the car's back half, smashed and crumpled. I glanced down, and here's how time works, how another three or four seconds in time, what that time carries and gets seared into the brain: I saw her leg. Her little calf, baby pudgy, maybe a shoe and sock, there in the crumpled wreckage. By her knee, her leg opened up, a neat wedge chunked out. There was no blood. Paramedic assessment clicking. No blood. So, detached. I shifted to my right, looked closer into the wreckage, tried to process what I saw, fit it into triage, mechanism of injury, extrication, treatment protocol, everything I'd learned. Bits of material, shirt, maybe, or perhaps belly or arm or other leg, I don't re-member how my brain parsed that because I was trying to figure out the hair. The blonde curls, gentle tendrils, soft, but parted and divided, headed all which way, and I think I blinked once or twice before I knew her tousled hair was mixed with her brain matter, spread on the scraps of wreckage, and I stood up then, and turned to my left and stepped back to my patients, step, step, step. A baby's leg that doesn't bleed. Blonde curls and brains.

I remember turning my back to the dead child, turning back to the living patients who still needed me, and thinking *Keep it together, Karen. You have people to take care of. Keep it together.*

So I walked, step, step, step, back to the patients I could help, to the baby's mother, telling myself to keep it together, when God touched me.

I do not mean this in a figurative sense. I mean, I felt the touch of God. I felt a tangible energy touch me, a lifeline, and it gave me strength and guidance, so unexpected, so powerful and beautiful. In that instant, I knew God had always known I was here, that I had never been alone.

I stepped back to the living, and the driver, who was only conscious enough to ask, again and again and again, "How's my tot? How's my tot?" and I said, "Everyone's being taken care of." I know we were stellar paramedics that day; I tell myself we took control of chaos and saved three of four lives in that wreck. I always have the urge to add, *for what it's worth.*

I think about her often. She was only a year old. I don't know anything else about her. I still see and smell and hear those seconds, looking at her wisps of hair, at her leg that didn't bleed, and feel my heart hammer inside my ribs. Perhaps she would be graduating college now, or tending her own children, if she hadn't been in that car, or if her mother hadn't lost control, or if the semi-truck hadn't been right where it was, traveling on the other side of the median in the other direction.

I wonder if she was frightened, or just startled at the sudden buck of the car as it careened across the median. Did she hear her mother and her aunt and her grandmother scream before the truck hit them? Sometimes, I think I see her, sitting in her car seat, baffled, but not quite scared yet, before the truck smashed the car and ripped her leg off and smashed her head and smeared her brains through her hair.

Sometimes I like to think she laughed, a child's delight at the bumping thrill in her tummy, laughed, laughed before she was snuffed out.

I did not imagine, then, that my desire to be a paramedic might also be as mortal as my patients. When I was first a paramedic, I believed I'd never lose the passion. In the middle of the night when I was on call, I could be out of bed, dressed, and running to my car before my pager had finished the dispatch. I remembered the first rescue call I ever went on. I didn't remember the last one, though, and I didn't remember many that came between the first and last calls. I wasn't aware of my passion's dissolution. I wonder sometimes if it gradually diluted with all those calls, was already thin and friable by the time I couldn't any longer tell you how many runs I'd been on or how many dead bodies I'd seen or how many car wrecks or farm accidents I'd responded to or how many heart attacks I'd worked.

Maybe my passion didn't dissolve gradually but lost the way when snow-storms slowed our response times until we were inconsequential. Or when another sober person was dead but the drunk driver who caused the accident was only walking wounded. Or maybe the passion spilled out at calls with dead babies. But while that day of our road trip may have been the beginning of the end of my passion, always, still, I feel the touch of some divine power steeling me through those crucial stepping seconds when I needed to keep it together for the sake of the other patients.

Perhaps it seems odd to think God was anywhere near that awful scene that afternoon. That God could be there as a baby was smashed and lives were shattered. Does it seem odd that I believe God gave me a metaphorical tap on the shoulder that day, that in all that chaos, in an instant, I had a spiritual revelation that has informed my life ever since? I believe I came to understand a lot about *God* or the *higher power* that day, although I don't know if I can really explain it.

Third: There's a certain peace to be had in believing God's watching over you. And with that conviction, for me at least, came the belief that things happen for a reason, or that something good eventually comes of something bad. Who would have thought when Paula died and left Lash motherless, anything good could come of that? But had that not happened, Bill and Janeen would never have married; they would not have moved to Ohio; I never would have met Lash, and how different and less rich would my life have been? So, I do believe that everything happens for a reason.

The year 2000 was the beginning of the end of many things. I lost two of my four baby horses to broken legs. I held each of them as they died, only hours into the promises of their beautiful new lives. And between early March when my first baby died and July when my second baby died, my mother's youngest brother sat down in his backyard, put a gun to his head and sprayed his brains across his garden.

Sometimes during that summer, I felt like my heart struggled just to keep beating. I tried so hard to understand why these things happen. But I couldn't find any reason, or grasp any consolation from my belief that everything hap-pens for a reason. I even wondered if God was punishing me for some reason, but I couldn't believe that God would punish me by killing my babies or having my uncle commit suicide. I had no answers, and I felt suffocated. And one eve-ning, as the sun was setting golden, and the mist curled warm and damp in the

folds of land, Danny, a local Amish man who used his Yankee business partner's farming equipment to make hay, made the third simple, profound statement. Danny had buried my first baby horse that had died, and he consoled me
now after my second baby had died. He sat on his tractor in the evening sun
and listened as I confessed my loss, my inability to understand how suffering
and dead baby horses and a suicide that would forever shiver through my family
could have reason. I wanted to believe it, I wanted to see it, I was trying so hard,
but I struggled and felt adrift.

Danny nodded slowly, stroked his beard thoughtfully, and said as a statement of fact—as if he had said spring follows winter—"Times like this, all you
can do is trust."

I feel the warmth of the sun even now that I felt that evening, when that
simple statement let me release my need to understand. I might never know,
and that's all right. Just trust. Such a simple statement. Pivotal.

So during Lash's final throes, it was so easy to ask where was God in this?
I don't think I have ever asked that question relative to Lash's illness and death,
but I heard it asked both directly and indirectly. Where was God in this, with
Lash still dying despite all the prayers, even those not prayed correctly? Where
was God in this?

Everywhere.

In a family who could be there to support, love, and care for Lash as she
died.

In Bill and Janeen selling their home in Florida and moving to Garrettsville just in time for Lash to get sick.

In Arnold coming back into my life right when he did, only a few months
before Lash found her lump. What made me decide I was not going to be alone
anymore, after all those years, right at this time? I do not think it was random.

In Lash and Anton building their dream house, even in the face of her
cancer, so that Lash did have her horse farm. She had her horses in her own
barn, rode on her own land, and in the end, died in the house she and Anton
had designed and built.

In the friends and family who cooked meals, cleaned the house, helped to
care for the horses and clean the barn and mow the grass and plant and garden.

The insipid suggestion that Lash didn't pray right perhaps just nurtured
an unease I had coddled since Lash was first diagnosed with breast cancer: that
she was angry with God. And how could I explain my fear to her; what could
I do, what could I say, even if I had the courage (or audacity) to broach the
subject with her? You're dying, but please don't be mad at God.

About a week before she died, after friends from work dropped off several days' worth of meals, prepared and frozen, and had helped clean the house and the barn, Lash and I sat on the couch in the living room.

I said, "You know, you're pretty lucky."

Lash looked at me steadily, grim. "I don't feel very lucky."

I may have said something about luck being relative, that for a dying person she was lucky, but I don't really remember. I just remember her eyes, sad, a little angry, a little hurt, and I felt that if she could direct that look at God, she would. The look said I don't deserve this. It was the look of one betrayed.

Lash never told me what to think or believe where God or religion was concerned, and I always felt at ease with and respected her in a spiritual context because she seemed at ease with and respected her own spirituality. But that same respect also impelled me, timorous and awkward, to express my concern about "where she was" with God. I don't recall exactly what I said or how I said it. But I do recall vividly how self-conscious I felt, as if I knew I was butting in where I had no business but was butting anyway.

Lash's expression softened. She gave me a crooked little smile then, and said, barely a whisper, "I'm OK with God."

I held her hand and smiled back, and we cried together for a while and we didn't talk about it again. But I did not believe then, and still don't believe now, that she was really OK with God. I think she was mad as hell at God, and she said that to ease *my* mind, and that generosity of spirit still moves me today.

People used to try and placate me with platitudes after Lash died: "She's with you in spirit." I hated that. Don't tell me that! She did not want to die, so the thought that her spirit is stuck somewhere between here and there does not comfort me. No, let her be gone if she has to be dead.

Sometimes I pictured Lash lying there in her coffin, in the pitch black, alone, cold, damp, lost, too dead for this world but not ready for…what? Heaven? Nirvana? Some utopia or other? It wasn't until several weeks after Lash was dead and lying six feet under the ground in her grave next to my grave, where neither of us should have been for decades, that a pearl of solace came to me, unbidden, unlikely, cathartic.

All summer, Joho had been slowly failing, his age draining the vitality from him. When it became obvious to us that his natural death was not far off, Arnold, the vet, and I made the decision to ease his exit. Six weeks after we buried Lash at Fairview Cemetery in Hiram, we buried Joho at the top of the hill in his pasture where he could look over his herd of mares and his children. It was a bitter December day, the end of a bitter year, the end of much of my life's directive forces. So much gone into the ground. So much buried.

It wasn't until years later, though, that it came to me like some kind of epiphany as I was driving home from work one afternoon that even if Lash wasn't OK with God, it didn't matter. Because God was OK with Lash. That day, I walked through the door and wailed into Arnold's chest tears of relief and joy, laughing and blubbering and sobbing, and wondered out loud how it was that it took me nearly a decade to figure out such a simple truth.

Hadn't Lash basically told me as much herself?

chapter sixteen

Dreamscapes

In the dream, Anton and I are preparing Lash's body in her casket, getting her ready for her funeral. How hard can two people cry? We are crying a lot. It was all over now—her suffering, our trying to ease her suffering. Wasn't it supposed to be easier? Why isn't it easier?

Anton stands on one side of Lash's coffin. I stand on the other. Anton runs his hand through Lash's short dark hair, only grown back a few inches after the first round of chemo. I look at her pale, pale face, pinched and thin and strained; my vision is tear-pool wobbly, making it look like her eyelids flutter.

We are selecting what Lash will wear for her service. "At least I'll be thin when people see me in my coffin. I won't be fat anymore," Lash had said, wry stab at nasty reality, months earlier. No, she certainly is not fat. Gaunt was more like it.

Had I promised her that if she didn't look good in her coffin, I wouldn't let it be open for her service? I had. Does she look good? No. She looks sick, exhausted, spent. But I am not prepared to close the coffin either. Because still she's beautiful, and really, I think she wanted it open anyway. Unless the cancer had eaten away her lovely face or something, which it had not. But the morticians had added nothing to it, such a difficult task if you stop to think about it, embalm someone then try to make him or her simply appear asleep. I didn't think it worked. Not for Lash. Not here. Probably not ever. Because Lash is dead, and you can't change that with trawls of foundation and makeup.

In this dream, her arm moves and my heart starts slamming in my chest. *Ignore that*, I tell myself. Anton hasn't noticed. So I try to ignore it. Lash is dead, and we are preparing her for her funeral. She is lying right there in her coffin, dead as a doornail. Except.

Except now she turns her head … it really moves. She's dead. We are preparing her dead body for her service, before we close the coffin lid, seal it shut, and bury her. So I continue with the preparations, because there's no going back, and even the thought of going back makes me feel panicky. *Please don't move anymore. You're dead. Dead people don't move.* Except.

Except now her eyes are open. She looks dazed, weak, but aware. Desperate, I try to talk to Anton as if this is not happening, to distract him, because we are preparing to bury Lash, and if I can just stick to what is supposed to be happening, maybe this will just go away, this unruly fact that Lash isn't acting so dead anymore. Hadn't I promise her that I would not try to make her live anymore when it was time for her to be dead? I had.

But now Anton has noticed that his dead wife isn't seeming so dead, and he's weeping strangely, maybe tears that come from the shock of sudden hope where there had been no hope; he's calling her name, helping her sit up in her coffin. I am rudderless, unmoored by this incongruity unfolding right beneath my hands and eyes. So, by the time she's sitting up, looking slowly around her, eyes heavy-lidded and dopey, asking what happened, her voice thin and tremulous but very real, I've given up trying to will her to stay dead. Too late for that.

I call the funeral-home people, call up the stairs for them.

"She's not dead, she's alive," I say, urgent and agitated.

"No, she's dead," says the director, coming down the stairs, his brows furrowed. But now he sees her; Anton is laughing and sobbing and helping her climb out of her coffin. She's unsteady on her feet, wobbly, but she's standing, leaning against her husband.

"No, she was dead," the funeral director is alarmed now. "She was dead! We embalmed her and everything."

Now Lash's parents, Bill and Janeen, are here, too, and everyone's around Lash, helping her walk toward the door; they all swarm in a frenzy of disbelief and joy and the sudden resurgence of her need for care, the frenetic treatments and medications and procedures that all stopped dead the moment Lash died.

I'm still standing by the empty coffin, just beyond the swarm's periphery, and I feel a pulse of that urgency, like ice or acid sizzling in my head. I say, "We need to call the doctor! They've embalmed her! We need to tell him, he needs to know she's been embalmed, it might change what we do now."

I don't know if anyone hears me. They're all crowding around Lash, blocking my view of her, escorting her from the room.

I had promised her I would be able to let her die when it was time for her to be dead. "Can you do that?" she had specifically asked. I had said yes. So when her death came, I had let her die, had done nothing, just looked into her fearful eyes while I held her hand, and let her go just as I had promised. Now she isn't dead anymore, and why am I not filled with glee and care renewed like everyone else? Why do I wish this were not happening? Why do I resist this so, resist it perhaps harder than I'd resisted letting her die?

Lash's posse writhes around her, leads her out of the room, away from her coffin; they're excited and frightened anew, the cares and desperation Lash's living brings back so thick around them it may choke them. I stand slack by Lash's vacant coffin and watch them go, watch Lash leave me again, ushered around a corner and down some dim hallway beyond my sight, and don't know how to feel, but however it is, it isn't right.

Waking from the dream did not bring relief that night; years of waking since have not brought relief either. For years, the dream, what it's trying to tell me, has haunted me. Had I helped Lash die when it was her time, as I had promised I would? Or had I not done enough to help her fight for her life? Was I so fixated on my own pain and grief, on the excruciating wait, wait, wait for The End, that I'd lost focus of what Lash needed and wanted?

Logic tells me I took care of Lash exactly as I'd promised, exactly as she'd asked me to. And yet I know all she wanted was to live; even as she sat in her bed, sucking in her last gasps, she stared at me with a clear, wide-eyed intensity so vital and aware, and she didn't quietly close her eyes and ease into her death. She watched us, fighting to keep her life, until even her heart shivered to a stop; then the life left her eyes as if someone had taken this from her entirely against her will, so her face drooped and her eyes dimmed and sagged, no peaceful repose.

I see this still in my mind's eye all these years later; I see and hear and smell and feel it all as if is happening now. I reside in the context of her agonal moments, and I can't stop asking myself if I should have done more than what I'd promised, that promise I'd made when she was less sick *to do nothing*, that promise to which I remained true. I held her hand and told her how much I loved her, thanked her for sharing her life with us ... and did nothing, nothing, to give the life in her eyes a little more time in her body. No CPR. No assisted breathing. No epinephrine. No resuscitation at all. I did nothing but sit and weep and watch her die and hold her hand until it had become cool.

Every time my mind goes to this place, I never change what I would do. I never override the logic, never mobilize the paramedic who could extend life, if only for oblivious moments. In every recreation in my mind, I yield to logic and Lash's express request, and do nothing. But the emotion never stops questioning, is always doubting, will remain implacable, I think, for as long as my brain retains the capacity to recall it.

Had I helped her die when she was ready, or had I let her die too soon? Sometimes I think I should have tried to save her, at least a little. But even as I think that, something wiser (or cold or pragmatic) has me shaking my head. I can always ask: should I have tried to save her, to give those bright eyes even just a few more minutes? I ask, and my action never changes, regardless of how often I relive her death. I had done nothing. Continue to do nothing. Will always do nothing. Yet, I keep asking.

And, here's the ugly crux of that ugly question: if I had tried to save her, forsaken the promise, even just to try and give her a few more minutes of life… if I had tried, for whose benefit would that have been?

For years after her death, when I dreamt of Lash, she was sick and dying. I would not call them nightmares; they were not frightening or disturbing beyond the fact of her illness. And in fact, I welcomed them, welcomed the REM-sleep-Lash, even if she was sick, dying, dead. Then, a few years ago, within one dream, her condition suddenly shifted.

In this dream, she's vibrant from the start. She says, "Now that I'm better, I want to find that horse I was looking at before I got sick. I want to see if he's still for sale, and if he is, I want to try him, and hopefully, he'll be my super dressage horse."

She looks at me steadily with her big brown eyes, and there is a positive intensity and energy flowing from her, a wellspring of enthusiasm to resume a project reluctantly abandoned, and I know that things are good. She glows with health, her cancer and death and all our anguish behind her now, and it is time to celebrate.

Giggling like school girls, we search the Internet, trying to remember details about the horse and his ownership, things that had first interested Lash about him that had impelled her to inquire about him years ago, right before she got sick and everything changed.

We type in keywords and phrases, and Google grey or gray warmblood or wmbld gelding seventeen hands or 17hh or 17h, and all the various iterations we can think of. We browse through equine sales web sites, and on dreamhorse.com, we find him, still out there, still available, waiting for Lash.

"That's him, that's him!" she says, poking the monitor screen, bouncing in her chair and yanking on my arm, even though I am sitting right next to her looking at the horse's image on the screen with her, laughing with her, basking in her delight.

So we are on the road again, not our annual excursion to the Swedish Warmblood or Trakehner inspections, but to go see Lash's dream horse in the flesh, to try him out. When we find the horse, actually meet him, he is everything Lash has ever hoped for. Handsome steel gray, tall and big-bodied enough to "fill out" Lash's long, long legs, a sweet and intelligent personality, and scopey, athletic gaits. Perfect.

In the barn aisle, as the owner grooms him and tacks him up and chats with us and answers our questions, Lash never stops grinning, and in the arena, when I watch her swing her leg over his back and settled into the saddle, it seems like a homecoming. They look good. The horse reaches around to nuzzle her leg, his expression kind and content. Lash leans forward in the saddle, stretches her hand out, strokes his face, then gathers up the reins and they move off down the arena track. The horse fits Lash perfectly, and after all those years of desperately loving horses that simply weren't big enough to fill out her legs, now she sits on her perfect match. I stand in the middle of the arena and watch the beautiful sight as she rides around me.

Lash looks over her right shoulder at me, her eyes glittering, her smile radiant. "He feels fantastic! He's *perfect*," she says.

Lash finally has the perfect horse. She is healthy again. Her smile glows out to me as she looks my way from the back of this big, kind, handsome, perfect horse, my smile glows back, the two of us giddy and grinning like goons, but what else can we do? Things are perfect. Health and delight flow from Lash, pour from her like a physical river, like the light and warmth of a summer afternoon washing downhill over cool grass, and I feel as if I breathe some new air, each breath filling me with that light, that warmth, easing and comforting some dark, cold thing that had come to rest in my core some time ago.

For the first time in the years since Lash has died, I feel her happiness again. For so long, she has been sick, even in my dreams after her death, she still was sick, until her illness seemed to root itself in my heart as part of her identity. But not now. Now it's behind her, not as if it never was, but as if she's grown beyond it, and she's spry and vibrant again. Ready to ride.

This dream does not fade after I wake, nor does Lash's happiness. It stays with me, and I feel it thrumming through my core like a tonic, like a good ride on a nice horse.

He feels fantastic. Perfect!

All day after waking from that dream I kept catching myself thinking about Lash beaming, riding her dream horse and smiling. And I'd smile. That feeling, that smile, stayed with me for weeks, months, even today. If my dreams are Lash's visits to me, then through this dream she's brought me the gift of revisiting her life—her true life, not relative to illness or death. Such a beautiful gift, to lift my heart and soul above darkness to see her truth. And it's like breaking surface in a gray sea and finally being able to breathe deep, then floating in calm waters, drifting finally to a warm bright sandy shore.

Lash riding her dream horse, every bit big enough for her. Lash happy and healthy, overflowing with enthusiasm, smiling back at me over her shoulder.

Which is how it always should be.

chapter seventeen

LOSS

A few weeks before Lash died, when I admitted I was well underway in the preoperative testing and approval process to undergo bariatric surgery, Lash grieved that I would be doing this without her. All our lives, she'd said, we'd battled the bulge, gained and lost weight together. *And now you're going to do this without me.* I don't think I ever found the words to really tell Lash that her illness, that she couldn't be *saved*, impelled me to pursue such drastic, risky measures to try and ensure my health. I wanted to be saved. If we had talked about that, we would have talked about that dream again, that nightmare, because it never, ever felt like a dream to me, and because when I'd told her about it, Lash had offered solidarity and commiseration. She knew how I felt; I didn't have to make excuses or try to explain.

In that nightmare, I lay in some kind of dream-paralysis on the gymnasium floor; lying near me, scattered all around, were fifteen or twenty men, all unconscious barely breathing, but alive. I was the only woman. The damp air was cool and still, and it was very quiet, but the calm didn't hide the inevitability of death if we didn't move. We needed to get out of the gymnasium, all of us, because some lethal thing was slipping toward us, and we would die if we were still there when it, whatever *it* was (a fog or mist or shadow), slid over us. But I couldn't move or even cry out for help, couldn't save myself or the others. The others were athletes: football, rugby, all big burly men, bulky, athletic. I was the only one in the gym who was conscious, who sensed that lethal thing moving, inertia propelling it toward me, even though I was struck dumb and mute. My terror was palpable, but I could not move, could do nothing to save myself.

Then suddenly rescue personnel were there, and their urgency sent a surge of hope through me. I was at the far end of the gym closest to the coming lethal fog and I watched as the rescue team hauled and wrestled the athletes' dead weight onto makeshift stretchers, lifting their massive, inert forms, one by one, through the only exit, a small chest-high window, and out into the light, to safety. *Please hurry, please hurry* I tried to will the rescuers, even though I could see they were going as fast and hard as they could; so I lay there and watched and waited, scared, anxious, relieved they were here to save me, terrified they were too slow. I knew they wouldn't stop, could see their determination to save us all. They worked methodically across the gymnasium. I watched them lift the football players, the boxers and weight lifters, the runners, to the window. I watched each big body hoisted high, disappearing into that safe light.

Finally, *finally,* I was the only one left to save; the lethal fog had begun crawling around the corner, into the gym, groping blind but deadly. It slid toward me like a slow incoming tide, and I rolled my eyes to watch it, heard my heart slamming in my ears, and waited for the touch of death. Then rescuers shoveled me onto the makeshift stretcher and dragged me across the gym, and I was under that window, that glorious shaft of life. I was overwhelmed with relief and gratitude, inhaled liberty through that porthole as the rescuers prepared to hoist me up and out to safety, just as they had done with all the others. All the hard bodies in this room had already passed through it; I had waited and watched our rescuers lift each and every one of them through that window, and now, after all the others were safely through, it was my turn.

My rescuers couldn't lift me. I was too heavy. They strained, sweating and gasping; they struggled but made no progress. I could do nothing to help. And the fog, aware of me now, knew I was there and was seeking me out, its prey. The rescuers watched the fog coming, and struggled, but they couldn't lift me. I was too fat. Too heavy. And when the only option my rescuers had left was to dive through the window and save themselves, they left me. With the death fog roiling toward me, there I lay alone and abandoned under the window to my salvation. They had left me to die, not that they hadn't tried. It was my own fault; I'd caused my own undoing. I was too heavy. Too heavy to be saved.

I woke then, the slow peeling away of sleep until I wasn't asleep anymore, but not much better off for being awake, not from this nightmare. Sometimes, my relief in waking up from dreams was exquisite, like the way it was when I'd dreamt I had huge over-sized feet that grew and grew until I could hardly move them. Everyone laughed at me and pointed, even my own mother, and I wept in fear as I tried to walk with monolithic flippers at the ends of my legs. When I woke up from *that* dream, I checked my feet; there they were, perfectly normal, and my relief had been enormous and buoyed by the humor with which I could laugh from this side of sleep.

But the dream in the gym came with me into the light of day; it felt so real my heart raced and sweat beaded along my hairline when I remembered it. I couldn't shake it and it dogged me, and surely such shamefulness glared from me for all to see—too fat to save, too fat to save too fat too fat too fat.

I had starved myself for days after that dream, but of course I started eating again. Lash was the only person I ever told about the dream, and I knew she knew my horror and shame. She did not dole out platitudes or try to talk reason and sense into me; she just listened, her expression grim. When I'd told her I was too heavy to save, they'd had to leave me to die, she'd nodded, her lips drawn into a tight line. She grabbed her thighs with each hand and shook them once, hard. The ripples carried down her legs and up her hips. *Too fat to save*, she said, and grimaced. We sat for a while, heads down with dejection, before we eventually, inevitably, gathered ourselves up to troll for fast food or an open diner.

We would diet tomorrow. There was always tomorrow.

Until there weren't tomorrows left for Lash anymore. I couldn't save Lash, and I couldn't save myself from my own obesity, but maybe a surgeon and his scalpel could. And if I felt guilty about trying to get myself saved when no one could save Lash, that guilt didn't stop me; it just made me want to go into the surgery prepared—not only for the operation itself but for the fact I would never again be able to eat the same way I had. I was ready to do that. I was ready to be saved.

I was morbidly obese, over 100 pounds overweight, heavy enough for insurance to concede my obesity was actually a disease, and gastric bypass surgery a sensible treatment. Fat enough, but only barely. A mere ten pounds lighter, and I wouldn't have been classified as diseased or a surgical candidate. I believe being on the barely-fat-enough end of the morbidly obese range was all to my advantage. I had less to lose, and even with my blood pressure and cholesterol levels too high, I was still relatively healthy. Because of all the physical work I performed every day on the farm, I was also more physically fit than many bariatric patients, which was all well and good. Still, if Lash hadn't gotten sick, hadn't died despite her pit-bull tenacity and desire to live, I wouldn't have been here at all.

Having undergone five knee surgeries during the late '80s and early '90s, I was familiar with the preoperative, anesthetic, and postoperative processes. I was also very aware of how acute immediate postoperative pain could be. But this was not an outpatient arthroscopic knee surgery. Make no mistake. This was a major surgery. I'd have an incision several inches long, and would remain in the hospital three to four days postoperatively. The very fact of my obesity made me an increased surgical risk. But I wanted my health, to have some control, and watching Lash die regardless of how intensely she wanted to live moved me to pursue this surgery. And as much as I was determined to move forward with this, to take charge of my life and health, my own emotions surprised me. I waved goodbye to Arnold and my mother, both of them blurred through a sheen of tears I didn't expect.

On the table, I shivered a bit, but not because of the chill. The anesthesiologist explained what he was doing before he did it, and as I felt the pre-anesthetic sedation weigh me down, I saw vividly in my mind's eye my own grave next to Lash's grave.

I love you Lash, I said silently, *but I'm not ready to join you yet.* And then the lights went out on the life I had known; or maybe it's more accurate to say I awoke to the same life, but re-routed to a different course.

Arnold and I kept a bariatric journal for the first year after my surgery, documenting my weight loss, taking pictures, recording the improvements in my blood pressure and cholesterol. On the first anniversary of my surgery, we looked at the entire journal, marveling and laughing at the changes from 262 pounds to about 165 pounds. And we laughed, too, at some of the things that had changed that I'd never associated with being heavy. I couldn't always just bump the truck door closed with my hip now; more often, I bounced off the door. Without the pounds to back me up, I couldn't move furniture around, shoving or dragging it where I wanted. Watching me try to physically bull my way through, my feet slipping in comic illustration of my ineffectiveness, sent Arnold into hysterics. My new disability was disconcerting, and tempered my own amusement with the realization that when I lost the pounds, I also lost a lot of what those pounds did to, and for, me.

I'd always been proud of my physical strength. Even as a paramedic when I was overweight if not yet morbidly obese, my strength served me well, instilling confidence I think, in my partners and patients alike. Partners commented on my weight-lifting prowess; even patients occasionally spoke about my physical capacity. One, a large, cranky, tattooed biker who probably topped six feet and 200-plus himself, chastised my partner about his constant litany of sexist comments, some of which seemed aimed at me in particular.

"Watch what you say, man," the patient had said, with all appropriate growl and intimidation his own size and demeanor gave him. "I bet she could set you on your ass no problem."

My partner and I both laughed, I not the least because what the patient said was probably accurate.

Others' appreciation of my strength pleased me; I'd always attributed it just being a big-boned woman, and not in the metaphorical sense. I was born big, with broad bones and thick muscles. Lash and I used to joke if we were horse breeds, she would have been a tall, fine-boned Arabian, and I would have been a bulldog of a quarter horse, maybe even a Belgian or other draft horse. Being strong was the one thing about also being big that I actually appreciated; I'd always attributed my strength to that innate physical quality, never giving any credit to the relative influence of the individual pounds themselves as I packed them on.

Now that I bounced off doors and couldn't budge a sofa, I wondered if the strength had really ever truly been mine, or only lent to me by proxy through my fat.

Still, I had no regrets having the surgery; it enabled me to lose the weight and keep it off, and to arrest and reverse regains early and more easily. It has served me very well, been the successful "tool" the surgeons all say bariatric surgery should be. Years and 100 or so pounds after I had my guts rearranged to help change my life for the better, I still have Indy, and most of my health, even if the farm and breeding are in my past now.

Sometimes I wonder if Lash would have shared in the delights and thrills and surprises of my weight loss, of my riding and showing successfully, especially if she continued with her own yo-yo weight loss and gains. Would the disparity have been a wedge? I don't think so. But I also don't think I'd ever have gotten onto the surgical table if Lash hadn't gotten sick and died in the first place, so perhaps it's a moot question.

chapter eighteen

Ashes to Lash

Recently, I had a discussion with Sarah's father, Tom, about how even the horrible things in life have positive impacts, though perhaps we can't fathom those ramifications at the time. This conversation was especially poignant coming as it did in the aftermath of Indy's second foal Rainier's death weeks earlier, and the grief and anger and gratitude and frustration and faith that swirled around it. Tom felt Rainier had served God's purpose, and so God had called him home. I'm not sure I believe there is such an explicit cause and effect, although certainly Rainier was a constant that wove the fabric of Lash's life into Tom and Sarah and Nancy's lives and kept that thread weaving for years after Lash had died with Arnold's and my lives.

Rainier may have been the tangible bond remaining between Lash and Sarah, but their connectedness preceded him. Perhaps the two shared some kind of intuitive only-child bond, some innate understanding of each other, of a "horse nut" little girl's life when that child has no siblings. Whatever, something was there everyone recognized and nurtured, so Lash and Sarah got to know and love each other, and I got to know Sarah and Nancy and Tom secondary to that something between Sarah and Lash.

Which is how it was that Tom and I would be having a deep theological discussion nearly a decade after Lash had died. A discussion I'd had before with Lash and others about how, if Lash's birth mother, Paula, had not died when Lash was four, Lash's father, Bill, would never have married Janeen, how the new family would not have lived in Ohio, how Lash and I would never have met, how Tom would never have hired Lash at Penske. Sarah would never have known Lash, would never have known Rainier, and so Rainier would not have gone from me to Lash, or from Lash to Sarah after Lash died. So Sarah would not have had this horse to grow up with, to help carry her through her adolescence, or be a constant between Sarah and the Nathers and me, increasing our own friendship going to horse shows together with Indy and Rainier, mother and son (Tom introducing Indy and me as Rainier's "birth mother"). Likely, Sarah would not have been so interested in dressage without Lash's influence nor had an interest in competition, but she did, was a talented rider, and Rainier had the quality and temperament to carry Sarah to national junior/young rider championships two years in a row. Sometimes I think Sarah was living and riding the competitive horse show life Lash always wanted, but was never able to fully immerse herself in.

And if Paula hadn't died, Tom would not have had Rainier to pacify him and give him solace when Sarah left Cleveland for college at Miami University, nor would the horse have been the constant in Sarah's life when she moved from Ohio to Washington DC for work after she graduated college. None of this would ever have come to be if a mother had not died so many years ago, leaving a four-year-old child and widowing her husband. If so much that is good and beautiful can come to have been from Paula's death, I have to believe that Lash's death, or Rainier's, must have some positive influence somewhere. But I don't see it yet, and in some ways I envy Tom his conviction in God's purpose for Rainier being complete, calling him home. Because at my most pragmatic, I think Rainier just took a bad step in pasture, shattering his leg and lives along with it. It happens. I've watched it happen in front of me, watched beautiful young lives with nothing but potential move on four legs, then hobble on three; perhaps this feeds the darker, niggling thought that something larger is at work, something that snaps the bones and ends the lives of the horses I have bred. Tom's conviction would be a comfort; this is no comfort. Nor is pragmatism.

Two weeks after Steorling produced Sukhoi—a delicate filly with no promise of the future size or substance that Lash had expected, counted on, that the genetic recipe should have ensured but failed to deliver—Lash stood in the field with Arnold and me. It was Good Friday—Friday, the *13th* of April in 2001—and Indy had perfunctorily stretched out in the sun-warmed grass and delivered her second foal into the bright afternoon. Nearby, Steorling grazed and Sukhoi frolicked, unmoved by the new addition to their little herd or how life had changed, was still changing. On April 2, Steorling had reproduced her too-small self in too-small Sukhoi, and even as Lash folded her six-foot-one frame to sit on the ground and help dry the new baby, she spoke in a hushed voice of the filly's lovely dark color, her exquisite face, her tiny white star on her forehead and white ringlet around her tiny hoof. Even as I smiled with Lash and delighted with her, I looked at the tiny filly; *too small, too small, too small* beat through my mind like a pulse. Although neither of us polluted the air that night by saying aloud the obvious, I know it must have been throbbing through Lash's mind as well.

Two days later, Lash found that lump in her breast and knew her life had changed. Then, perhaps, she stood outside the foaling stall and looked at Steorling, who never grew tall enough, and diminutive Sukhoi, and said out loud, "Too small, too little, too late."

When Lash ambled down into the pasture, she walked past where Steorling grazed with Sukhoi and joined Arnold and me by Indy and her foal. The new colt, his near black coat drying, was contemplating gravity and the ground and the new big world, and Indy, having devoured all of the grass within her reach, had hefted herself back to her feet and was alternating between nuzzling her new baby and eating the grass he sprawled across.

Lash and I helped the colt in his attempts to stand, and Lash laughed and smiled and beamed at the baby, because even if you're only thirty-four and you've just been diagnosed with breast cancer and your life is shattering around you, new life like this shines through that fog for a while and everything glows. So Lash stood there in the field on a Friday afternoon, and Rainer, his black coat drying in the breeze, leaned against her, absurdly huge, a baby who had no business being so much bigger than Sukhoi, and Lash looked up from him, looked across the field to her tiny filly, back to me, and laughed.

"Hey, you got my horse," she said, and I laughed with her, even though I felt the sting behind the words, the inequity that Sukhoi did not embody the sum of her genes, all of which should have made her big, *big*, much bigger than she was, or that Rainier should unfold from his little mother with such long, long legs hoisting his hefty, solid body nearly to Lash's waistline.

So we swapped babies. I suggested it a couple weeks after Rainier's birth, and I admit now (although I didn't then) that I was motivated in part by guilt. It wasn't fair that Lash had cancer and I didn't. It wasn't fair that I had three foals that year, all of which were far larger than Sukhoi. It wasn't fair that Lash dreamed and hoped and finagled to buy or breed a horse big enough for her, that the ferocity of her love and devotion to her horses and her hopes didn't matter. It wasn't fair. Life's not fair, trite and true, but I could do something about *this* inequity. *Let's make a trade,* I suggested. I had a breeding farm, and Sukhoi had Olympic champions on her dam's side as well as her sire's side—on paper she was genetically superior to any of the three babies I had that year. *So, take your pick*, I told Lash: Alberta, tall bay filly out of Mysty, or Venice, a hefty, tall chestnut full sister to Indy, or Rainier. I hinted that from a business standpoint, Rainier was most saleable for me—a colt, big, and just about black. Popular. Saleable. Plus, everything about him was quality: his conformation, his gaits, his temperament. It would be good to have a baby like him on my sales page.

But Lash wanted Rainier, not one of the fillies, and I knew that, so we made it official, signed the papers, sent the certificates off to the registry in Sweden, and finally, finally, *finally*, Lash had the horse she was supposed to have.

Would we have swapped if Lash hadn't just been diagnosed with cancer? I don't know. Perhaps not. But her diagnosis, the sudden potential finity of her life, spurred Lash into actions and decisions she may have otherwise left open-ended. Now she tightened her grip on what she wanted, what was important, and narrowed her focus. She and Anton had just sold their house in Mantua, were looking for a temporary living situation while they built their dream house and barn when they'd found the lump, changing their future.

"Maybe you should wait a year to build," I had said early on. "Focus your energies on treatment and getting better, and worry about building afterwards."

"No," Lash said, clear and certain. "I've waited my whole life to have my farm. I'm not going to let cancer keep me from it. We're not going to wait to see what happens."

So maybe that's how it was with the horses too. Lash hadn't been able to love Tabriz into being big enough or quality enough. She had gambled with Steorling, buying her as a weanling, knowing she was smaller than her full siblings, but counting on the filly's gene pool and her own determination to overcome, and when that failed, breeding Steorling to Joho—a match that should have been fortuitous but instead produced Sukhoi, small and fragile. Perhaps, if Lash had gone through that spring with two normal breasts, she would have bathed Sukhoi in the same forceful love and determination that had failed to perfect Tabriz or transform Steorling into a mare with the size and quality her breeding should have ensured. Perhaps having cancer lent her a pragmatism that just enabled her to acknowledge Sukhoi's limitations, to shift her love and hope off the little bay filly and let it settle onto the big black colt. So Sukhoi stayed at home in the pasture, small and weedy, while Rainier grew and flourished, buoyed and supported Lash's love, floated her dreams, and did not disappoint.

Tom and Nancy ferried Sarah out to Hiram and later to Parkman on weekends to be with Lash, and Sarah and Lash played with Rainier, groomed him, trained him. Lash taught Sarah about raising a baby, eventually leaving to her or Anton some of the more physical aspects of working with a youngster when chemotherapy made her too weak or sick to do it herself. Lash never hid her illness from Sarah. Indeed, she talked with the girl about how Sarah could continue with her equestrian passion after Lash died and helped prepare her for it.

At Lash's memorial, Sarah, barely fifteen years old, stood in front of hundreds and spoke in eloquent eulogy of Lash's impact on her life. She spoke of Lash's spiritual journey, of God's purpose, and I wondered as I listened to her if she were too young to really comprehend what she was saying, if she were simply repeating what she'd heard in her own home and church and life; did she truly feel it in her soul, understand it? Or did she just think she did? I didn't understand it, and I had almost twenty-five years on Sarah. I saw then, still see now, the small, mean, dark place where that thought resides, but I don't relinquish it. Still, I see now in Sarah, many years later, the same spiritual tenor as she confronted losing Rainier, and I wonder if the years have stained the clarity of her belief.

She seemed to grieve with a purity I found reassuring. She grieved for the horse, for herself, her parents, for Lash. "He was my last connection to Lash," Sarah said the night Rainier died, only hours after she and Tom and Nancy had to make the awful decision to euthanize the ten-year-old, standing with a broken leg in his pasture. Incongruous, it occurred to me as Sarah and I spoke, that Rainier was in her life years longer than Lash had been. Even through Sarah's grief, profound and visceral, that connection to Lash remained paramount. "We're having him cremated," she told me, "I want to bring him home to Lash."

Tom told me later Sarah had decided years earlier that at the end of Rainier's life, he should go back home, back to Lash. No one expected that to happen so soon, or so tragically. And something about the *how*—that he should break his leg—worms its way into me, places him with Sandusky and Cyprus. When my baby horses die, they break their legs. In 2000, in March when Sandusky broke his leg and then in July when Cyprus broke his, Lash was there, physically holding me, helping me bear the grief, the shock and improbability of losing two of my four foals that year, and losing them to broken legs. In all my years with horses, I'd never lost a foal, and I'd never had a horse with a broken leg. Broken legs are rare, a far rarer way for a horse to die than disease or other injury, but perhaps that was my curse, or the curse of my foals, and the excruciating minutes where I embraced their suffering before the vet arrived and pumped barbiturates into their veins. Waiting for the vet, I had shifted into medic mode, splinted and bandaged their fractures, trying to stabilize those broken bones to ease their pain, or to change the courses of their lives now that it was too late. Still I can smell their blood, and the sweat and milk dripping from their dams, standing over their prostrate babies. I can still hear the cries of those mares, calling, calling, calling for their dead babies, no amount of drugs sedating them beyond their anguish.

Lash helped me bury my foals, but not my grief or guilt or fear of cursedness—things you can't bury because they don't die like foals, but acquire their own sentience and live on and on. In the next two years, she shored me up emotionally when my mares foaled; she sat on the ground by the pasture gates the first few times I put a mare with her new baby out to help keep an eye on everything, to help me make sure these new babies didn't break their legs, that they would live. Even as her own life was fading, ending much too quickly, she still invested herself in taking care of me, helping me take care of my dream, helping keep it alive.

Yet I still count my dead babies' birthdays each year, still think, *if he had lived, he would have been—*

And now Rainier. My Good Friday baby who became Lash's baby, and later Sarah's baby, who broke his leg and now comes home to Lash again as ashes. Was there something inherent in being one of my babies that doomed Rainier? Was some insidious seed planted when that black colt slipped onto the sunny grass on a Friday the 13th? Was he doomed to this fate, some curse to be born in my field, or on my farm, or to my ownership?

I don't speak of these thoughts, because they seem at once paranoid and selfish and pagan, and probably come from that same small dark place that questioned young Sarah's capacity to understand the spiritual message in her eulogy.

Rainier came back to Ohio to Tom first. "Forty-three pounds of ashes," he told me. They will keep some. Sarah will as well.

I will go out to Parkman, to two different farms, owned now by people I do not know, to ask if we can spread some ashes. I'll drive up the long drive I haven't traveled since Anton sold the farm and moved a year or two after Lash died, and I'll ask the people who own the farm now, *May I put some ashes here in this field, where he spent his first two years?* Tom and Nancy and Sarah and I think it feels right to leave him in the places where he lived. And in the end, we will leave some of him over Lash's grave, and my grave next to hers. A decade after he was born here in Ohio, years after Lash went into her grave and Rainier went to spend his life with Sarah, he will be back in Ohio, back with Lash, his ashes spread over her final real estate, settling through the grass, sinking into Lash's earth. Back with Lash, where he belongs, Sarah says.

Someday soon, before the cemetery, I'll pull up the long driveway I haven't traveled since before Anton sold the farm. I'll ask the folks who live there now, *May I put some ashes in your fields?*

Then I'll pull into a driveway I pulled out of for the last time several years ago. I'll step out onto ground that in the late '90s was a hayfield where I put my home and horses and built a barn and fencing and friable dreams. I'll go knock on a door that used to be mine.

May I put some of his ashes in this field here, where he was born ten years ago? I'll ask. I run the script over and over in my mind.

Some part of me doesn't feel I should have to ask, but it's not my place anymore. We sold the farm years ago. Over the years after Lash died, then Joho, I slowly stopped breeding; I sold all my horses except Indy, and she I boarded elsewhere, where I could ride and socialize. Then there was no longer really a reason to keep the farm and look out over my empty fields, or toward my empty barn, or up the hill into the trees, where if things had been different, Lash would have been looking back toward me across horse-rich fields.

So it's not my farm anymore. If I am to take any part of Rainier back there, I need to ask.

And that, I suspect, will be the easy part.

chapter nineteen

Bye to the Farm

In 2006, I sat at the dining room table on the farm, smoothing out the rumpled diagrams and sketches I'd made years ago at my father's insistence. *Mark where the utilities are buried*, he'd said. *It'll be very useful if you ever sell the place.* I'd laughed at him outright, told him we all knew I'd never sell the place, but I conceded mapping where things were buried was a good idea regardless.

So with the barn only partly constructed, and the cement foundation for the house setting, we'd measured the trenches cradling electric and phone from the dirt road to the house. Then measured from the house to the barn, marked where the utilities left and entered each building, how deeply they were buried, where the trenches curved, and that the water line sat directly below the electric line from the house to the barn. I marked the wellhead (even though it would be obvious to anyone looking for it) and where the water line was trenched from the well to the house. I marked where the septic tank was buried, where the leach field marched in rows back and forth down the hill behind the house. ("Don't want pasture over this. Horses'll tear the crap out of it," the contractor said. We'd laughed at his wordplay, but he'd stared at us, his expression just this side of a scowl.)

I did this on a sunny April morning in 1997, recording this birth of my farm, putting down for history what I would forget even though I was certain I would always remember. Writing it all down in case I ever were to sell the place, this culmination of years of work and hope, my dream farm, which I knew I would never sell.

I'd signed the papers for a construction loan that would convert to a thirty-year mortgage on my thirty-fifth birthday. There seemed some kind of significance that I'd sign them this day and make my last mortgage payment on my sixty-fifth birthday, the day I would retire. My future's course seemed locked and loaded, set, organized, no surprises—just the time to be lived and the work to be done. Signing for that seemed the most apropos of birthday presents.

I remember the day I moved to the farm, my first night there alone, after everyone had tired of the excitement of moving day and left for their respective homes. It was just my Border Collie Bristol, the horses, and me on the property, inhabiting the farm for the first time, beginning the rest of my life living in the reality of my lifelong dream. And I remember the ungrounded sense of not feeling *at home* so much as trying to *learn to* feel at home. I remember taking care of the horses in the evening as if going through a daily routine, although none of us had ever gone through this process here, on this farm. I remember going to bed that first night, wondering if it actually *was* bedtime or if I'd learn bedtime here was really earlier or later. I remember not sleeping well, surprised at hearing Amish buggies on the road all through the night. I listened for the sounds of my horses in the barn, assessing and sorting the noises into envelopes of normal bumps and bangs, or nuisance fiddling with buckets or bickering with neighbors. I listened to my house, for it to tell me its quiet night stories. I listened to Bristol, who at first lay by my bed, then got up and padded to the window, then padded into the living room, then padded back into the bedroom; she was alert and aware, but not unsettled—learning the farm just as was I.

I'm sure I slept, and I don't remember getting up the following morning. That first maiden night on the farm was the only time there when I wondered, just a little, where I was, stepping from my past and poised, leaning into my future, reaching my foot forward, feeling in the dark for my first toehold onto my future's ground.

On a sunny April morning in 2006, I'd remembered making the drawings, searched them out, and was preparing to retrace them to make tidy, more official-type renderings we could show potential buyers. The papers were crumpled, smudged with mud, crisped from their early life stuffed in pockets, or spread out on the ground or against the side of a barn or hood of pickup truck, maybe rocks or boots or tape measures holding the papers flat and still in the breezes. In a mix of pen and pencil, I had drawn a rough topography of the farm. Farmington Road at the top. The house sketched, scribbled out and re-sketched closer to the road, then re-sketched again to reflect how it sat at an angle to the road, aligned with the slope of the hillside and broadside to the best views; the barn a rough rectangle a little way from the house. Four straight lines outlining the 8 ½ x 11 sheet of paper. Crude arrows pointing to the lines and figures, identifying them: *West fence line. East fence line. Barn. House.* I remember having laughed identifying those obvious structures. I had laughed, too, when I'd drawn a rough plus mark with the letter "N" at the top, and under it, scrawled, *map not to scale.*

I sat at the dining room table, my hands spread across the papers, and I looked out the windows and over my pastures, lush and mowed and empty. Weeks earlier, Nova, Indy's yearling colt, had stepped from the Ohio dirt of this farm into a trailer that would take him to his new home in Missouri, and with his departure, Donley Farm East was horseless. The previous fall, at weaning time, I had moved Indy to Cornerstone Farm, a local boarding stable, leaving Nova at home with his uncle Monterey and Studly, a visiting pony. I always found weaning easier on the babies when I took the mares away—out of sight, sound, and smell—and left the foals at home in familiar surroundings with their buddies. Some months later, I'd bring the mares back home.

But I never did bring Indy back. It was 2005, and she was nine years old. I'd lost a lot of weight, and I kept her at Cornerstone where, now that I was thin enough to ride again, I could do so in the indoor arena when the weather was bad. Cornerstone was where I could socialize, where my trainer came to give me lessons, and to coach Indy and me in competition.

During the late fall of 2005, I gave Monterey away when his pre-vetting exam showed questionable foot issues; when he left the farm for his new home in Pennsylvania, it was just Studly and Nova. When I sold Nova in 2006, Studly went back to his owner. So in 2006, less than a decade after my immortal dream had risen up out of the grass in the fields there, Donley Farm East was barren.

Only Joho still was there, would stay there forever, buried deep at the crest of the hill in his pasture, where he'd stood keeping watch over his mares. I didn't want to leave him there. When the backhoe dug his grave, it never occurred to me that I'd ever leave the farm, so I'd never expected to leave him.

There had been a lot I didn't expect, back when I signed those papers on my thirty-fifth birthday.

I looked down at the crude topographical drawings in front of me on the table, inhaled the slightest hint of sun and mud and dampened paper drying in the brightness of young hope and realization, and I wondered when the dream had died. I think it happened slowly, so I didn't really see it for a long time. I think it was dying even as I physically downsized myself, even as I "downsized my breeding operation" and openly decided to breed only two mares a year, then one, then maybe none at all. Silver was gone to Pennsylvania to be a Pony

Club horse after weaning Monterey in 2002; so also eventually went Ro. Mysty I had sold to a breeder in the Midwest in 2003.

I used to laugh and tell people I had no desire for children, but if I ever heard the clock ticking, I'd just breed one of my mares. Nova was in fact the result of such a spontaneous decision, maybe an ember-flare from my dream as it died, when I decided one summer to breed Indy to Amorex, a Swedish stallion I loved. So Nova was conceived because Indy was in season, and for that moment, I felt all the old, familiar impulse to breed horses. But Nova was the last, and I knew that, even as he gestated, turning and moving in Indy's womb, even as he slipped out onto the straw on a warm May afternoon, even as Indy welcomed and nurtured her third colt, born at Donley Farm East like each of his brothers before him, even as I basked in the tide of exhilaration and joy, of discovery and new life, all the things that had breathed life into the dream in the first place, even then I knew he was the last.

Decades before, when I trained to become a paramedic, I had a passion to come to the rescue, to step in and make a difference, take control of chaos, and save lives. I discovered the first time I performed CPR that it was just like we practiced on Annie-the-manikin, except for the airway and the ribs. In a real live dead person, the airway is flaccid, much harder to manage than Annie's. And with a real live dead person, when you do chest compressions, you feel the patient's ribs and cartilage snap and crack under your palms. Your first impulse is to pull back. But you don't. You push through it to the heart of the matter, because you must. It's the only way.

When I was first a paramedic, I believed I'd never lose the passion. In the middle of the night, I could be out of bed, dressed, and running to my car before my pager had finished delivering the dispatch. It makes me think of my passion for the farm, for breeding and raising horses, that dream I spent years attaining, could not imagine ever leaving behind. I remember the first rescue call I ever went on, just as I remember my first night on the farm. I don't remember the last rescue call, though, any more than I remember the last night I spent on the farm, and I don't remember most calls that came between the first and last call. I wasn't aware of my passion's dissolution. I wonder if it gradually diluted with all those calls, was already thin and friable by the time I couldn't any longer tell you how many runs I'd gone on, or how many dead bodies I'd seen, or how many car wrecks or farm accidents I'd responded to, or how many heart attacks I'd worked.

How does passion die? Does it whither in fragments with dead babies or impotence to repair what is shattered? Is it smothered in the ashy dust of burnout? Does dispassion worm and slither its way into the life of passion, poison it without you even seeing it? And then there's this: would seeing it make any difference? I don't remember my early passion dying, although I do remember a late surge of that passion—maybe the last surge of it. I had finished a shift, the details of which are lost to me, and someone asked how my day was.

"I had a great day," I said, and remember smiling broadly, feeling that smile all through me. "I had a great day, saving lives."

I wonder: does enough death, in the wrong doses at the wrong times, suffocate passion so dreams dry out and scatter like chafe on a breeze? I wonder now, sometimes, years away from the farm, if its dream would have died if Lash had lived. Somehow I don't think so. I think it was connected to her, even if I didn't recognize how deeply, and without her, it thinned and frayed, lost its structure, evaporated.

Over the years, I've come to know that even if I don't fully understand, there was more to my farm-dream's demise than just Lash being gone. Sometimes, I think I have hold of what may be the reasons, the answers, but when I try to touch them, feel their nature and understand, any answers I think I might have grasped slide through my fingers like powdered bone and dust, the serpentine vapors of dreams. And even if I can't close my fist around some formed seed or stone, can't palpate its veracity or weigh its import, still from the intangible and indefinite I learn. Because even as bone dust and dream vapor answers slip through my fingers, I feel the breath of their stories, hear sighing confessions in their whispers as they pass, catch a hint of scent or taste, just fleeting but enough to make me want to turn my head and look again. And maybe the distance of years wends threads together until I can begin to discern their nebulous structure, see how they spread and curl under and around everything like vining ivy, touching, connecting, twining, encircling. So the weight of *why* shifts, clinging less to Lash and rebalancing outward over this nebulous net, finding mass in details not of Lash.

Now I can begin to see how things shot through the dream, things that happened beyond Lash's influence, or after she was dead, and I begin to see how the dream's fabric frayed with the cumulative terminal effect of all those shots. When I open myself to that, I know I can't put it all on Lash, nor is it fair to her or me, or even to the dream, for me to try to anymore. Yes, my dream died in part with Lash. But only in part. There was more to it than that.

It was also two lovely foals in 2000, the embodiment of my hopes and dreams and love, lying broken-legged on my farm, the skin yawning open to show the blood and ugliness of shattered bones. Foals whose broken legs I splinted with all the skill of any paramedic, even though I knew as I tended them that all my care and expertise meant nothing, because there was no repairing the damage. Their blood smeared my own shins, and I remember that angered me; I should have been able to prevent their injuries, and if any blood had to be spilled at that farm, it should have been my own, not theirs.

Some of it was two foals that should have thrived, which with all my care and love and effort, should have grown and blossomed, bolstering my dream, shoring it up, sweeping it along upon their sloping shoulders and well-set, arching necks, with their sheer quality, with their bright eyes and keen temperaments, babies anyone could love. But I failed them, and all I could do was hold their broken bodies in my lap as the vet ended their precious lives, because by then, killing them was the best I could do for them.

And it was the filly a year later, lame from a stone bruise, so her limping skewed the pressure on the rapidly changing growth plates in her knees—just that fast, a matter of weeks—so her legs bowed and warped and she would never be sound-legged enough to ride. Or maybe her deformity had really nothing to do with a temporary sore foot and uneven weight-bearing. I've seriously questioned if I made some monumental error in my feeding and nutrition or management. I gave her away to a good home, where she's produced lovely, sound, straight-legged foals and has a good life.

And I think it was in part the promising two-year-old that had a routine abscess in her front foot in early 2004, a setback that should not even have warranted a memory these years later, but which defied treatment for weeks until the vet feared the infection would invade the bone. We took the two-year-old to the veterinary hospital for surgery on the foot, only to find the horse had a seriously contracted tendon from weeks holding her leg with her knee and ankle bent, favoring her infected foot. She eventually recovered from both the infection and the contracted tendon, but in my darkest thoughts, I suspected the very fact of my ownership was like a curse on her, threatening her soundness and survival. So she, too, I gave away.

Over the course of the years, I bred some extraordinary horses, the kind of horses upon which I'd framed and built my dream, and I sold a couple "big horses" that managed to survive my care and stewardship, including Mackinac, Indy's first foal. Those successful sales validated my dream, gave credence to my presumption that I could breed top quality sport horses, and that people would pay top dollar for them too. But those sales were the exception, and usually, I let guilt or fear or shame overrule any kind of business sense. I hugely undersold some top quality youngsters, anxious to find them new homes, move them away from my custodial care or curse. I simply gave away more horses, some perfectly sound, than I sold. And how could the dream thrive if I failed to embrace the businessman-like attitude I needed to make pragmatic business decisions and sell what I produced, even if it was imperfect?

Some of the dream died when Joho died just months after Lash's death, almost as if he were following her, and perhaps he was. He wouldn't have been on my farm at all without her, because if Lash had not bluntly suggested I tap into the equity I already had in the farm and property to purchase him, such creative financing would never have occurred to me. I would never have moved beyond pining over his for sale ad in a horse magazine had Lash not been sitting in my living room that day, had not said, *You should buy him*, had not pointed out exactly how I could do that. Tackling that financial folly was my move and my responsibility. But its conception was Lash's. So in that regard, she was as responsible for Joho coming to live his final years at Donley Farm East as I was. If that is true, and I believe it is, then there's a certain logic that Joho's presence in my life and on my farm was tied to Lash, that he would follow her rather than stay with me.

I don't know why it took me years to recognize that Joho's decline mirrored Lash's, or to see it beyond especially sad timing of the inevitable. Each month, every year of fertility and vitality he gave me seemed a gift, because at twenty-one, he was an old horse when I bought him, at an age where his death would not raise eyebrows but rather elicit small nods acknowledging a long life with a timely end. As he entered his mid-twenties, with no decline in his vigor and virility, his age became a bragging point; where before I had felt defensive of my decision to buy a breeding stallion his age, had felt the need to extol his continued breeding-shed vitality, I now touted the latter, highlighting it by telling it all in context of his age. He was moving beyond the years where his death fell into the timely-end-small-nod age and more toward the raised-eye-brow-wow-he-was-old age.

So when it became harder and harder to keep weight on the old stallion, I saw it as the beginning of his age catching up to him, the start of his end. That it began slowly the summer of Lash's initial diagnosis, that his condition and then his morale deteriorated more rapidly the following summer when Lash herself was actively dying, seemed to me only particularly cruel chance timing. Now, looking back, the connection between Lash's decline and Joho's seems clear beyond coincidence, glares so obvious I'm stunned not to have seen it for so many years.

But I didn't see that logic, or even consider it, for years. In the winter of

2002 into 2003, I knew only that I missed Joho, felt his absence, even though he was an old stallion, had already given me more time, more foals than I should have expected or perhaps deserved.

One thing I knew, although I assigned it to grief at the time, was this: my heart wasn't in it the way it had been when Lash was there, bolstering the dream. Maybe with Arnold in my life I could let the dream go, even though he shared in the joys of the farm and was content to stay there—with or without horses. I didn't trust that idea for a long time though, suspecting grief contributed to it, although guilt layered it like sheets of shale, one layer fracturing and crumbling just to reveal another sheet of stone. It feels arrogant to even put into words the thought that Arnold came into my life because Lash would be leaving it. The concept is at once insulting to both of them, diminishing the significance and impacts of them as individuals; and shames me, as if by considering the concept I bloat my own self-importance.

And yet…

When we actually sold the farm in late 2006, moved our lives from its empty fields, it didn't really feel like abandoning a dream. Lash was years gone. Anton had sold their farm and moved away to Cleveland two years previously. Joho was long dead and buried. And the dream that had wrought the farm, given it vision and shape and purpose, had been shot through, friable, its substance dissolved. So leaving by choice was easier than if it had been forced, if the dream were alive and well, but the financial or physical capacity to keep the farm were not.

But I would be lying if I were to say we left and never looked back. Both Arnold and I drove past the farm a few times a year, always stung with displeasure at some disrepair or un-mowed fields or junk left lying around. Even knowing it wasn't ours any more, and we had no right to judge, we couldn't help ourselves so eventually we stopped driving past. Sometimes, instead, I'll think about sitting on the back porch in the dusk, watching a pasture full of healthy and content mares and foals, or Arnold and I will reminisce about tag-team mowing the pastures, barn swallows swarming around us, gorging on the bugs our mowers had stirred to flight. Or we'd laugh at how we don't miss breaking ice out of frozen water buckets every winter, or how amusing it had been watching the cats trek through two feet of snow to and from the barn.

Of the dream, only Indy remains now—that little mare Lash pointed out to me was my equine soul mate before I was even aware of it myself. Indy, Joho's daughter, a smaller, feminine version of her father, conceived early, early in my dream, Indy who was born in a shed and lived at the farm I leased in Garrettsville before we moved to Donley Farm East. Indy, who left Donley Farm East years ago and lives still at Cornerstone Farm. Indy, who gave me three extraordinary babies, then shifted from broodmare to riding horse, and carried me to regional championships and national Swedish Warmblood All-Breeds awards three years running. Indy, who after populating my breeding dream, served as mount for my dreams—pipedreams, I often thought in my obese years—of riding and showing, of competing at a national level. Indy, idle now in her pastures and stable, content to be a pasture potato and occasional seat for me when I have the urge to swing a leg over a horse's back.

Of all the first seeds of my horse farm dream, of all those seeds that had been sown and grown and harvested or ruined young or plowed under or simply left to go fallow in the fields, only Indy remains, older now and getting gray, but no less here than she's ever been.

Everything is finite. I know that. Even so, I believe Indy will always warm my palms with her breath and my soul with her presence, regardless of which side of the Rainbow Bridge she stands on.

Indy, my lovely little mare, who has been with me over two decades, perhaps transcends the dream. Or maybe she never was *of* it, but rather came before, stepped into it, strode through it, stepped out, and is with me still because she is, as Lash said, my soul mate. She is with me always.

After Lash.
After Joho.
After the farm.
After the dream.

Appendix A:

The Birthday Bullet List for Lash

1978-ish

- Walking from Hiram to the farm on 700 that summer, because I wasn't old enough to drive yet.

- Backing the car down your parents' driveway with you and Caroline (who was facing backward) both screaming "left" "right" and your mother having to pull the car out of the mud with the Bronco. Repeatedly.

- Sleeping in the barn waiting for Kara to foal. You and Caroline galloping around "event courses" in the hayloft all night until I got pissed off and went home.

- Riding Sugar up Rt. 700 bareback, at a full gallop, because I said, "see how far you can get before I catch up to you" in the car. I didn't think you were going to go hell-bent-for-leather straight up the center line. Your resultant close encounter with a phone pole, my throwing you in the car, and following Sugar home (Sugar, again, at a full gallop), yelling "loose horse" out the window (long after she'd already gone by, and there was no one around to hear anyway).

- You and me throwing malted milk balls at the screen at Garrettsville Cinema—but only after we'd stuffed our faces and couldn't eat any more of them.

- Winging cookies out of the car window while yelling "biodegradable" as we had fits of willpower–again, only after we'd already stuffed our faces and were full.

1980-1981

- Sitting in the art room at Crestwood High School, looking at a map, planning our cross-country horseback ride. "Hang a right at Georgia."

- You changed your name from Leslie to Ashley, my reluctance to comply, the birth of "Lash." Pretty cool nickname, actually.

1982-1988

- The really tall guy–Anton–whom you met while in high school and had a crush on–but he had a drug problem or something, and he graduated and moved away. I figured you just had the hots for him because he was taller than you.

- I leave for Virginia Intermont College–you leave for Sweden. For a year. You bring me a Swedish wooden horse–I could never remember what they're called, but it's still on my mantle.

- I came back to Hiram College. You left for ATI. You lived off campus and moved in with Kent.

- You dump Kent.

- You buy Tabriz.

- You go to Miami University.

- You date Chris. And Jason. And take up fencing.

- You do the modeling thing for a while.

- I do my paramedic training.

1990

- Anton, MIA for years out in California, shows up on your doorstep at your parents' house in Hiram while he was in Ohio on a visit to Jack and Judy.

- You visit Anton in California; you send me a postcard that says, "I'm in California. Now, I'm in heaven."

- Anton leaves California and comes back to Ohio. He lives with you for a short while in your room in your parents' house in Hiram (amazed me–that would not have happened in MY parents' house, ha, ha).

- You and Anton get an apartment in Kent.

- Anton works at Giant Eagle and takes classes at KSU.

1991

- You visit me in Garfield Heights. We go out to dinner at "our place"– Denny's–until we encounter terrible service and never go back. We decide that if we were black, we would have very easily believed it was racial discrimination (there was a big discrimination lawsuit against Denny's at the time).

- You call and ask if I would be your maid of honor. Of course I say yes.

October 5, 1991

- Mario's in the morning. Fun at first, then stressful because they over-booked. The hair guy asks, "are you in the wedding party?" You reply, "I'm the bride." Trying to keep you and Anton from seeing each other at the spa.

- I send you two off to the church while I bluff my way through Mario's shoddy bookkeeping (I tell them you have a cancelled check for the payment–which is a bluff–but fortunately, it was also true, though I didn't know it).

- Getting dressed in the basement of the church. The ceremony. The reception and dancing to "Love Shack." You two leaving late in the evening for your honeymoon.

1992 - 1994

- Chris calls and asks if you were married. You tell him yes. Touché.

- You and Anton buy the house in Mantua.

- Anton rescues Feivel from a Dumpster.

- You enroll at Ashland Theological Seminary for your M.A. in pastoral counseling.

- Attempts to breed Tabriz to Martini. No luck.

1995

- You give up on breeding Tabriz.

1996

- You fly down to Florida to look at Martini babies and visit your folks. You and your mom visit Valhalla Farm. You choose Steorling.

- Steorling comes north.

- Steorling and Tabriz at Milt's in Garrettsville with my horses.

- Field trips with Indy and Steorling.

1997

- Chino dumping me on my side. You take me to the E.R.

- Selling Chino. Mare shopping for me. Buying Mysty.

- Finding the land in Parkman. "I can't afford it," I say and won't even look at it. You shanghai me out there.

- Putting offers on the land. We're next-door neighbors!

1998

- You find your job at Penske Logistics and leave Hummel.

- You get me into Penske.

1999

- Joho's for sale. I say I wish I could buy him. You say "You can. You have equity in your home." Insane, but I get a home equity loan and buy Johanniter. He arrives on January 29, 1999.

- Breeding Steorling to Hailo. Steorling's in foal!

- The trip with Steorling to Louisville for the inspection; staying at The Columbine B&B and having crepes with fresh fruit for breakfast

(Nettie stays at the farm and takes care of the horses for me). The disappointing inspection results. You're crushed, again. You so desperately want everyone to love Steorling like you do. The pride of Steorling's behavior on the trip.

- Showing NODA walk-trot shows. Earning Achievement Certificates.

- Steorling loses pregnancy.

- Finding Bristol in the chicken barn—my not hearing the old crooked man right when we go to pick her up.

- You, me, and Anton going to Mountaineer on the spur of the moment to watch Roanoke in her last race before we bought her.

- Helping me move Ro, Indy, Mysty, and Silver to the new farm.

- You suggest I contact Arnold. I refuse.

- Donating Tabriz to Crossed Sabers.

2000 – early 2001

- Breeding Steorling to Joho.

- Sandusky's birth and death.

- Mackinac's birth, my anxiety, your reassurance and support.

- Savannah's birth.

- Cyprus' birth and death.

- Showing at NODA—you and Steorling win the adult amateur training level championship.

- You again suggest I contact Arnold. I again refuse.

- I finally contact Arnold, we meet again, get back together.

- Bringing Steorling to my house to foal.

April, 2001

- Sukhoi arrives.

- The following Saturday, you and Anton find a lump.

• Rainier is born in the field at 3:30 in the afternoon of Good Friday. You look at him and say, "Hey, you got my horse."

• Your house finally sells, and you move into my parents' basement to save money before you build your house.

• Exams, biopsies, surgery, staging. Sentinel node biopsy, injection of radioactive dye. Anton dubs you "Glowing Boob Girl."

• Buying wigs. Cost covered by insurance. "Dr. Spiffy's" script–"total cranial prosthesis for chemotherapy-induced alopecia."

• We trade Sukhoi for Rainier–maybe he'll be tall enough for you.

• Chemotherapy.

• The Grand Haven Recognized Breed Show. Rainier wins his class with a score of 79.8 percent.

• You look lovely bald, with your elegant dinky little head.

• Your birthday, and the big honking rock you got on your left hand for your tenth anniversary.

• Groundbreaking party for your new home in Parkman.

• The renewal of your vows with Anton.

• End of chemotherapy, beginning of radiation therapy.

• End of radiation, Christmas!

2002

• Trade Steorling for Sampson.

• Building your house and barn. Putting up fencing in the freezing cold.

• Moving your horses. The first turnout session. How beautiful!

• Moving you in to your new house in March. Again, how beautiful.

• Tours of the house to all and sundry. Anton likes to point out "the twins' room." Startled looks from family and friends (desired effect achieved).

- Finally, finally, finally we are living right next door to each other on our horse farms.

Early May, 2002

- You take care of the farm while Arnold and I go to NYC.

May 9, 2002

- Routine follow-up with Dr. Spiffy. Blood draws, etc. He says go ahead and get pregnant.

May 13, 2002

- Dr. Spiffy calls with the lab results.

May 17, 2002

- Transvaginal ultrasound. Anton and I come into the exam room with you. Technician is disconcerted at first.

May 19, 2002

- CT scan.

May 21, 2002

- Mack's OCD surgery. Your appointment with Dr. Spiffy to go over the test results. Liver involvement.

May 24, 2002

- Liver biopsy, confirms metastatic breast cancer. Slow, painful convalescence from the biopsy.

May 31, 2002

- Monterey arrives at 11:30 a.m. I call you, you're able to drive down and watch the delivery–and take pictures.

June, July, August, 2002

- Chemotherapy again. You tell Dr. Spiffy, "I don't want the fat chemo this time. I want the skinny chemo."

August 19, 2002

- Repeat CT scan. Progression.

August 23, 2002

Dearest Lash:

What do I do for you on this day? I have no idea. But I've thought over the last many weeks about what you have meant to me. You have been the sister I never had. You are my dearest friend, my soul mate, my confidant, my advisor, my partner in crime, hilarity, delight, and anguish. I could not think of anything to do for you on this, your 36th birthday, other than remember our lives growing up together. And even though you were there for it all, I wanted to share it with you. I'm sorry I can't do more. I love you, I will always love you, and you will always be a part of me and my life. Your friendship has been, is, and always will be priceless to me. What a wonderful gift that is! I am honored and grateful. I will love you always.

Our Equestrian Timeline

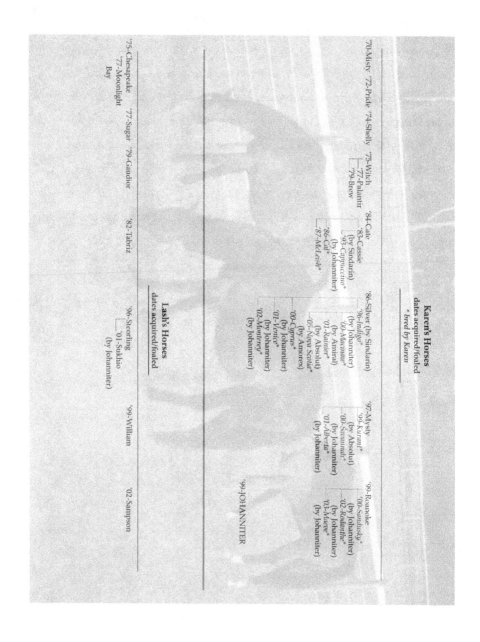

Karen's Horses
dates acquired/foaled
* bred by Karen

'70-Misty '72-Pride '74-Shelly '75-Witch
  '77-Palantir
    '79-Brew

'84-Cate
'83-Cassie
  (by Sindarin)
  '93-Cappuccino*
'86-Cal*
'87-McLeisir*
  (by Johanniter)

'86-Silver (by Sindarin)
  '96-Indigo*
  (by Johanniter)
  '00-Macnair*
  '01-Amiral*
  (by Amiral)
  '01-Rainier*
  (by Absolut)
  '05-Nova Scotia*
  (by Amorex)
  '00-Cyprus*
  (by Johanniter)
  '01-Venice*
  (by Johanniter)
  '02-Monterey*
  (by Johanniter)

'97-Mysty
  '99-Kurmt*
  (by Absolut)
  '00-Swannah*
  (by Johanniter)
  '01-Alberta*
  (by Johanniter)

'99-Roanoke
  '00-Sandusky*
  (by Johanniter)
  '02-Rolanthe*
  (by Johanniter)
  '03-Mieze*
  (by Johanniter)

'99-JOHANNITER

Lash's Horses
dates acquired/foaled

'75-Chesapeake '77-Sugar '79-Gaudior '82-Tabriz '96-Sterling '99-William '02-Sampson
'77-Moonlight Bay
  '01-Sukhio
  (by Johanniter)

Appendix C:

Photo Gallery

I've often wondered, if Lash and I were such compatriots in our love of horses and riding, if we spent so much of our lives together with horses, how it is I have so few pictures of Lash and me together? For the majority of my horse pictures, we were not both in the photographs because more often than not one or the other of us was holding and posing the horses, trying to get them to stand with their weight evenly distributed over all four legs, their ears up and attention forward, necks arched just so, while the other stood behind the camera, waiting, poised to click the shutter when everything was just right. We wanted good "conformation shots" for my farm advertising or we could use to show off our horses to others. Getting good horse photos can be deceptively difficult; horses can be as bad as (or worse than) people in taking "bad pictures," and for each good shot there were probably ten "crap" pictures. In the days prior to digital cameras, when a roll of film yielded only a few dozen photos and it was expensive to develop those photos, we didn't "waste" time or money trying to get pictures of us together with our horses. This is an oversight I regret.

As it is, the photos I do have of Lash, pictures she appeared in because she happened to be in the frame when I pressed the shutter, are perhaps more honest, less posed, more reflective of our time together. I find a small beauty in that—that she was there on the periphery of so much of my life, not always in the picture, but nearly always helping orchestrate it.

For years and years, decades, I had stacks and bags of photos, crap pictures with horses in unbalanced positions or lips twisted or half-cocked ears or lighting all wrong or just not inspiring. I remember many pictures I know captured Lash in whole or part—her hand or leg stretched out to hold the horse, leaning her body back to try and get out of the photo's frame or her walking through a field. Or Lash riding a horse, squinting into the sun, scowling or unflattering photos adding ten or twenty or forty pounds… I remember these pictures, I remember taking them, seeing them, flipping through them over the years, but they're gone now. When did I decide, in some spontaneous and ill-conceived moment of organization and economy, to throw out all those "crap" pictures? I don't remember throwing any of them away; all I remember is rebuffing the tug of resistance, turning my ear away from the little voice murmuring keep them keep them keep them. Surely, I cannot have thrown these all away after Lash had died. Surely not then. But I don't remember.

Now, I riffle through bags and boxes, and I solicit pictures from Bill and Janeen and Anton and Nettie and Laura. I invade my parents' house and delve into spider-ridden basement boxes, trying to ferret out just a few images, light captured on paper, now perhaps mold and mildew-smudged and dim. When I come across one, a sudden blink, I catch my breath, clutch it, and bring it back into the light, however small or peripheral or oblique her image. I think I'll always be searching for more boxes and bags, treasures sequestered in corners or nudged over time from view, always I'll be rummaging, hoping, expectant.

1. Karen at five or six years old, late 1960s, in her natural, inborn element … with a horse.

2. Lash started riding at a young age, too, before she and Karen ever met.

1

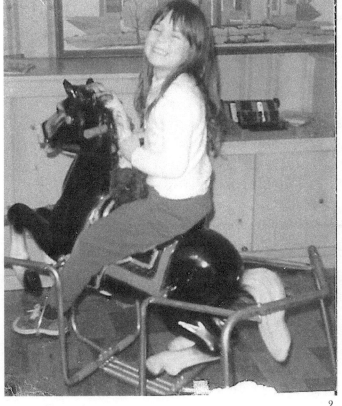

2

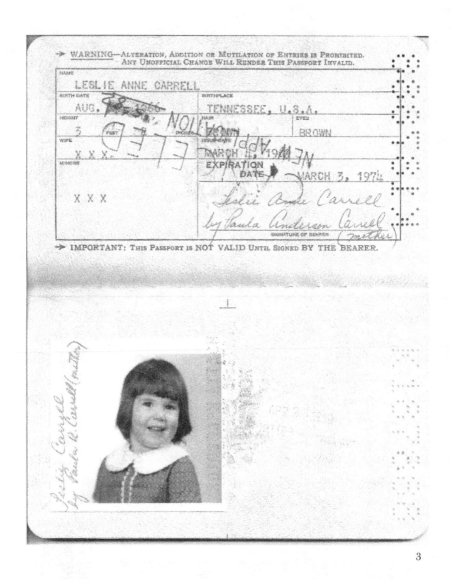

3. Lash's first passport.

4. Janeen at Hiram College in 1968. Hiram College Lantern yearbook photo.

5. Lash with Paula, her first mother—circa late '60.

4

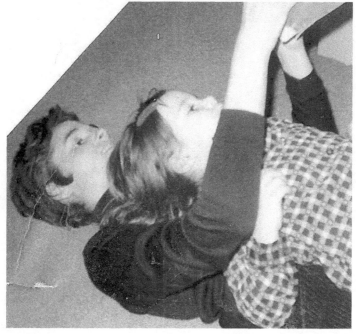

5

6

6. Bill, Janeen, and Lash, early 1970s.

7. Circa 1971, in the front yard in Hiram with (left to right) Misty the pony, Karen, Greg, Ted, and Puff the dog.

8. Lash with Gaudior—a big-enough horse for her—in the late 1970s.

7

8

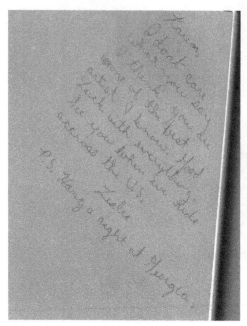

Carrell, Leslie

Karen Donley

9

9. *Crestwood High School yearbook, 1981, when Lash, a freshman, was still Leslie, Karen was a senior, and they both still dreamed about riding their horses across the nation.*

10. *Lash during one of her modeling stints.*

11. *Lash had fun modeling, even if she never felt she was thin enough.*

10

11

12

13

12. Even "too thin" wasn't thin enough, because Lash still had those legs that kept going and going...

13. At one point when they had both lost weight, Lash convinced Karen to pose for a "glamour shot" so they could model together. Lash took the picture in her front yard, but that was the closest Karen ever got to any career in front of a camera.

14. Karen during a brief, brave flirtation with riding racehorses, summer 1982, Hawkeye Hill Racing School, Commiskey, Indiana.

15. Lash with Tabriz, whom she couldn't love into being big enough.

14

15

16

17

18

16. *When they first got back together, Lash visited Anton in California. She sent Karen a postcard: "I'm in California. No, I'm in heaven."*

17. *Karen trying to help Lash secure her pillbox hat and veil and get ready to walk down the aisle to marry Anton Habsburg, October 5, 1991.*

18. *Karen with Lash and Anton Habsburg at their wedding October 5, 1991.*

19

20

21

19. Nettie on Cappuccino, Lash on Tabriz in the fall of 1996 at a hunter pace at South Farm, Middlefield, Ohio. Cappuccino, the first Swedish Warmblood Karen bred, was at three years old already bigger than Tabriz, Lash's first Trakehner mare that didn't grow tall enough to fit her.

20. Lash and Anton for a formal dinner.

21. Lash and Anton at her graduation with her Master's in Pastoral Counseling.

22

22. *Karen and Lash, with Steorling as a weanling. Steorling had just arrived in Ohio from Florida, and Lash would spend the next three years trying to grow the filly big enough through the sheer force of her love.*

23. *Karen and Lash at the Mid-Ohio Dressage Association recognized breed show, getting ready to show their two-year-old fillies Indy and Steorling. July, 1998.*

24. *Karen presenting Indy in the two-year-old fillies class at the Mid-Ohio Dressage Association 1998 recognized breed show. Bob Tarr photo.*

23

24

25

25. *(Above) The Donley Farm East fields, Parkman, Ohio, April, 1998, with the barn just started under construction. Looking west from Lash and Anton's property line; the small pine trees mark DFE's west property line (before the white house).*

26. *(Below) Donley Farm East fields September, 1998, with the mares in their pasture. Looking southeast from the back porch of the house toward Lash and Anton's property (the tree-line upper left and all of the woods).*

26

27

28

27. *The barn of Donley Farm East from the back porch of the house. Circa 2004.*

28. *Donley Farm East doormat with the Swedish Warmblood logo—a "farm warming" gift from Lash. Karen kept the door mat when she and Arnold sold the farm and still uses it in their (non-farm) house in a village, years after Lash died.*

29

30

29. Lash standing behind Johanniter, fall 1999.

30. Mysty with Kurant, her first foal and the first foal born at Donley Farm East, March, 1999. Johanniter watches from his pasture in the background.

31. Lash watches Mysty with Kurant—the first foal born at Donley Farm East—end of March, 1999.

32. Karen riding Johanniter in the fields at Donley Farm East, fall 1999.

33

34

33. Karen with Johanniter in the fields at Donley Farm East, fall 1999.

34. Sandusky with his mother Roanoke a few hours before his death, early March, 2000. The first Joho foal born at Donley Farm East, he broke his leg at one day old and was euthanized.

35

36

35. *Indy gives birth to Mackinac, her first foal, at the end of March, 2000, less than three weeks after Sandusky's death. Mack (by Olympic Swedish Warmblood stallion Amiral) was Joho's maternal grandson. Lash (left) and Karen (right) in attendance with Indy when she delivered Mack.*

36. *Lash helping Karen get pictures of Mack when he was about six weeks old—a "crap" picture, mostly because of the... well, pile of manure in the background.*

37

38

37. Mysty with Savannah, her second baby, May, 2000. Savannah was the only Joho foal born at Donley Farm East in 2000 to survive.

38. From left to right: Roanoke, Silver (shortly before delivering Cyprus) and Mysty nursing Savannah, summer 2000 at Donley Farm East.

39

40

39. Nettie with Cyprus in his first hours, early July, 2000. Cyprus was Silver's second foal, and was Indy's full brother.

40. Silver with Cyprus in the pasture early July, about an hour before Cyprus broke his leg, becoming the second foal to die at Donley Farm East in 2000.

41

42

41. *Steorling as a three-year-old, October, 1999.*

42. *Steorling with Sukhoi, her too-small Johanniter filly born at Donley Farm East just days before Lash found the lump in her breast, April, 2001.*

43. *Lash gives too-small Sukhoi a kiss on the nose. She had undergone a biopsy but not yet started chemotherapy at this point.*

44. *Lash showing Steorling the fall before she got sick.*

43

44

45

46

45. *Arnold with Indy in the field a few hours before she delivered Rainier, April 13, 2001. Steorling with her too-small filly Sukhoi are in the background.*

46. *Anton with Tom and Sarah Nather in the early construction of Lash and Anton's new barn.*

47

48

47. Karen with Rainier and Indy shortly after he was born in the field, April 13, 2001; a few weeks later, Lash and Karen swapped Rainier for Sukhoi.

48. Indy with Rainier at about three days old. After trading too-small Sukhoi for Rainier, Lash finally had a baby who would grow up big enough for her, although she died when Rainier was only a year and a half old, and didn't get to see him grow up or ride him.

49

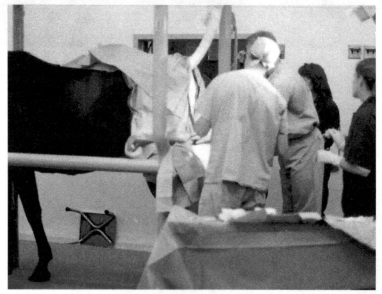

50

49. *The view across the Donley Farm East fields and Karen walking the fence line spring, 2002. Lash and Anton's house is still visible in the trees on the opposite hill. They finished building the house and moved in March of that year, seven months before Lash died.*

50. *Roanoke at Ohio State University, fall of 2000, undergoing surgical repair of the rectovaginal fistula she sustained delivering Sandusky. The surgery was successful, and she conceived and delivered two more Johanniter foals at Donley Farm East.*

51

52

51. Fat, fat the water rat... Arnold and Karen in New York City, May, 2002. In January 2003, Karen had gastric bypass surgery and lost about 100 pounds.

52. Roanoke with her two-week-old filly Rodanthe in the fields at Donley Farm East. Rodanthe was Roanoke's second foal, conceived after Roanoke's surgery and delivered without incident in April, 2002.

53. Lash sitting by the gate watching Silver and her newborn filly Venice, June, 2001. Lash had started chemotherapy and cut her hair short before it started falling out. By mid-summer, she was bald.

54 Silver nuzzles her new filly Venice, June, 2001.

55. Silver the day before she delivered her last foal, Monterey, in May, 2002. Lash and Anton's house is still visible through the leafing-out trees on the hill. Lash had just undergone a liver biopsy, confirming her breast cancer's metastases.

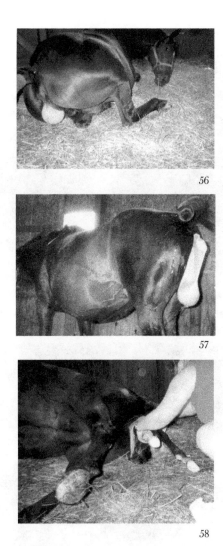

56

57

58

56. *Silver delivered Monterey during the middle of the day in May, 2002. Lash sat in a chair in the doorway, too weak to stand, and took pictures of the colt's birth while Karen attended the delivery. The birth is just beginning; this is the amniotic sack. Foals are born in a "diving" position. The foal's front feet have not yet appeared.*

57. *Silver stood up again to reposition herself; Monterey's first foot is visible in the amniotic sack just beneath her tail.*

58. *Silver lay down again and continued the delivery. Monterey's front feet and nose are out (his head is below his legs here, gravity pulling his nose toward the straw). Karen helps guide the colt's shoulder through Silver's pelvis by giving light traction to the colt's leg.*

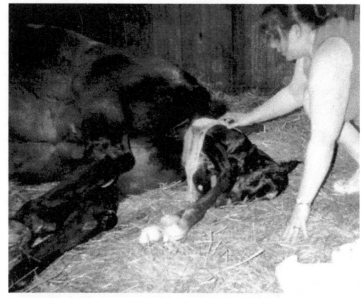

59

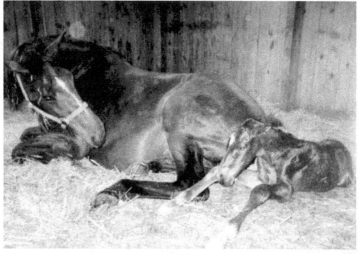

60

59. *With Monterey's shoulders out, the hardest part of the delivery is done. Karen moves the amniotic sack away from the colt's face and head so he can breathe.*

60. *As soon as she has finished pushing Monterey out, Silver rolls onto her chest and looks around at her new baby, nickering to him. Only a few minutes old, Monterey has already rolled onto his chest and is holding his head up; within moments, his floppy ears will gain tone and stand upright.*

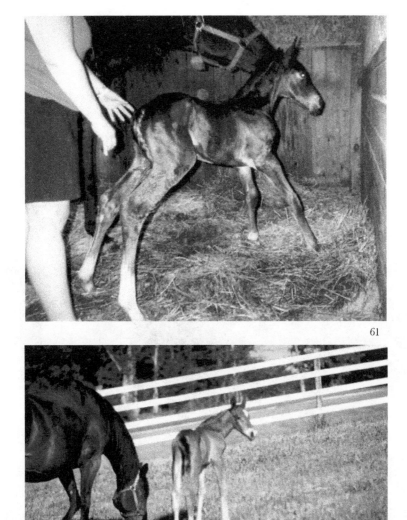

61

62

61. *At one hour old and before he's even dry from his birth, Monterey is on his feet, albeit unsteadily. Silver dotes on him, and Karen stands behind him to stabilize him.*

62. *Silver and Monterey out in the front pasture at Donley Farm East, May, 2002. Monterey is one day old.*

63

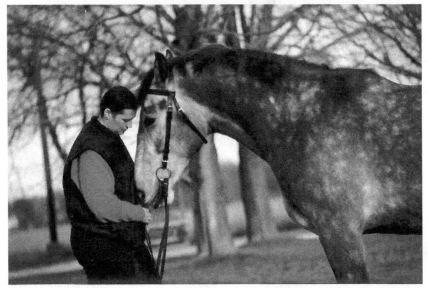

64

63. Lash standing in what would become the kitchen of their new house. She is bald from the first round of chemotherapy.

64. Her hair not even an inch long after finishing her first round of chemo, Lash spends time with Sampson, a "big enough" riding age horse for whom she traded Steorling.

65

66

65. *Determined to have a horse to ride that was big enough, Lash traded Steorling for Samp-son, a draft-cross gelding (Rainier was still too young to ride). The spring and summer she died, she rode him in the arena she and Anton built on their farm next door to Donley Farm East. This was the last time she rode, August, 2002, two months before she died.*

66. *Lash riding Sampson in the arena on their farm in August, 2002, two months before she died. The house and barn of Donley Farm East are on the hilltop in the background.*

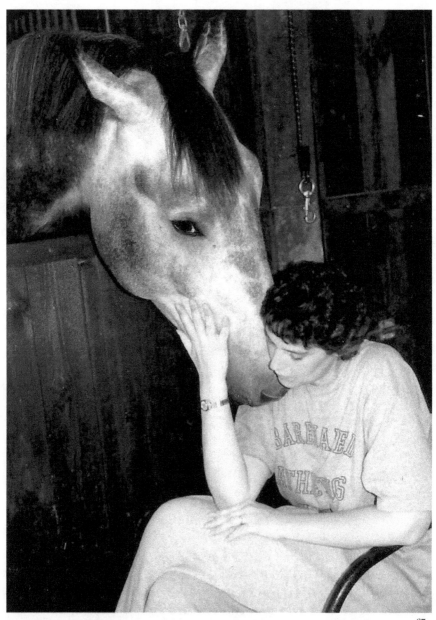

67

68

67. *Lash sitting in the barn with Sampson a few weeks before she died.*

68. *Anton and Lash sitting on the back porch of their new house only a few weeks before Lash died.*

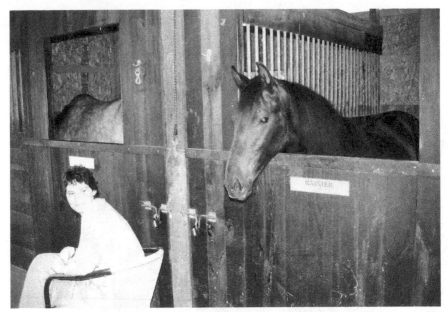

69

69. Lash, too weak to stand for very long, still enjoyed sitting in her new barn with her horses—Sampson, the large gray draft cross for whom she traded Steorling, so she would have a "big enough" horse to ride before she died; and Rainier, for whom she traded too-small Sukhoi. Rainier is only a yearling in this picture; Lash died before he was old enough to ride.

70. Anton with William, the Clydesdale he and Lash bought for him in 2000 before Lash got sick.

71. Anton with Fivel, the "Dumpster kitty," late 2000s.

70

71

72

73

72. *Maeve, Roanoke's third Johanniter foal, at one day old in the front pasture at Donley Farm East, April, 2003. Maeve was the last Johanniter foal born at Donley Farm East, arriving the spring after Joho's death.*

73. *Maeve, the last Johanniter foal born at Donley Farm East, at one day old with her mother Roanoke, early spring 2003.*

74

75

74-75. Indy with her third foal, Nova Scotia, the last horse born at Donley Farm East, born in May, 2005.

76

77

78

79

76. *Karen and Arnold at their wedding, May 22, 2004.*

77. *Bill and Janeen Carrell with Lash's portrait at Karen and Arnold's wedding reception, May 22, 2004.*

78. *Karen, Anton, and Arnold at Karen and Arnold's wedding reception, May 22, 2004.*

79. *The bracelet Janeen gave to Karen the night Lash died – and Lo, I am with you always.*

80

81

82

83

80. *Indy at ten years old during her 2006 show season. Bob Tarr photo.*

81. *Karen in the dressage show ring, summer, 2006. After weaning Indy's third (and last) foal, and losing almost 100 pounds after bariatric surgery in early 2003, Karen rode, trained, and showed Indy for several years, earning United States Dressage Federation Swedish Warmblood breed championships or reserve championships at training and first levels in 2006, 2007, and 2008. Bob Tarr photo.*

82. *Karen on Indy and Sarah Nather holding Rainier at a Grand Haven Stables recognized show, summer, 2006. Mother and son, having lived on different farms from the time Rainier was weaned in late 2001, did not seem to remember each other.*

83. *Sarah with Rainier after her high school graduation, 2006, shortly before she left for college at Miami University.*

84

85

86

84. *Sarah on Rainier at the USDF Region 2 Championships near Cincinnatti, September, 2006. Sarah was a freshman at Miami University, and left school for the weekend to compete in the show.*

85. *Anton came to watch Sarah show Rainier at the USDF Region 2 championships at Paxton Farm, September, 2006.*

86. *Karen sharing some quality time with Indy, summer 2008. Julie Feather photo.*

87

88

87. Karen sitting on her own grave site next to Lash's grave, October 24, 2010, eight years after Lash died.

88. Lash's gravesite on August 23, 2011, what would have been her 45th birthday, nearly nine years after her death. The hydrangea tree survived the buck-rub from the prior fall.

Photo courtesy of the author

Karen Donley-Hayes's work has appeared in *The Journal of the American Medical Association, Bartleby Snopes, Blue Lyra Review, The Quotable, The Healing Muse, Pulse, The Saturday Evening Post* online, and others, and has been anthologized in *Chicken Soup for the Soul: My Cat's Life; The Heart of All That Is: Reflections on Home;* and *Blue Lyra Review Anthology.* She and her husband, Arnold, live in Garrettsville, Ohio. *Falling Off Horses* is Karen's first book.

Karen's debut young-adult novel, *Shoalie's Crow* will be released by MilSpeak's imprint, Family of Light Books, in spring 2024.

Thank you for supporting the creative works of veterans and military family members by purchasing this book. If you enjoyed your reading experience, we're certain you'll enjoy these other great reads.

American Delphi

BY M.C. ARMSTRONG

During America's summer of plague and protest, fifteen-year-old Zora Box worries her pesky younger brother is a psychopath for sneaking out at night to hang with their suspicious new neighbor, Buck London, who's old enough to be their father. Their father, a combat veteran, is dead—suicide. Or so everyone thinks, until Buck sets Zora and her brother Zach straight, revealing their father as the genius inventor of a truth-telling, future-altering device called American Delphi.

Salmon in the Seine

BY NORRIS COMER

One moment 18-year-old Norris Comer is throwing his high school graduation cap in the air and setting off for Alaska to earn money, and the next he's comforting a wounded commercial fisherman who's desperate for the mercy of a rescue helicopter. From land-lubber to deckhand, Comer's harrowing adventures at sea and during a solo search in the Denali backcountry for wolves provide a transformative bridge from adolescence to adulthood.

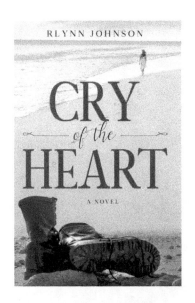

Cry of the Heart

BY RLYNN JOHNSON

After law school, a group of women calling themselves the Alphas embark on diverse legal careers—Pauline joins the Army as a Judge Advocate. For twenty years, the Alphas gather for annual weekend retreats where the shenanigans and truth-telling will test and transform the bonds of sisterhood.

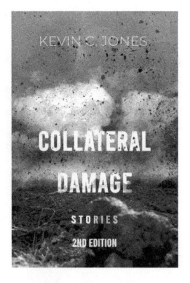

Collateral Damage
2nd edition

BY KEVIN C. JONES

These stories live in the real-world psychedelics of warfare, poverty, love, hate, and just trying to get by. Jones's evocative language, the high stakes, and heartfelt characters create worlds of wonder and grace. The explosions, real and psychological, have a burning effect on the reader. Nothing here is easy, but so much is gained.

—ANTHONY SWOFFORD, author of *Jarhead: A Marine's Chronicle of the Gulf War and Other Battles*

Sub Wife

BY SAMANTHA OTTO BROWN

A Navy wife's account of life within the super-secret sector of the submarine community, and of the support among spouses who often wait and worry through long stretches of silence from loved ones who are deeply submerged.

The Fine Art of Camouflage

BY LAUREN KAY JOHNSON

A young woman's coming-of-age in the military against a backdrop of war, viewed through her lens as an information operations officer who wrestles with the nature of truth in the stories we hear from the media and official sources, and in the stories we tell about ourselves and our families.

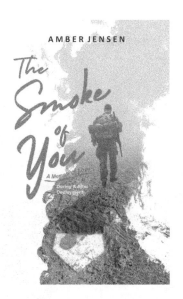

The Smoke of You

BY AMBER JENSEN

A young couple's love and marriage are tested during and after a military deployment with the National Guard to Iraq that results in a battle with chronic pain and the slow-burning challenges of married life. A story of selfless love and self-discovery, of hardship and hope, *The Smoke of You* will resonate with anyone who has ever suffered, and still bravely loved.

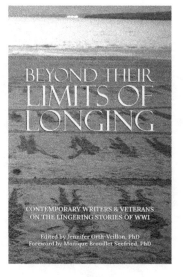

Beyond Their Limits of Longing

EDITED BY
JENNIFER ORTH-VEILLON, PhD

In America, WWI became overshadowed by WWII and Vietnam, further diluting the voices of poets, novelists, essayists, and scholars who unknowingly set a precedent for the sixty-two successive, and notable, war writers who appear in this collection to explore the complexity both of war's physical and mental horrors and of its historical significance in today's world in crises.

CPSIA information can be obtained
at www.ICGtesting.com
Printed in the USA
BVHW041533060723
666783BV00004B/721

9 798985 794144